THE ALDINE EDITION
OF THE BRITISH
POETS

THE POETICAL WORKS OF THOMAS CHATTERTON

THE POETICAL WORKS OF

THOMAS CHATTERTON

WITH AN ESSAY ON THE ROWLEY POEMS BY THE

REV. WALTER W. SKEAT, M.A.

LATE FELLOW OF CHRIST'S COLL.

CAMBRIDGE

AND A MEMOIR BY EDWARD BELL, M.A.

TRIN. COLL. CAMBRIDGE

VOL. I.

LONDON

GEORGE BELL AND SONS YORK STREET

COVENT GARDEN

1875

AMS PRESS
NEW YORK

Reprinted from the edition of 1875, London
First AMS EDITION 1968
Manufactured in the United States of America

Reprinted from a copy in the Collections of the Harvard College Library.

Library of Congress Catalogue Card Number: 68-59008

AMS PRESS, INC.
New York, N.Y. 10003

TABLE OF CONTENTS OF VOL. I.

II. Poems written in 1769.

III. Poems written in 1770.

IV. Miscellaneous Poems, &c.

Page

POLITICAL AND OTHER LETTERS.

PREFACE.

HE present edition of Chatterton's Poetical Works is no mere reprint. A good deal of labour has been expended in endeavouring to improve the form in which they have hitherto been offered to the public. The first volume contains Chatterton's Acknowledged Poems, together with a selection from his prose works and letters, including all that are of general interest or which seemed worthy of being reprinted. At p. 362, a list is given, accounting for all the pieces not included in this selection, with references to the magazines, &c., in which they first appeared. At p. 375, amongst the Additional Notes, will be found a sufficient abstract of the contents of the Chatterton MSS. now preserved in the British Museum. The improvements effected in this volume are these, viz.: the arrangement of the poems, &c., in chronological order, as far as such order could be ascertained; the correction of several misprints by reference to the original sources made use of by Southey and Cottle, as far as was practicable; a complete revision of the punctuation, which in the editions of 1803 and 1842 is frequently so imperfect as to destroy the sense; and the addition of notes explaining where the various poems and pieces first appeared in print. The last of these improvements supplies the critical reader with references, such as will enable him in every case to ascertain the actual source of information, and to test at pleasure the correctness of the text. Such references are supplied but very scantily and vaguely in the edition of 1803, and in that of 1842 seem to have been frequently suppressed. A few notes have been added, and their number might have been largely increased, but it did not seem desirable to explain at length all the details referred to in the course of the Political Poems.

In the compilation of the Memoir prefixed to this volume, the principal authorities which have been consulted are Barrett's "History and Antiquities of the City of Bristol," Dean Milles's edition of the "Rowley Poems," Sir Herbert Croft's "Love and Madness," (ed. 1780,) and Dix's "Life of Chatterton," (ed. 1837,) especially the appendices in the last-named book; other authorities are also referred to in the footnotes. But, chiefly, the writer desires to acknowledge his obligations to Professor Wilson's "Biographical Study" of Chatterton, published in 1869; this excellent volume is the first attempt of any importance to combine the various materials relating to Chatterton's history into a complete and harmonious whole, and its author's careful and appreciative work has necessarily in a very great degree lightened that of any succeeding writer on the subject.

The second volume contains the so-called "Rowley Poems," together with several pieces in pseudo-antique spelling, which also had their whole and sole origin in Chatterton's fertile brain, although he unfortunately was at great pains to disavow the authorship of most of them. At p. 315, a list is given of all the pieces which have not been here reprinted. The Additional Notes at the end of the volume account for the original sources of all the poems, and give exact references to the pages in which they have been printed in the four editions of Tyrwhitt (1777), Milles (1782), Southey and Cottle (1803), and Willcox (1842). In the case of all the longer and more important poems, the very necessary method has been adopted of modernizing the spelling as far as possible, so as to render them at last, after the lapse of a century, accessible *for the first time* to the general public. The principles which have guided me in this attempt are explained in the Essay prefixed to the second volume, in which the question of the authorship of the Rowley Poems is reconsidered, and the whole matter carefully explained.

WALTER W. SKEAT.

Cambridge, July, 1871.

THE LIFE OF THOMAS CHATTERTON.

THE city of Bristol, in respect either to its antiquity, or to the historical distinction to which its annals bear witness, has few equals in the British Isles. And even in this nineteenth century, if the rapid growth of many other large towns has somewhat diminished its relative political importance, it continues to hold a high place amongst the great centres of commercial activity. At the same time it retains abundant traces of an early greatness: it is still rich in the traditions, and crowded with the visible memorials of bygone times; sufficient in themselves to establish for it a certain renovated importance, founded as it were on the ruins of that which has gone.

Of such a nature must be the importance which the old city acquires for all who yield to the never-failing interest attached to Chatterton's history; and such it had for Chatterton himself. The thread of his story as written in his works is interwoven with associations which carry the reader back from Bristol of his own day, to that of three centuries before, when England was divided in the civil wars of the Roses: sometimes to a period still more remote. All the past history of his native town had an interest for him; and to the result of its influence on his mind we owe the redeeming features in a picture, which in other respects has but few points of attraction.

At the south side of Bristol, connected with it by a bridge which spans the Avon where it flows past busy wharves and warehouses to join the broad waters of the Severn, is situated the suburb of Redcliff. The eminence from which it gained its name was once separated from the city by the walls which just skirted its northern declivity; but now, as in Chatterton's time, an unbroken street leads by a gentle and continuous ascent from the river banks to where the brow of the hill is nobly crowned by the church of St. Mary Redcliff.

This edifice, as remarkable for its size as for the elaborate beauty of its architectural detail, has justly gained a more than local fame. The slender shafts, the profusely embossed vaulting, the clear-story of unusual depth and lightness, the unique north porch, exhibit the grandeur of mediæval architecture in its more advanced stages of development; and with that most striking feature, "the noble ascent by a great many steps"[1] characterize

[1] Camden. By the alteration of the level of the street on the north side of the church, this feature has unfortunately been in a great measure destroyed. The plates in the "Essay on Redcliffe Church," by John Britton, F.S.A. shew the building as it existed in Chatterton's time; or be-

it, in spite of the deformity of the incomplete spire, as one of the finest parish churches in England.

With the history of the foundation, building and completion of St. Mary's, are associated the names of three munificent mayors of Bristol: Simon de Burton, Wm. Canynge the elder, and his grandson the second William Canynge: but it is the last alone who is popularly regarded as its founder. The name of this distinguished citizen is still famous in the municipal annals of Bristol; he was no less than five times mayor of the city which he was also chosen to represent in Parliament. Later in life, if tradition speaks truly, he took holy orders; and ultimately became Dean of the College of Westbury, where he died. Two effigies in St. Mary's Church, one in magisterial robes, the other in the priestly vestments, perpetuate his memory in either capacity. But the wider immortality of his name and history is due to the poet in whose fancy he seemed to stand out as a central figure; and in whose works all that is most worthy of remembrance owed its inspiration to the influence of the church whose foundation popular tradition, with perhaps only partial truth, has assigned to William Canynge.[1]

That the church should from the first have awakened an interest in Chatterton, is due to cir-

---

fore the restoration, which has now been going on for many years, was commenced.

[1] To what extent Redcliff Church was indebted to this family may be seen in Pryce's "Memorials of the Canynges' family," ch. VI. where the questions relating to its foundation and rebuilding are fully discussed.

cumstances not wholly accidental. "For time out of mind" as it was said, his family had been connected with it, though but in an insignificant capacity. There is evidence that for at least one hundred and twenty years, the office of sexton of St. Mary's had been held uninterruptedly and in a direct line by the Chatterton family. The last of the name who succeeded to this humble heritage was John, who died in 1748. The post then fell into the hands of his son-in-law Richard Phillips; for his son Thomas, the father of the poet, seems to have aspired to a higher position than that which had contented so many generations of his forefathers. This Thomas, after having filled the place of writing-master in a classical school, was appointed "Sub-chaunter" in Bristol Cathedral and obtained also the mastership of the Pile Street Free School, which was situated a few yards from Redcliff Church. He was a man of peculiar character, and intellectually above the station which he occupied. Fond of reading, and specially given to antiquarian studies, with considerable musical ability, and, it is said, "not totally destitute of a taste for poetry" he had apparently some foreshadowing of the versatile genius which was developed so much more highly in his extraordinary son. The pride which was so strongly marked a characteristic of the latter was also inherited: "All the family," says one who knew them,[1] "were proud." But not-

[1] Mrs. Edkins, who afterwards resided with Mrs. Chatterton, and whose valuable account of the poet's early years, given as an appendix to Dix's Life of Chatterton, will necessarily be frequently referred to.

withstanding the mental superiority of the elder Chatterton, his habits were dissipated; he was a frequenter of the tavern, an inconsiderate and unkind husband; and it can scarcely be supposed that his early death at the age of thirty-nine is to be regretted on account of the beneficial influence which he might have had on the character of his son.

By this event, which took place on the 7th August 1752, his widow, who was only twenty-one years of age, was left penniless with a daughter aged two, and her old mother-in-law, who also lived with them; and on the twentieth day of the following November, this family was increased by the birth of a son who on the first day of the next year was baptized in St. Mary's Church, by his father's name Thomas.

Mrs. Chatterton had hitherto remained at the small dwelling which was provided for the master at the back of Pile Street School, but she now removed to a house opposite to the Upper Gate on Redcliff Hill, and still very near to the church. Here she established a small dame's school, and also took in needlework, in which she was assisted by her friend, Mrs. Edkins, who resided with her, and who, from the birth of her son, entertained for him an affection scarcely less than his mother's.

Mrs. Chatterton appears to have been a woman of simple if not weak character, but though little more than a girl at the time of her bereavement, she met her troubles with the patience and courage which such natures sometimes shew in an unlooked-for manner. Though liable now and then to a sudden flash of temper, she was in general more than ordinarily kind and affectionate towards her children; and was but ill fitted for controlling the wayward spirit of the highly gifted being whom she had brought into the world.

To the eyes of his friends the early years of Chatterton were far from conveying any manifestation of unusual precocity; and such indications of the dawn of any extraordinary intellectual power as did appear, were completely misunderstood. He would sit alone for hours crying, or remain silent in a fit of abstraction, which was attributed to stupidity. He is described by his sister[1] as dull in learning, not knowing many letters at four years old. Waywardness, inability to acquire the merest rudiments of education, and a distaste for the ordinary amusements of children only aroused a fear that he was deficient in intellect.

At the age of five years he was placed at the school in Pile Street of which his father had been master, and which was then conducted by a Mr. Stephen Love. Here however he showed no improvement, and was soon remanded to his distressed mother as incapable of receiving instruction. "Many were the uneasinesses," says Mrs. Edkins,

[1] Afterwards Mrs. Newton; in whose letter to Sir Herbert Croft, who prosecuted a timely inquiry into the poet's life a few years after his death, many interesting particulars have been preserved. These were published in the strange and almost forgotten publication entitled "Love and Madness."

"that his singularities cost his mother, and until he was six years and a half old they thought he was an absolute fool."

But, on the other hand, we have, even as early as this a glimpse of what afterwards became the predominating impulse of his life. His sister recalls as a distinguishing characteristic of his childhood "a thirst for pre-eminence." "Before he was five years old," she says, "he would always preside over his playmates as their master, and they his hired servants." A trifling anecdote, resting on the same authority, shows at a not much later period, the same impulse in a still more recognizable form. A friendly manufacturer of earthenware had promised to present Mrs. Chatterton's children with two little bowls; and on the boy being asked what device he would like to have painted on his, he replied with precocious grandiloquence, "Paint me an angel with wings and a trumpet to trumpet my name over the world."[1]

Mrs. Edkins also tells us of his early ingenuity in mechanical matters, which, when very young, he would turn to account in the execution of various little domestic repairs. It is evident, therefore, that his friends formed but a hasty estimate of his childish capacity. Indifference or natural distaste to the ordinary routine of an infant's education, are not surprising in one whose short career at every state presents a psychological phenomenon; it is

---

[1] See the "Life," by Dr. Gregory, prefixed to Southey and Cottle's edition of Chatterton's works, p. vii. *note.* The same anecdote in a somewhat different form was published in the Public Advertizer, June 8, 1772.

not wonderful that listless dreaminess and fits of abstraction accompanied the development of a mind remarkable in the highest degree for the intensity and vividness of its imaginative power. But to the humble-minded guardians of his childhood, those "moody fits," as they called them, were suggestive of nothing but mental deficiency in comparison with other children of his age; and, as the failings of an only son, were all the more deeply mortifying to the poor widow.

But between the ages of six and seven, the tardy alteration suddenly took place. Mrs. Chatterton was one day tearing up for waste paper an old music folio, which had belonged to her husband, when the illuminated capitals with which it was ornamented took the boy's fancy. As his mother expressed it, "he fell in love with it," and by its means she had no difficulty in teaching him his letters. In less than due course the power of reading was also acquired by the help of a large blackletter bible; for with characteristic originality "he always objected" his sister says, "to read in a small book." His mental cultivation may now be said to have commenced, and henceforth its progress was rapid. No sooner could he read with facility than he devoured everything that came in his way; and his mother's fears for the soundness of his intellect were replaced by anxiety lest he should injure his health by too constant study. "At eight years of age he was so eager for books that he read from the moment he waked, which was early, until he went to bed, if they would let him."

When not absorbed in reading, or in a fit of abstraction, he showed himself an affectionate and attractive child, with a quick but shortlived temper. His appearance was pleasing; and his grey eyes, one of which it was noticed was brighter than the other, were remarkable for their brilliancy. The strong family affection which he evinced as a child, and which remained unimpaired throughout his life, goes far to rescue his character from some of the worst accusations, which too many prejudiced critics have not hesitated to advance. But the want of an appreciative friend and instructor, capable of sharing in his emotions, and sympathizing with his thoughts, tended to encourage habits of reserve and secresy to which he was by nature only too prone. When reproved for crying without any apparent reason, he would say, to avoid an explanation, that his sister had beaten him. He would fall into reveries from which he could scarcely be aroused; and then he would start and ask what they were talking about; sometimes, after such a mood, he would "snatch up a pen and write incessantly."[1] To avoid interruption and the disturbance which his mother's little school no doubt caused him, he soon appropriated a small attic lumber-room: here it was his delight to lock himself up with books and materials for drawing, for which he had a natural taste; and even at meal times it was difficult to persuade him to come down.

When Chatterton was about seven years and nine months old, an important change took place

[1] Dix's Life of Chatterton, App. p. 300.

in the course of his life. His mother obtained for him a nomination to Colston's Hospital, the Blue-coat School of Bristol, and on Aug. 3rd, 1760, he became one of its scholars. This institution was founded in 1708, by Edward Colston, a Bristol merchant, who, having partly by inheritance, and partly by successful trading, become possessed of an enormous fortune, devoted a large portion of it to the benefit of his native city in this and other charitable works. The building which he purchased for the school was situated in St. Augustine's Back, and occupied the site of a demolished monastery of the Friars Carmelite.[1]

The founder's rules provided for the clothing, maintenance, and religious education according to the principles of the Church of England of one hundred boys; and further enjoined that each in due course should be apprenticed in some respectable trade or calling. The routine was strict; throughout the year all were required to be in bed by eight o'clock, and absence from school was only permitted on the afternoons of Saturdays and Saints' days. The dress of the scholars was almost identical with that worn at Christ's Hospital, London, of which foundation Colston was a governor; the metal plate on the breast of each boy bearing the figure of a dolphin, the founder's crest. They were further distinguished by short-cropped hair, in perpetuation of the monkish tonsure.

It may well be imagined that this institution,

---

[1] The school has since been removed to Stapleton, a short distance from Bristol.

excellently adapted as it might be for the training of tradesmen and clerks, was deplorably inadequate to deal with such a mind as Chatterton's. The boy who had hitherto had unrestricted opportunities of indulging in fancies, or busying himself with studies which were already far removed from the occupation of ordinary children of his age, was likely to find the meagre curriculum and close restraint of a charity school almost insupportably irksome and unsatisfying. Though he had contemplated the prospect of going to school, and, as he thought, of gaining increased opportunities of acquiring knowledge with eager joy, experience of the bare reality speedily disenchanted him, and his dissatisfaction expressed itself in the not unreasonable complaint that "he could not learn so much at school as he could at home, for they had not books enough there." He grew gloomy and reserved, and made few friends at school. There however he was destined to remain for nearly seven years of his life, and it does not appear that he neglected the ordinary school work. By his tenth year the usher reported him as having made considerable progress in arithmetic, which was probably the only branch of the prescribed education in which he had by that time much to learn. At the same time he neglected no opportunity of increasing his knowledge in more congenial subjects. The small sum which his mother allowed him as pocket money enabled him to borrow books at a circulating library, which he would read in the hours when his schoolfellows were at play. And whenever Saturday afternoon or an occasional Saint's day brought round its welcome release from school boundaries, he would hurry home and spend the remainder of the day in reading or drawing. Sometimes he would write at the window-sill in his mother's little schoolroom, but more frequently he would retire to his attic study, and, locking himself in, remain till he was with difficulty induced to come downstairs to tea. His abstinence in matters of eating and drinking was remarkable; he would often go the whole day without food, and frequently refused to eat any animal food on the ground that it impaired the intellect. In the later years of his life, a tart and a glass of water often formed his dinner. But of tea he was always fond, and usually drank six or seven cups.

Amongst his early studies, antiquities, and especially the surroundings of mediæval life, were the favourite subjects; heraldry seems especially to have had a fascination for him. He supplied himself with charcoal, blacklead, ochre, and other colours; and with these it was his delight to delineate in rough and quaint figures, churches, castles, tombs of mailed warriors, heraldic emblazonments, and other like belongings of the old world, in which his imagination seemed to revel.[1]

It is not difficult to divine the sources in which such tastes had originated. From his earliest childhood he must have been familiar with the church of which his uncle, Richard Phillips, was

[1] Many rough drawings of this nature are preserved amongst the Chatterton MSS. in the British Museum.

sexton, and in whose shadow he had been born and lived. In the silent aisles and transepts of "that wonder of mansions," as he calls it, he, no doubt, began to realize, amongst the tombs of the long-departed Bristol worthies, that romance of mediæval life which has gained him a place amongst English poets. And to the same end there were other influences, which even at home were not absent; to trace these, however, we must go back to his father's lifetime.

Over the hexagonal porch which forms the principal entrance on the north side of St. Mary's Church there exists a small chamber commonly called the Muniment Room. Here there stood six or seven chests in which in past times had been deposited a large collection of parchments and parochial documents, dating probably from the completion of the building. To one of these, designated as Master Canynge's coffer, peculiar value was attached. It had been secured by six locks, the keys of which in process of time were lost; so that when (about seventeen years before Chatterton's birth) an examination of the church muniments was instituted by the Vestry this and the other chests were forcibly broken open.[1] Of the parchments which they contained all those which had reference to the church or were considered otherwise of value were removed to a place of security, while the remainder were left loose and became the prey of any one who liked to help himself. There were probably not a few depredators, one

[1] See Dr. Wilson's "Chatterton," p. 130.

of the least scrupulous being Chatterton's own father, who was in the habit of taking large quantities at a time, and applying them to covering school books and other common uses. He had helped himself so unsparingly that at the time of his death there still remained in the house a sufficient quantity to fill two boxes, which the widow took with her to her new abode. These continued to supply the household with thread-papers, dressmakers' patterns and other trifling requisites; and in this way it happened that old parchments and their antique caligraphy became familiar objects to the boy's sight. There is no distinct evidence as to the precise time at which he first learned to attach any particular value to these documents; but it appears that when he discovered in answer to his enquiries that they had come from the church, he resented the manner in which they were abused and destroyed, and whenever afterwards he found any parchment with writing upon it, he would seize and carry it off to his attic.[1]

To these circumstances may be traced the sentiment which seems to have predominated in Chatterton's mind, especially during the earlier and more thoughtful period of his life. With him a love for antiquity was innate, and, as we have seen, was manifested even at the first steps in his education. His associations with St. Mary's created in him an enthusiastic attachment, not only to the church itself, but for every person and object even remotely connected with its history, and it was

[1] See Dean Milles's Rowley Poems, p. 7.

under the influence of this sentiment that that remarkable literary fiction, the Rowley Romance, was first imagined.

This creation is embodied in a series of writings most of which are ascribed by their real author to the pen of one Thomas Rowley, a priest, who is stated by him to have lived in the fifteenth century. They are in both prose and verse, the latter consisting of dramatic, lyrical, and descriptive poems, in many cases of great beauty, and the former of letters, historical and architectural notices, and other miscellaneous writings, which though fragmentary and imperfect are sufficient to develope a connected and well conceived story.

Its central figure, as we have before said, is a real character, the opulent and benevolent William Canynge the younger, who as the foremost citizen of Bristol and the frequent occupant of its civic chair, ruled the city as prudently as might be in the troubled times of Henry VI. and Edward IV. But it is to his private rather than to his public life, to the traditional rather than to the historical character, that the story introduces us. In this wise Canynge appears endowed with all human excellencies:

> Noble as kings if not of kingly blood;

as the God-fearing merchant piously devoting a large portion of his fortune to the foundation of a church; or as the enlightened patron of art and literature, gathering round himself, Mæcenas-like, a few select and cultivated minds; or sometimes entertaining with princely hospitality, at his dwelling of the Red House, a larger circle of his fellow citizens.

Amongst his chosen associates appear Dr. Carpenter, Bishop of Worcester, Sir Thibbot (or Theobald) Gorges, a knight of ancient family residing on a neighbouring estate, and John a Iscam, a Canon of St. Augustine's Abbey in Bristol.[1] Of these the last is represented as a poet of some repute, while the other two, like Canynge himself, are not incapable of inditing on occasions an appropriate song or stanza. But the genius of the plot is Canynge's friend and father-confessor, the poet-priest, Thomas Rowley. He and his patron, it appears, had in boyish days been schoolfellows at the Priory of the Friars Carmelite; "here," says Rowley, in his "Lyfe of W. Canynge," "did begin the kindness of our lives; our minds and kinds were alike, and we were always together." The friendship thus begun was never interrupted; and in aftertime the poet, as parish priest of St. John's, still remained the confidential friend and adviser of the wealthy merchant.

After the death of his beloved wife Joanna, Canynge devoted himself to the patronage of literature, and to forming collections of MSS. and antiquities. In these pursuits, the services of his friend were in constant requisition; and when too any extraordinary occasion gave rise to festivities at the Red House, it was Rowley's poetical talent which supplied the fine dramatic interludes, in which their author with the host and his most

---

[1] See vol. ii. p. 275, *note*.

distinguished guests would each personate a character.

When Canynge had become well advanced in years, King Edward IV., who was already considerably indebted to him pecuniarily, sought to impose on him a second marriage with a lady of high family; whereupon Canynge, seeing no other means of avoiding this uncoveted distinction, took orders hastily and retired to the College of Westbury in Gloucestershire, where he remained for the rest of his life. In conjunction with Rowley he made considerable improvements in the buildings of this foundation, and ultimately became its Dean. Rowley concludes his account as follows, "hee deceased yn M.CCCC.LXX.IV. of the age of seaventy-two. Hys Worke I shalle ne blazon the Eyen wylle atteste yts Worthe—hys Mynde, knowledge & Lore hys hylten Epistles wyll Shewe, & the moe soe as hee dyd ne entende the same botte forre pryvate Syghte."

Such is the bare outline of the fictitious narrative which may be gathered from the various Rowley MSS., and which their author would have had the world believe, as it did in part, to be genuine. The letters, historical notices, and other matter in which the story is embodied, are written with a graphic simplicity which is itself attractive; the incidents are at first sight natural, and the circumstantial gravity with which they are related is occasionally relieved by touches of satire and broad humour.[1] But the very completeness and interest

[1] See vol. ii. pp. 25, 251, 272, 274, &c. An example from the prose MSS. will be found at p. 222; see also Dr. Wilson's biography of Chatterton, ch. viii. p. 154.

of the story, and the manner in which the various MSS., though professing often to be fragmentary, are made to confirm and supplement one another, might alone have sufficed to disprove their genuineness.

Rowley and his contemporaries were however only flitting as indistinct figures through his mind during the earlier years of his residence at Colston's Hospital: and the first verses which can be assigned to Chatterton's pen are in no way indicative of either the subject or the style of his finest works. The occasion to which they are referred is his confirmation, which took place at the commencement of the year 1763, when he was still only ten years old. The ceremony seems to have made for the time a deep impression on the boy, and the serious thoughts arising from it found expression in verse. During leisure hours at school, "the week he was door-keeper," says his sister, he wrote a paraphrase of the ninth chapter of Job and of several chapters in Isaiah. He composed also some lines "On the last Epiphany, or Christ coming to Judgment," which he apparently thought worthy of publication, for they were sent to the editor of Felix Farley's Bristol Journal, and appeared in that paper on January 8, 1763.[1]

From the date at which these compositions were produced, Chatterton's relations noticed a change in his manner, and in the habitual reserve and gloominess which had marked his demeanour since he went to Colston's Hospital. "He had been

[1] See vol. i p. 1.

gloomy," says Mrs. Newton, "from the time he began to learn, but we remarked he was more cheerful after he began to write poetry." About this time he received from his sister a pocket-book as a New Year's gift, which some time afterwards he returned to her filled with writing, chiefly verse. It is probable that it was from this same book that Sir Herbert Croft transcribed the short satire called "Apostate Will," which was long regarded as Chatterton's first attempt in verse. It is remarkable as proving an early and innate facility in this style of composition.[1] It is seldom that the quickness of temper, acuteness of observation, and readiness of expression, which are the distinguishing qualifications of a successful satirist are found in conjunction with that intensity of imaginative power which was the noblest quality in Chatterton's mind. It is to this comprehensiveness of his powers, the speedy versatility with which he would turn from the higher avocations to which his genius prompted him, to play the unscrupulous part of an eighteenth century satirist that so much misconception as to his works and hence to the real character of their author has been due.

The date appended to "Apostate Will" is April, 14, 1764, but some months before this he had made another appearance in the columns of Farley's Journal, as an anonymous satirist. It appears that one Joseph Thomas, churchwarden of St. Mary's Redcliff, had caused a beautiful stone cross, which had stood for centuries in the church-

---

[1] See vol. i. p. 7.

yard, to be removed as an obstruction, and had, at the same time, levelled the churchyard and obliterated the graves, applying the superfluous clay so obtained to the manufacture of bricks, which was his trade. In these acts of barbarism he only followed the example of the Dean and Chapter of the Cathedral, who, in the same year, had given their sanction to the removal of the ancient High Cross of the city, because it "interrupted gentlemen and ladies from walking eight or ten abreast"[1] on one of the walks of the College Green, where it then stood. Accordingly in December, 1763, and January of the following year, several satirical comments on this proceeding appeared in the Journal, one of which in verse was entitled "The Churchwarden and the Apparition; a Fable." Though these verses were never directly authenticated, there can be no doubt as to their author, when the opening lines are compared with those of "Sly Dick," another satirical fragment written by Chatterton about the same period.[2]

In the same paper in which the verses in Churchwarden Joe appeared, there was a humourous letter signed "Fullford the gravedigger," complaining of the disturbance which had been made in the churchyard, and the impossibility there was of recognizing the graves. The signature is interesting as being suggested, we may fairly suppose, by the surname of a Lancastrian knight who was executed at Bristol by Edward IV. In one of the prose

---

[1] Barrett's History of Bristol, p. 475.

[2] See vol. i. pp. 4 and 6.

Rowleian documents printed by Barrett (p. 44), "England's Glorye revyved in Maystre Canynge," Chatterton mentions "Syrre Charles Bawdwynne a Fulforde, commonlie cleped Baudynne Fullforde, his Bonde toe the Kynge Henrye to take the Erle of Warwyke's Life or lose hys hede, whych he dyd not perfourme, butte loste his heede to Kynge Edwarde;" which real historical incident is commemorated in "The Bristowe Tragedy, or the Dethe of Sir Charles Bawdin."[1] If the assumption as to the authorship of the letter is correct, and there is scarcely room to doubt it, it proves that Chatterton was already familiar with the subject of that spirited ballad, which in some respects is one of the best of the Rowley poems.

In these instances the objects of his satire were legitimate enough; it would have been well if its use had been limited to such fitting occasions. But though it was reserved for the latest period of Chatterton's Bristol life to exhibit the unbounded license which he would allow his pen, the juvenile poet was not long in learning to make it a weapon of offence in more strictly personal causes. It is said that one of the masters of the school, probably Mr. Warner, the headmaster, became the object of his attack, and that having one day discovered Chatterton finishing some such obnoxious composition" he corrected him severely for it." The punishment was probably neither forgotten nor forgiven, and the attacks were renewed after the pupil had become the apprentice of the attorney Lambert.

---

[1] See vol. ii. pp. 1—18.

Dr. Gregory[1] relates how "a very abusive anonymous letter" received by his old schoolmaster was traced to Chatterton by the paper on which it was written, and how Mr. Lambert on a complaint being made vented his irritation by the infliction of a few blows.

Hitherto, then, Chatterton's relations with Colston's Hospital do not appear in a satisfactory light. But notwithstanding the insufficiency of its training to his mental requirements, he owed to it one advantage. If he did not obtain learning he at least gained a friend. Amongst his schoolfellows he had not many intimate companions, though such few as he had were, his sister says, "solid lads." But in the year 1763, probably towards its close, Chatterton was first brought into contact with the usher of the school, Thomas Phillips by name, the possessor, apparently, of considerably more talent and natural refinement than is usually met with in persons of the same social position. Thistlethwaite, another of his pupils and, it would appear, one of the "solid lads" above referred to, describes him shortly as one who "notwithstanding the disadvantage of a very confined education possessed a taste for history and poetry."[2] The possibility of gaining other independent testimony to his character was unfortunately prevented by his premature death, but if we may accept as evidence the elegy by which Chatterton has perpetuated their friendship, after due allowance for partiality and

[1] In the Life prefixed to Southey and Cottle's edition of Chatterton's works, p. xix.

[2] See Dean Milles's Rowley Poems, p. 454.

extravagance or crudeness of expression, we may still infer that Thistlethwaite's meagre praise does him far less than justice.

That Phillips was accustomed to compose verses, which he sent to Felix Farley's and other Journals, is about all that we know of his literary efforts; what was their merit and how far they justified Chatterton's somewhat grandiloquent designation of their author as "great master of the boundless lyre" has not been ascertained. They had, at all events, a perceptible effect in exciting amongst his elder pupils similar tastes, which, further encouraged by a spirit of emulation, resulted in numerous contributions to the journals of the day, and, in after years, gained for some of these literary aspirants, such as Thistlethwaite and another named Fowler, some little local fame. It is not inconsistent with the natural pride of Chatterton's character and the consciousness of superior powers that he held aloof from these literary contests; but he was, we may believe, no less amenable to the beneficial influence of Phillip's friendship. Purity and earnestness of character, healthful frugality and moderation in habits, were among the characteristics of the latter, which produced an impression not easy to be effaced. His death took place in the autumn of 1769, probably after all constant intercourse between him and his pupil had ceased, and the elegy in which their friendship is commemorated was written at a time when far different interests and less harmless associations had already exercised a deteriorating influence on the mind of the poet.

The year 1764 is important as being that to which we must assign the first indication of the actual existence of any of the Rowley poems; and the promulgation of that fiction which has hitherto invested the renown of its author with an unworthy ambiguity. Since he first went to school his intellectual progress had been rapid; he had read with unflagging industry, employing for this purpose the hours allotted to play. Between the ages of eleven and twelve he gave his sister "a catalogue of books to the number of seventy" which he had read—works principally on history and divinity. Such eager acquisition of knowledge did not impede, but rather stimulated the rapid development of his creative powers; and we have evidence that before he was twelve years old he had produced one of the finest of his pseudo-antique poems. The statement rests on Thistlethwaite's authority, who had no motive either for dissembling the truth or speaking with a certainty which he did not feel. The following is his statement contained in the letter to Dean Milles before referred to.

Going down Horse Street, near the school, one day during the summer of 1764, I accidentally met with Chatterton. Entering into conversation with him, the subject of which I do not now recollect, he informed me that he was in possession of certain old MSS. which had been found deposited in a chest in Redcliffe Church, and that he had lent some or one of them to Phillips. Within a day or two after this I saw Phillips, and repeated to him the information I had received from Chatterton. Phillips produced a MS. on parchment or vellum, which I am confident was *Elenoure and Juga*, a kind of pastoral eclogue, afterwards published in the Town and Country Magazine for May, 1769. The parchment or vellum appeared to have been closely pared round the margin, for what purpose or by what accident I know not, but the words were evidently entire and unmutilated. As the writing was yellow and pale, manifestly (as I conceive) occasioned by age, and consequently difficult to decipher, Phillips had with his pen traced and gone over several of the lines (which as far as my recollection serves were written in the manner of prose, and without any regard to punctuation) and by that means laboured to attain the object of his pursuit, an investigation of their meaning. I endeavoured to assist him, but from an almost total ignorance of the characters, manners, language, and orthography of the age in which the lines were written, all our efforts were unprofitably exerted; and although we arrived at an explanation of, and connected many of the words, still the sense was notoriously deficient.

For my own part, having little or no taste for such studies, I repined not at the disappointment; Phillips on the contrary, was to all appearance mortified, indeed much more so than at that time I thought the object deserved; expressing his sorrow at his want of success, and repeatedly declaring his intention of resuming the attempt at a future period.

From this matter-of-fact statement we may infer that Chatterton, before he was twelve years old had already planned in outline the deception which he intended to practise on the public; and moreover that he regarded it as essential to his design to include his most intimate friends amongst his dupes. The degree of culpability herein incurred may be variously estimated. It can scarcely be denied that a system of concealment, though commenced with no guilty end in view, must gradually have produced a habit of deception, and tended more and more to blunt all moral feeling on this point. For Chatterton had no sooner matured the design of figuring behind a literary mask and putting forward his own compositions as mediæval relics which he had discovered, than he saw in each new acquaintance an additional opportunity of testing the probability of his success. But before branding the boy of twelve as simply an impostor and forger, it is at least just to consider whether a large portion of the blame should not be attached to those with whom he was brought into contact, and whose obstinate credulity made them almost voluntary victims.

Though reserved and slow to associate with his schoolfellows, he had no difficulty in making friends when it suited his purpose; even under circumstances which ordinarily would have forbidden success. Eager for knowledge, ambitious, and already partly conscious of his intellectual power, he naturally preferred the society of those who were superior to himself in age, education, and social position. But the mental calibre of Bristol's foremost citizens seems in few instances to have been great, and the observant boy was not long in gauging it. His later satires show for how few of these patrons he entertained feelings of unmixed respect.

One of the earliest of these was Henry Burgum, who with his partner George Catcott, carried on the business of pewterers in a house close by Bristol Bridge. He was a man of humble birth who had come to Bristol when a boy, and had by some natural ability and energy of character, attained a respectable position among his fellow citizens. But he still betrayed unmistakable signs of his original condition of life, which the very qualities that had assisted in raising him, only exhibited in higher relief. As is frequently the case, his chief aspirations were directed to the most unattainable ends; to be thought of good family and high mental culture were the principal objects of his ambition. With the latter in view he is said to have studied Latin, Greek, and music, and to have affected a general patronage of art and literature; though at the same time he was both coarse in manner and speech, and unable to speak the English language correctly. Nevertheless he was not without a certain rough generosity and kindness of disposition, which had effect in modifying even Chatterton's caustic satire.[1]

How the young charity-boy, now in his fifteenth year first made his acquaintance, is not known; but, probably on some Saturday in the spring of the year 1767, he called at the pewterer's establishment and announced to Mr. Burgum, that he had discovered amongst some old parchments belonging to Redcliff Church, an emblazonment of the coat-of-arms of the *de Bergham* family and had succeeded

[1] See Epistle to Rev. Mr. Catcott, vol. i. p. 73.

in tracing the descent of its present representative from one of the noblest of ancient English houses. The delighted tradesman was eager to see this proof of his real nobility, and accordingly in a few days he received a piece of parchment, on which was emblazoned the heraldic achievement in question. This was accompanied by a copybook in which were transcribed two pieces of poetry, (The Tournament and the Gouler's Requiem,) in sham-antique diction, and a pedigree entitled "Account of the family of the de Berghams, from the Norman conquest to this time, collected from original records, tournament rolls, and the Heralds of March and Garter's Records, by Thomas Chatterton."[1] This document traced the family from one Simon de Seyncte Lyze alias Senliz, Earl of Northampton, who had come over with the Conqueror, and terminated, for the present, with Sir Alan de Bergham Kt. who lived, it was said, in the middle of the thirteenth century. It was apparently verified by numerous marginal references to various authorities — Roll of Battle Abbey, Ashmole's Order of the Garter, Monasticon Anglicanum, Collins, Garter, March, Rouge Dragon, Original Charters, Rowley, etc. etc.—many of which were, it need not be said, in themselves quite apocryphal. One of the most noticeable names introduced was that of Radcliffe de Chatterton of Chatterton, a hypothetical ancestor, we may suppose, of the young herald himself; and which alone, had Burgum been less vain and credulous, might have aroused his suspicions.

---

[1] See vol. ii. p. 308.

But it was passed over unnoticed, and the gratified scion of this noble stock testified his delight by presenting the boy with five shillings. In a few days he was furnished with a "Continuation of the account of the family of the de Burghams," starting with the son of Sir Alan, one Sir John who was fond of tilting, and who is, by a suspicious coincidence, one of the characters in The Tournament, the poetical interlude inscribed in the first copybook. The pedigree was now brought down to the reign of James II. at which point it seems to have occurred to its young fabricator that it would be prudent to stop. As additional collateral evidence of its authenticity, to this portion was appended a few lines of ancient poetry, entitled "The Romaunte of the Cnyghte," said to have been composed about the year 1320, by John de Bergham, who is described as one of the greatest ornaments of the age in which he lived.

The whole account was accepted unsuspectingly by Mr. Burgum, and it was not until some little time afterwards when he submitted the document to the College of Heralds, to be ratified, that he learnt that the pedigree was entirely a fabrication, and that there never had been a de Bergham entitled to bear arms.

Such credulity as Burgum's may be pardoned in consideration of the ignorance from which it partly resulted, and the whole affair may be regarded as little else than a practical joke; but others of Chatterton's friends and patrons are less excusable because less ignorant. Such a one especially was Mr. William Barrett, a surgeon of considerable reputation in Bristol, and known as one of the most indefatigable antiquarians in the district. He was at this time engaged in preparing for the press a volume on the History and Antiquities of Bristol; and with the assistance of his friends, was busily searching for and obtaining possession of all the old deeds and records likely to aid his design. There is some obscurity about the precise time and circumstances of his making Chatterton's acquaintance, but the friendship was probably commenced by the latter, while still at school. Barrett's house was situated near Colston's Hospital, and would be passed by the boy as he made his way home on Saturday and saints' day half holidays. Attracted no doubt, by the surgeon's reputation for antiquarian learning, he would easily find some method of commending himself to his notice, possibly by the offer of communicating some parchment from the store which he had secured and preserved in his attic study. However commenced, the acquaintance grew rapidly, and led to relations not common between individuals so different in age and station. Barrett appears to have admired the boy's earnestness and conversational power, and as he himself told Sir Herbert Croft, "used often to send for him from the charity school, which is close to his house, and differ from him in opinion, on purpose to make him earnest and to see how wonderfully his eye would strike fire, kindle, and blaze up."[1] But Barrett's character was not such as to allow of the relations which were established between him and Chatterton being of any real ser-

[1] Love and Madness, p. 241.

vice to the latter. Jacob Bryant, a contemporary, and the most plausible of all the believers in the authenticity of the Rowley Poems, calls him[1] "a gentleman of consummate candour and goodness," but Barrett's own work, the volume on which he was at this time engaged, and which was not published till some twenty years afterwards, sufficiently justifies us in forming no very favourable estimate of his mental qualities. From this he appears as a cold and narrow-minded pedant, as self-sufficient and credulous as he was deficient in any faculty for appreciating the real genius of the boy with whom he was now brought into contact. Chatterton soon became aware of the nature of the mind with which he had to deal. At the time he left school (July 1, 1767,), the friendship was probably still new, but during the two years that their intimacy continued to increase, he did not hesitate to make the surgeon a dupe to his strange talent for fabrication.

It is by no means to be assumed that in his dealings with Barrett, he was actuated in the first instance by mercenary motives; nor was this a case like the transaction with Burgum, in which he made his favourite study and powers of invention a source of momentary amusement, and trifling pecuniary advantage to himself. His intercourse with Barrett was probably for long uncontaminated by any dishonourable designs. In the conversation, pursuits, and well-stocked library of the antiquarian, he no doubt found much to interest

[1] See Bryant's Observations on the Rowley Poems, p. 545.

him; while in the relics of the spoils of St. Mary's muniment room he possessed ready means of gratifying a patron to whom any old document was an invaluable gift.

It was an event soon to be narrated, the opening of the new bridge at Bristol, which probably first made him aware of the profitable use to which he might turn his own inventive faculties, and from this time it is to be feared that his conduct towards Barrett become less innocent. In other matters Chatterton cannot justly be accused of any unusual want of truthfulness; on the contrary his general habits and conduct ill accord with the character of an habitual liar; and his sister described him, apparently on good grounds, as "a lover of truth from the earliest dawn of reason."[1] But in purely literary matters this could scarcely be said; and whatever the cause, whether ignorance, want of thought, or the example of other literary men, in the wholesale production of pseudo-antique writings, he appears neither to have acknowledged nor felt any moral responsibility whatever. Accordingly he produced one after another numerous documents, purporting to be copies of parchments which had been preserved in the Muniment Room of St. Mary's Church, which Barrett accepted with the grossest credulity, and incorporated into his volume. They consisted mostly of prose works relating to the history, architectural remains, and antiquities of Bristol, supposed to have been compiled by the imaginary Rowley for his patron Canynge. But

[1] Love and Madness, p. 144.

in addition to these there were also two fine poetical compositions, "The Parliament of Sprites," and the two sections or rather versions of "The Battle of Hastings." Of the latter the first portion was produced as a fragment of a metrical translation by Rowley from a poem "wrote by Turgot the Monk, a Saxon in the tenth century," and on it the real author had inscribed the words "the remainder of the poem I have not been happy enough to meet with." Its incompleteness caused Barrett, apparently for the first time during the continuance of their dealings, to ask for the original MS. Chatterton, unable to evade his request, admitted that he had written it himself "for a friend," but that he also had the copy of another translation by Rowley. On Barrett's desiring to see this he after some time produced the greater part of the second poem, and in compliance with repeated inquiries for the remainder, he brought, again after some interval, the twenty concluding stanzas, all of which were received without suspicion.

This transaction is noteworthy, as shewing under what extenuating circumstances Chatterton persisted in a course of deception. There needs no plainer proof of Barrett's weak credulity, of his total want of appreciation of the extraordinary talent of the young poet than it affords. He repeatedly told Mr. Bryant that he considered Chatterton's powers "by no means shining;"[1] but putting aside the injustice of such an estimate, the fact that he should continue to regard a youth

[1] See Bryant's Observations, p. 560.

who could compose such a poem as the Battle of Hastings as a mere copyist, or that he should even fail to perceive that one capable of such a fabrication was also the probable author of much simpler compositions, is a manifestation of stupidity which transcends all similar displays, too frequent in the history of untried genius. No suspicion, however, seems to have crossed his mind till years afterwards, when as he drew to the conclusion of his work the question as to the authenticity of the Rowley poems began to be seriously agitated amongst the learned men of the period, and he felt so far unsure of his position as to leave "the judicious and candid reader to form his own opinion."[1]

It was seemingly Chatterton's fate to be constantly associated with men of less than ordinary judgment or mental capacity, and in the individuals with whom he next came into contact he was not more fortunate.

In tracing his connexion with Barrett we have gone somewhat beyond the course of events. On the first of July, 1767, the same day on which he left Colston's Hospital, he was apprenticed to Mr. John Lambert, an attorney. The fee of £10 was paid by the trustees of the school, in return for which his master undertook to teach him the trade of a scrivener, providing at the same time lodging, board, and clothing. He had chosen the occupation himself, and in any case the change in life to most charity boys would have been a welcome one.

---

[1] History of Bristol, p. 647.

Mr. Lambert's business was not extensive, and the apprentice was frequently left in sole charge of the office. All that was required of him when not engaged in more immediate work was to copy out legal precedents, a task which to a boy of idle disposition would have given unlimited opportunities for laziness. To Chatterton, who was never idle, it gave increased facilities for literary work, which he did not fail to turn to account.

But this new life soon grew irksome to him. His position in the house was less that of a clerk than of a servant; he was required to take his meals with the domestics and to sleep with the footboy, indignities to which, proud and ambitious as he was, he was not likely to grow reconciled.

Mr. Lambert's behaviour, too, was not conciliatory. He was a strict and irritable man, of little refinement, and incapable of discovering anything in his apprentice beyond an office drudge. He accused him, probably with much reason, of a "sullen and gloomy temper, which particularly displayed itself among the servants." He looked with a jealous eye on his literary labours, and if he on any occasion found him engaged on unprofessional work he would seize the paper and tear up what he angrily denominated his "stuff." Mrs. Edkins, who, however, was likely to be anything but impartial, described his conduct as brutal. But except on the single occasion on which he corrected Chatterton for sending an abusive letter to his former schoolmaster, he had no definite complaint to make against him. That the office work was not totally neglected is proved by the existence of three hundred and seventy closely written folio pages of precedents in Chatterton's neat handwriting. Mr. Lambert admitted that though the footman was frequently sent into the office to see whether Chatterton was there, he never found him absent from his post, and on no occasion but once, when he was known to be at his mother's house, did he stay out beyond ten o'clock, the hour at which he was expected to be within doors. His evenings were for the most part spent at home; "he was seldom," says Mrs. Newton, "two evenings together without seeing us." Other evenings were passed in the society of several young men, more or less of literary tastes, with whom he speedily made acquaintance. For this change in his circumstances brought him more in contact with city life, and gave him a greater choice of companionship. At Colston's Hospital besides the usher Phillips, he had made few friends, and the only schoolfellow with whom he appears to have been on intimate terms, was his bedfellow Baker. This lad had now emigrated to Charlestown, but still kept up some correspondence with Chatterton. The young poet was in fact of considerable service to his absent friend, in assisting him to prosecute a love affair with a certain Miss Eleanor Hoyland of Bristol, by composing short poems, sonnets, etc., which Baker transmitted to the young lady as his own.[1]

Chatterton himself did not remain altogether unsusceptible of the attractions of Bristol belles.

---

[1] See several short poems to Miss Hoyland, vol. i. pp. 13—20.

"Till his fifteenth year," his sister tells us "he was remarkably indifferent to females." "One day," she says, "he was remarking to me the tendency severe study had to sour the temper, and declared he had always seen all the sex with equal indifference, but those that nature made dear. He thought of making an acquaintance with a girl in the neighbourhood, supposing it might soften the austerity of temper study had occasioned." This girl was a Miss Rumsey; but the correspondence so commenced had not been carried on many months, when Chatterton heard that she was engaged to be married to his friend Fowler.[1] The injured vanity consequent on this discovery is discernible in the following letter to his friend Baker.

March 6th, 1768.

Dear Friend,

I must now close my poetical labours, my master being returned from London. You write in a very entertaining style; though I am afraid mine will be the contrary. Your celebrated Miss Rumsey is going to be married to Mr. Fowler, as he himself informs me. Pretty children! about to enter into the comfortable yoke of matrimony to be at their own liberty: just apropos to the old saw—but out of the frying-pan into the fire! For a lover, heavens mend him; but for a husband! O

---

[1] It seems doubtful whether this marriage ever came off. See "The Advice," vol. i. pp. 82-84, where Fowler is called *Pitholeon,* and the lady is advised to be sincere. In the letter dated May 14, 1770, p. 344, we still hear of "Miss Rumsey."

excellent! what a female Machiavel this Miss Rumsey is! . . . . . . O mirabili! what will human nature degenerate into. Fowler afore-said, declares he makes a scruple of conscience of being too free with Miss Rumsey before marriage. There's a gallant for you! why a girl with anything of the woman would despise him for it. But no more of him. I am glad you approve of the ladies in Charles-Town; and am obliged to you for the compliment of including me in your happiness; my friendship is as firm as the white rock when the black waves roar around it and the waters burst on its hoary top, when the driving wind ploughs the sable sea, and the rising waves aspire to the clouds, teeming with the rattling hail. So much for heroics. To speak in plain English; I am, and ever will be, your unalterable friend. I did not give your love to Miss Rumsey, having not yet seen her in private, and in public she will not speak to me, because of her great love to Fowler; and on another occasion. I have been violently in love these three-and-twenty times since your departure; and not a few times came off victorious. I am obliged to you for your curiosity, and esteem it very much, not on account of itself, but as coming from you. The poems, &c. on Miss *Hoyland*, I wish better, for her sake and yours. The TOURNAMENT I have only one canto of, which I send herewith; the remainder is entirely lost. I am with the greatest regret going to subscribe myself, Your faithful and constant Friend, 'till death do us part,

THOMAS CHATTERTON.

Mr. Baker, Charles-Town, South Carolina.

At the same time it is apparent that his sentiments towards women were not as yet of a nature to involve him in any serious attachment. He no doubt speedily made a large circle of respectable female friends, amongst whom we may infer from his London letters[1] he enjoyed considerable popularity. To many he addressed verses, but the affected style of all his acknowledged love poems plainly shews them to have been little more than complimentary attentions. His feelings were simply those of a precocious boy of fifteen, anxious to assume the position of a man; and though he evidently liked female society, sentiment was always subordinated to his own studies or the more congenial society of intelligent companions.

Amongst these was James Thistlethwaite. He had left school and been apprenticed two years before Chatterton, and their friendship was for a time broken off, but through an accidental meeting it was now renewed. Both were already in the habit of contributing verses to the public journals, and there was sufficient community of interest between them to establish what was, at least in Thistlethwaite's estimation, a close intimacy.

Lambert's office when he first received the Bluecoat boy as his apprentice, was in a house situate on St. John's steps, a locality which has since been considerably altered, but it was shortly afterwards removed to a building in Corn Street opposite to the Exchange. In the same house were several

---

[1] See vol. i. pp. 344, 345, 346, &c.

other apprentices, amongst whom Thomas Palmer an heraldic engraver, whose professional knowledge Chatterton probably found interesting and useful, was his chief friend. With these and two other acquaintances named Tipton and Capel, he frequently spent the evening in the office. Another friend was named Cary, who though a tradesman with a small business, was a man of some little literary ability.[1] He was probably older than the rest of his associates; whilst Smith,[2] Fowler, Capel, Tipton and others, whose names are mentioned in his letters or poems, were youths of about his own age. All these had literary tastes in common, and were probably as intellectual companions as Chatterton could find amongst his fellow townspeople.

His private studies about this period were most multifarious, and his avidity for reading on all subjects undiminished. Thistlethwaite would sometimes call at the office during the day-time and has described how he would find him engaged in studying by turns, heraldry, antiquities, metaphysics, mathematics, astronomy, music, and even medicine. In the latter subject he, indeed, asked Barrett to give him some instruction, but the

---

[1] Cary wrote an elegy on Chatterton's death, published in the Town and Country Magazine for October, 1770, p. 551.

[2] There were three brothers of this name mentioned in connexion with Chatterton, William, Peter, and Richard; the first was his principal friend. It is to him that the strange letter commencing "Infallible Doctor" (see vol. ii. p. xxxi.) is addressed; and the Elegy, p. 261 of this vol. was composed under the mistaken supposition of his death.

surgeon objected. A few years later he endeavoured as will be seen to turn what little medical knowledge he had acquired to some practical account.

He disliked however to be interrupted during the daytime, and there is no doubt that at this period of his life, during undisturbed office hours, he composed the greater number of the Rowley Poems.

The actual knowledge required for their composition was not so great as might be and has been supposed. Chatterton's memory was an extraordinary one, and it enabled him to make a very little study go a long way. The number of books he had read, wholly or in part, was no doubt enormous; and amongst them were Shakespeare, Pope, Dryden, Gray, and other poets of his own day; but his acquaintance with Chaucer and Spenser was evidently only superficial. The copy of Speght's Chaucer, which he is known to have borrowed from a bookseller, was chiefly useful on account of its Glossary.

For many books which would otherwise have been inaccessible, he was no doubt indebted to Mr. Barrett's library; amongst them are mentioned Skinner's Etymologicon Linguæ Anglicanæ, and Benson's Saxon Vocabulary. Of the latter, however, he appears to have made but superficial use.[1] The two books

[1] See Mr. Skeat's Essay on the Rowley Poems, in vol. ii. especially § 10. Chatterton's acquaintance with Latin was little less superficial than with Anglo-Saxon. The existence of various Latin quotations from obscure authors in the Rowley poems was made an argument in favour of their

which were most serviceable to him were Bailey's and Kersey's English Dictionaries, which gave a large number of old English words, though many of them were wrongly spelt. From these he compiled a counter glossary of modern words, followed by their supposed old English equivalents.[1] His method of working, as we may judge from several *unantiquated* pieces preserved amongst the MSS.,[2] was to write down the composition in modern English, and then by the aid of the glossary, to transmute it into the pseudo-antique dialect. The mechanical labour involved was no doubt very considerable, and from this point of view alone, the Rowley Poems are instances of extraordinary industry. The periods during which he was busy at some new piece seem to have been marked by unusual gloominess and reserve. Palmer describes him as sometimes for days together, going in and out of the house without speaking to anyone and seemingly absorbed in thought. After such occasions he frequently called some of his associates into his room, and read them some portions of Rowley.[3] For he made no mystery of the existence of the poems, though to none of his most intimate friends did he trust the true secret of their authorship.

---

authenticity, till Mr. Tyrwhitt discovered them in Cato's Distichs and Sentences of Publilius Syrus, which were sometimes used, in one volume, as an elementary school-book. See Tyrwhitt's "Vindication," in reply to Milles and Bryant, p. 208: quoted in vol. ii. p. 254, *note*.

[1] The MS. Glossary is twice mentioned by him in letters. See vol. i. pp. 343, 348.

[2] See vol. ii. pp. 296, 299.

[3] Dix's Life, p. 30.

It is remarkable that those who considered themselves mostly in his confidence, Thistlethwaite, Cary, and Smith, were the firmest disbelievers in his ability to compose such poems. Smith describes how he would read them to him: "'Come,' he would say, 'you and I will take a walk in the meadow. I have got the cleverest thing for you that ever was. It is worth half-a-crown merely to have a sight of it, and to hear me read it to you.'"[1] But Smith was convinced that he had no intention of claiming it as his own. At home, too, the name of Rowley was familiar, and his sister says that once when a relative named Stephens from Salisbury visited them the year after he left school, he talked of nothing else. There is no reason to suppose that if he had had one friend capable of fairly appreciating his own peculiar tastes and aspiration, he would have withheld his confidence. To his mother and sister he in fact acknowledged the authorship of the "Bristow Tragedy," and of the poem on "Our Lady's Church." His confession to Barrett of having written the Battle of Hastings, No. 1, "for a friend"—a very considerable admission—has already been noticed.

It was through a local event of some importance that the Bristol public in general was made familiar with Chatterton's story about the old parchments.

Seven years before, the old gothic bridge which had crossed the Avon since the days of Henry II., and whose roadway was crowded with buildings

[1] Bryant's Observations, p. 530.

overhanging the river, had been condemned as insufficient for the increasing traffic of the city, and the new one which supplanted it was now approaching completion. By the month of September, 1768, it was sufficiently advanced to allow of its being used by foot-passengers, and in the following November it was thrown open to general traffic. During this interval of two months the following letter appeared in the columns of Felix Farley's Bristol Journal.

MR. PRINTER,

The following Description of the Mayor's first passing over the Old Bridge, taken from an old manuscript, may not at this time be unacceptable to the generality of your readers,

Yours, &c.,
DUNELMUS BRISTOLIENSIS.[1]

It was accompanied by the description referred to, giving an account, in antique diction and orthography, of the procession and public rejoicings which had signalized the opening of the old bridge.

This remarkable communication naturally excited considerable interest and curiosity, and many inquiries were made as to who was its sender. The printer, however, could only state that it had been left at his office by a stranger. But before long Chatterton again called there, and, of course, did not escape examination in respect

[1] This letter is given as printed by Dr. Wilson from the journal in which it appeared. It slightly differs, as does the appended "Description," from the original MS. reprinted in this edition: see vol. ii. p. 279.

to the manner in which he had acquired the document. He gave an evasive answer, and, when threatened, a haughty refusal to account for its possession; but milder arguments at length elicited the statement that he was employed to transcribe the contents of certain ancient manuscripts by a gentleman, who also had engaged him to furnish complimentary verses, inscribed to a lady with whom that gentleman was in love. This was probably an extempore invention, suggested, we may suppose, by the engagement which he was under to his friend Baker, of Charlestown, to supply him with poems of that nature.[1] He further stated afterwards, that the description was transcribed from a parchment, which his father had taken from the muniment-room of St. Mary's Church. This explanation, strange as it may seem, was accepted without further question, and with less scrutiny than Chatterton himself had anticipated. In this matter he seems to have had a confidant; as appears by the following account.[2]

Mr. John Rudhall, a native and inhabitant of Bristol, and formerly apprentice to Mr. Francis Gresley, an apothecary in that city, was well acquainted with Chatterton, whilst he was apprentice to Mr. Lambert; during that time, Chatterton frequently called upon him at his master's house and soon after he had printed this account

---

[1] In the letter to Baker, March, 1768, he says, "The Tournament I have only one canto of, which I send herewith; the remainder is entirely lost." Cf. note 1, p. 332, of this volume.

[2] See Dean Milles's Rowley Poems, p. 436, *note*.

of the bridge in the Bristol paper, told Mr. Rudhall that he was the author of it, but it occurring to him afterwards that he might be called upon to produce the original, he brought to him one day a piece of parchment, about the size of a half-sheet of foolscap paper; Mr. Rudhall does not think that anything was written on it, when produced by Chatterton, but he saw him write several words, if not lines, in a character which Mr. Rudhall did not understand: which, he says, was totally unlike English, and, as he apprehended, was meant by Chatterton to imitate or represent the original, from which this account was printed. He cannot determine precisely, how much Chatterton wrote in this manner, but says, that the time he spent in that visit did not exceed three-quarters of an hour; the size of the parchment, however, (even supposing it to have been filled with writing), will in some measure ascertain the quantity which it contained. He says, also, that when Chatterton had written on the parchment, he held it over the candle, to give it the appearance of antiquity, *which changed the colour of the ink, and made the parchment appear black and a little contracted;* he never saw him make any similar attempt, nor was the parchment produced afterwards by Chatterton to him, or (as far as he knows) to any other person. . . . .

Mr. Rudhall had promised Chatterton not to reveal this secret, and he scrupulously kept his word till the year 1779; but, on the prospect of procuring a gratuity of ten pounds for Chatterton's mother, from a gentleman who came to Bristol in order to collect information concerning her son's history, he thought so material a benefit to the family would fully justify him for divulging a secret, by which no person now living could be a sufferer. It ought to be mentioned that Chatterton soon after broke off his acquaintance with Mr. Rudhall, improperly resenting by a challenge some good advice which Mr. Rudhall had given him, in a point very essential to his temporal and eternal happiness; and the propriety of that advice too soon appeared in the subsequent fate of that unhappy youth.

The credulity of the Bristol literati did not, however, require any corroborative testimony of the authenticity of the account, and the story of the discovered parchments gained general credence with the few who had any interest in such matters.

One of the most unquestioning believers was Mr. George Catcott, the partner of Henry Burgum, and whose acquaintance with Chatterton was probably due to this affair. He was a man of very different stamp from his partner; he was the son of a clergyman, and had some pretensions to education and what in the last century was considered refinement, but if his failings were less vulgar and common-place, his character was no more entitled to respect. An inordinate vanity and love of display, combined with a total insensibility to ridicule, allowed him constantly to exhibit himself in an absurd light. Of this propensity Chatterton has commemorated two especially ludicrous examples. More than a year before the new bridge was opened, it was sufficiently advanced to allow of its being crossed by the aid of some planks laid on the unfinished arches, and it occurred to Mr. Catcott that to be the first to perform the passage of the bridge would be a desirable honour. Accordingly on the 6th of June, 1767, after the payment of an extraordinary toll of five guineas, he was allowed to perform the feat on horseback. On a previous occasion he had signalized himself by ascending the unfinished spire of the Church of St. Nicholas, which had been rebuilt, and placing beneath its topmost stone a pewter plate engraved with a Latin inscription recording the circumstance.[1]

It was probably rather from vanity than from any more genuine motive that he affected a taste for literature, and especially for such as had a flavour of antiquity. He had a large collection of books, of which he is said to have boasted that none were less than a hundred years old. It is in this biblomaniac capacity that we are chiefly concerned with him, for it is owing to his indefatigable eagerness in securing the supposed transcripts of Rowley's poems that so much has been preserved that might otherwise have perished with their ill-fated author. Amongst these he received the masterpiece of the collection, the dramatic interlude of Ælla, another transcript of a portion of the Battle of Hastings, of which Barrett also possessed a copy, the fine ode entitled "Songe to Ælla, Lorde of the Castel of Bristowe ynne days of Yore," the spirited ballad on the "Dethe of Syr Charles Bawdin," and other smaller pieces. All these were produced, according to Catcott's own account, before Chatterton was sixteen years of age. What

---

[1] See vol. i. p. 187.

amount of remuneration he received for them we do not know; some were probably freely given. In any case, the poet cannot be accused of forming an exaggerated estimate of the value of his own compositions when he presented the following characteristic account.

Mr. G. Catcott to the Executors of T. Rowley, Dr.

	£	s.	d.
To pleasure recd. in readg. his Historic works.	5	5	0
" " " Poetic works.	5	5	0
	10	10	0

That hitherto he had been ill supplied with money, is scarcely to be doubted. It is not probable that he found Barrett a very liberal patron, and he apparently had difficulty in supplying himself with what to him were almost necessaries of life. One of Lambert's causes of complaint was that he made use of the office paper for his own compositions, and Miss Edkins states that she sometimes lent him money to buy some.

His dislike for his master and for his profession was not lessened by his introduction to Catcott, and the clearer prospect of literary success. "He would often," says Mrs. Newton,[1] "speak in great raptures of the undoubted success of his plan for future life .... His ambition increased daily. His spirits were rather uneven, sometimes so gloomed that for many days together he would say very little and that by constraint; at other times exceeding cheerful. When in spirits he would enjoy his rising fame; confident of advancement, he

[1] Love and Madness, p. 145.

would promise my mother and me should be partakers of his success."

And as his aims grew more definite, his present occupation became more unbearable; the chain which bound him to office life was one which lengthened at every step, and a year and a half of his apprenticeship had not elapsed before he made his first effort to gain a decided footing in the literary world. He had already entered into correspondence with the editor of a London Magazine. The first evidence of this fact is to be found in the November number of the Town and Country Magazine for 1769, where one of the notices to correspondents is the following: "D. B. of Bristol's favour will be gladly received." Under this signature (the initials of his pseudonym Dunelmus Bristoliensis, there soon appeared contributions on heraldry, imitations of Ossian, and other papers. He now determined to make an attempt to introduce Rowley to the world. Accordingly, on Dec. 21, 1768, he addressed a letter to Dodsley the publisher in Pall Mall, which ran as follows:—

Sir,—I take this Method to acquaint you, that I can so procure Copys of several Ancient Poems; and an Interlude, perhaps the oldest dramatic Piece extant; wrote by one Rowley, a Priest in Bristol, who lived in the Reigns of Hennry 6th and Edward 4th.—If these Pieces will be of any Service to you, at your Command Copys shall be sent to you by

Y^r^ most obedient Servt,

D. B.

Please to direct for D. B. to be left with Mr. Thos. Chatterton, Redclift Hill, Bristol.

The publisher, it is supposed, did not answer this letter, and in two months Chatterton made another attempt, writing this time in his own name. He stated in exaggerated terms that after some trouble he had discovered the tragedy of Ælla, of the existence of which he had heard, but that its present possessor declined to allow him to copy it except on receiving a guinea, which sum Chatterton requested the publisher to advance.[1] In a postscript he added :—

My reason for concealing my name was lest my master (who is now out of town) should see my letters, and think I neglected his business.

Then, after an extract from the poem as a specimen, he concludes :—

The whole contains about 1000 lines. If it should not suit you I should be obliged to you if you would calculate the expense of printing it, as I will endeavour to publish it by subscription on my own account.

The simplicity and want of knowledge of the world shewn in these letters seem surprizing in one whose intellectual prematurity was so remarkable; and the publisher probably thought that his correspondent, who in the character of an unknown apprentice whose master was out of town requested the advance of a guinea, was insane. And indeed it is scarcely conceivable that Chatterton should have made such a request, unless it were directly necessary to his object. Mr. Catcott, by his own account, had already received the MS. of Ælla, for which it is

[1] See the letter, vol. ii. p. 20.

possible that he gave the supposed transcriber this sum; and for which Chatterton, if Dodsley had exhibited any desire to come to terms, would have endeavoured to reclaim it. But the specimen sent does not seem to have impressed the publisher with the merits of the work, sufficiently to induce him even to answer his correspondent; and the disappointed author was left to devise some other means for accomplishing his plan.

About three years previously the "Castle of Otranto" had been published, and had no doubt been read by Chatterton, for whom it would possess an additional interest as purporting to be translated from a mediæval Italian MS. When, after considerable success, a second edition was called for, Horace Walpole, its real author, declared himself. The mere fact of his having successfully carried out a scheme similar to that which had long formed the most cherished object of Chatterton's ambition was sufficient to turn the young poet's thoughts to him: while the high if undeserved reputation which he enjoyed in the domains of art and literature seemed to point to him as a modern representative of the ideal Canynge, and to augur for the pseudo-Rowley as powerful and appreciative a patronage as he could dare to hope for.

But the method which he adopted in order to bring himself under the great man's notice was not less clumsy and self-destructive than his attempt to open negotiations with Dodsley. He carefully prepared a document supposed to be transcribed from an original MS. entitled "The Ryse of Peyncteyne yn Englande, wroten by T.

Rowleie, 1469, for Mastre Canynge." This was of course a leaf from the Rowley Romance, devised specially to appeal to Walpole's tastes, just as his earlier ventures had been adapted for Burgum's or Barrett's.

It was accompanied by this letter :—

Sir,—Being versed a little in antiquitys, I have met with several curious manuscripts, among which the following may be of service to you in any future edition of your truly entertaining "Anecdotes of Painting." In correcting the mistakes (if any) in the Notes you will greatly oblige

Your most humble servant,
THOMAS CHATTERTON.

Bristol, March 25th, Corn Street.

The notes referred to are explanations of the allusions or phraseology, and the first note, which in fact contained the gist of the whole missive, ran as follows:—"T. Rowlie was a secular priest of St. John's in this city; his merit as a biographer, historiographer is great, as a poet still greater: some of his pieces would do honour to Pope; and the person under whose patronage they may appear to the world will lay the Englishman, the antiquary, and the poet, under an eternal obligation."

In another note was given as a specimen of poetry the little ode beginning "Harte of Lyone shake thie sworde," ascribed to "John second abbot of St. Augustine's," and the last contained an offer of other similar MSS.[1]

---

[1] See vol. ii. pp. 282-287.

This letter did not fail to produce the desired impression upon its recipient, who at first, at any rate, accepted its statements without question. He replied as follows[1]:—

Arlington Street, March 28, 1769.

Sir,—I cannot but think myself singularly obliged by a gentleman with whom I have not the pleasure of being acquainted, when I read your very curious and kind letter, which I have this minute received. I give you a thousand thanks for it, and for the very obliging offer you make me, of communicating your MSS. to me. What you have already sent me is very valuable, and full of information; but, instead of correcting you, Sir, you are far more able to correct me. I have not the happiness of understanding the Saxon language, and, without your learned notes should not have been able to comprehend Rowley's text.

As a second edition of my Anecdotes was published last year, I must not flatter myself that a third will be wanted soon; but I shall be happy to lay up any notices you will be so good as to extract for me, and send me at your leisure; for, as it is uncertain when I may use them, I would by no means borrow and detain your MSS.

Give me leave to ask you where Rowley's poems are to be found? I should not be sorry to print them; or at least, a specimen of them, if they have never been printed.

The Abbot John's verses that you have given me, are wonderful for their harmony and spirit, though there are some words I do not understand.

You do not point out exactly the time when he

[1] See Letters of Horace Walpole, edited by P. Cunningham, vol. v. p. 152.

lived, which I wish to know, as I suppose it was long before John Ab Eyck's discovery of oil-painting. If so, it confirms what I had guessed, and have hinted in my Anecdotes, that oil-painting was known here much earlier than that discovery or revival.

I will not trouble you with more questions now, Sir, but flatter myself from the humanity and politeness you have already shown me, that you will sometimes give me leave to consult you. I hope too, you will forgive the simplicity of my direction, as you have favoured me with none other.

I am, Sir, your much obliged
and obedient humble servant,
HOR. WALPOLE.

P.S.—Be so good as to direct to Mr. Walpole, Arlington-street.

Chatterton lost no time in replying. His second letter is dated March 30, the day on which he received the answer to his first. Only the concluding portion is preserved, a piece at the beginning having been carefully torn off.[1] Its contents, however, may be inferred from the account of the transaction which Walpole afterwards published.[2] The affable manner in which his first letter had been answered probably induced Chatterton to be more unreserved as to his real position. He "informed me," says Walpole, "that he was the son of a poor widow, who supported him with great difficulty; that he was clerk or apprentice to an attorney, but

[1] See vol. ii. p. 346.

[2] See Dix's Life of Chatterton, p. 135, *et seq*. This vindication was also published in the Gentleman's Magazine, vol. lii. pp. 189, 247, 300, 347.

had a taste and turn for more elegant studies; and hinted a wish that I would assist him with my interest in emerging out of so dull a profession by procuring him some place in which he could pursue his natural bent." Appended to Chatterton's letter was another MS. entitled "Historie of Peyncters yn Englande, bie T. Rowley."[1] It was of a similar nature to the former composition, and made mention of several unknown poets, with a few specimens of their work. In a postscript he replied to Walpole's question as to the date of Abbot John, and announced his intention of copying out Rowley's works and sending them; while a second specimen, the ode entitled "War," was enclosed.[2]

Whatever may have been the real contents of the letter, they were such as to arouse some suspicion on Walpole's part, and the specimens were sent to his friends Gray the poet, and Mason, who at once pronounced them to be modern fabrications. He thereupon wrote a letter of advice to Chatterton, recommending him to give his attention to his profession, and telling him that "when he should have made a fortune, he might unbend himself with the studies consonant to his inclinations." Chatterton, in reply, curtly reiterated his confidence in the authenticity of Rowley's poems, but concluded—"Though I am but sixteen years of age, I have lived long enough to see that poverty attends literature. I am obliged to you, sir, for your advice, and will go a little beyond it by destroying all my useless

---

[1] See vol. ii. pp. 288-292.
[2] See vol. ii. p. 266.

lumber of literature, and never using my pen again but in the law."

There is reason to believe that Barrett was consulted by his protégé in these proceedings. In the British Museum there are two drafts of a letter from the latter to Walpole, one of which is in the surgeon's handwriting, but both endorsed, apparently by Chatterton, "never sent." In place of either of these, the following was despatched,[1] no answer having been received to the last one:—

Sir,—Being fully convinced of the papers of Rowley being genuine, I should be obliged to you to return me the copy I sent you, having no other. Mr. Barrett, an able antiquary, who is now writing the history of Bristol, has desired it of me; and I should be sorry to deprive him, or the world indeed, of a valuable curiosity which I know to be an authentic piece of antiquity.

Your very humble servant,
THOMAS CHATTERTON.

P. S. If you wish to publish them yourself, they are at your service.

On the receipt of this, Walpole, by his own account, was about to set out for Paris, and either forgot to return the MSS. or detained them purposely in order to have them copied. He remained away some time, probably forgetting all about

---

[1] This is also in the British Museum. It is a condensed copy of the two drafts, which are longer and less curtly expressed, though the same in general effect. We may infer that it is Chatterton's final copy of a letter concocted by himself and Barrett jointly.

Chatterton; but after his return he received the following very justifiable, but in his opinion "singularly impertinent" letter.

Sir,—I cannot reconcile your behaviour to me with the notions I once entertained of you. I think myself injured, Sir; and did not you know my circumstances, you would not dare to treat me thus. I have sent twice for a copy of the MS.—no answer from you. An explanation or excuse for your silence would oblige.

THOMAS CHATTERTON.

July 24th.

"This," says Walpole, "I flung into the fire, and snapping up both his poems and letters without taking a copy of either, for which I am now sorry, I returned all to him, and thought no more of him or them."

So ended Chatterton's second attempt to make his poems known to the public; and for its abrupt failure and for the evil influence which it undoubtedly exercised on the remainder of the boy's life, Walpole did not fail to receive more than a full measure of blame.

That he should be charged with the catastrophe which ultimately occurred, because he might by different conduct have arrested it; or that he should be stigmatized as inhumane because he was not exceptionally charitable is, however, obviously unjust. Walpole's most prominent characteristic was what his admirers call an "exquisite sensibility of taste," but which, in plainer terms, amounted to selfish fastidiousness in trifling matters.

His conduct was regulated by a reference to the opinion of the world, or of that limited portion of the world constituted by the society in and for which he lived. That he would risk his reputation by any flagrant act of inhumanity was as unlikely as that he should trouble himself by any act of unselfish generosity.

If his exquisite taste had enabled him to discern Chatterton's genius, if in assisting him he could have hoped to add to his own fame, he would, no doubt, have done it; but his previous blunder in the case of the author of Ossian had made him suspicious of all literary adventurers. A more noble-minded man might have felt excusable anger at the impudence of the attempted and partly successful deception; but if he could have overlooked this, as Walpole at first professed to do, his sympathy would have extended to something more than cold advice followed by neglect. Walpole was not capable of this. He says, in his defence, "Though I was far from treating him either with contempt or neglect, he did not seem totally unworthy of both, as I could consider him under no aspect but that of a youth who endeavoured to impose upon me." At the same time the condemning fact must not be ignored that to save himself from the charge of credulity, of which his first answer to Chatterton convicts him, he did not hesitate to deny explicitly on several occasions having received a letter which he undoubtedly did receive.[1]

---

[1] See two letters to Hannah More, and one to the Countess of Ossory, (Letters of Horace Walpole, edited by P. Cunningham, vol. ix. pp. 221, 231, 380,) in which he denies

Such was the unsatisfactory termination of a venture on which Chatterton had probably entered with much confidence; and though his pride forbade any outward expression of mortification, there can be little doubt that the course of future events was greatly influenced by the baleful effect of disappointment on his mind. In a letter to a relative, Mr. Stephens of Salisbury,[1] he refers to the correspondence with Walpole as to an unimportant literary dispute on the age of a MS., and anticipates that they may "publicly engage" in the columns of some periodical. But though this expectation was not verified, numerous satirical and bitter allusions to Walpole in his future writings show that he neither forgot nor forgave the cool indifference with which he had been treated.[2]

Chatterton, as we have seen, possessed all the qualities for a successful satirist; and he did not hesitate to give them full scope. He even allowed his powers to carry him further than his own judgment in calmer moments approved; so that not only public characters, but also those who, but for this, were willing enough to be his friends, found their

having received Chatterton's first two letters. Also in Gent. Mag. vol. lxii. pt. i. p. 398, Dr. Farmer, Master of Emm. Coll. Cambridge, writes that his friend Mr. Steevens gave him the following information: "Mr. Walpole has authorized his friends to declare that he never saw those letters from Chatterton, which Mr. Barrett has printed, till they appeared in the new History of Bristol. Mr. W. also expresses his apprehensions that, after his death, some pretended answers to them will be produced." Apprehensions well grounded, seeing that his own answer to one at least was in existence.

[1] See vol. i. p. 332. [2] See vol. i. p. 32.

failings mercilessly exposed to the ridicule of the youth's rather large circle of acquaintance.

Conspicuous amongst such victims is the Reverend Alexander Catcott, who by his brother's means had become acquainted with Chatterton during the preceding year (1768), in the course of which the reverend gentleman had entered on the living attached to the Temple Church, situate at no great distance from St. Mary's Redcliff.

He was a man of higher attainments than his brother, and had the reputation of being one of the best Hebrew scholars of his day.[1] But his chief interest lay in theological and scientific speculation, and at this period he was at work on a second edition of his "Treatise on the Deluge and Structure of the Earth," which he had published some years before. In him Chatterton probably found the most highly cultured man whom he had yet met, while the vicar was no less susceptible than others to the attractions of the boy's bright intellect and eager thirst for knowledge. The acquaintance in consequence rapidly ripened, and Chatterton was soon a frequent visitor at his new friend's house, where a well-stocked library and a valuable geological collection would doubtless have the greatest interest for him. To Mr. Catcott he was also indebted for an introduction to the Bristol Library.

But in the relations between the two there was no foundation for any permanent friendship. The vicar was prejudiced and narrow-minded; he professed to despise poetry, and was, in fact, indifferent

---

[1] See Dr. Wilson's "Chatterton," p. 192.

to all literature which did not bear upon his favourite subjects of speculation. Chatterton, acute and self-confident, was not likely to show deference to one whom he found to be naturally his inferior. As soon as Catcott's theories had lost the interest of novelty, he began to criticize them, to oppose dogmatism with rationalistic arguments, and finally to ridicule the philosopher. How regardless he was of all restraint in expression, or of respect for his social superiors, is shewn in his "Epistle to the Reverend Mr. Catcott," dated Dec. 6, 1769; and in the "Exhibition," written early in the following year, he speaks of him with still more licence.[1] Some allowance must undoubtedly be made for the prevalent style in literature, and the debased taste of an age in which Churchill was the popular satirist; and that Chatterton was sensible of allowing his pen too great licence, is evident from a postscript to the Epistle, dated Dec. 20, 1769, in which he attempts to modify the opinions he had expressed. He wrote, "Mr. Catcott will be pleased to observe that I admire many things in his learned remarks. This poem is an innocent effort of poetical vengeance, as Mr. Catcott has done me the honour to criticize my trifles. I have taken great poetical liberties, and what I dislike in verse probably deserves my approbation in the plain prose of truth." Postscript as well as Epistle were no doubt sent to the vicar, but the former had naturally no effect in moderating his rather justifiable wrath, and the acquaintance was brought to an abrupt conclusion.[2]

---

[1] See vol. i. p. 131. [2] See vol. i. pp. 66-75.

Amongst others satirized in the same effusion George Catcott came in for no little ridicule; but he was less sensitive than his brother, and appears to have considered himself rather flattered than otherwise. There is, or was, a copy of the poem extant with elaborate notes in his handwriting, complacently explaining the allusions to his own foolish exploits.[1] Some of the victims of Chatterton's satire, however, did not always allow him to escape with impunity. Mrs. Edkins relates how "going one evening after dark over the Drawbridge (across the Froom, a tributary of the Avon) he was knocked down" and beaten by some one, who threatened, with an oath, "to spoil his writing arm."[2]

It was not possible that during the past two years the connexion between Lambert and his apprentice should have become less irksome to the latter. Though the attorney had as few occasions as possible for justly finding fault, he was well aware that much time was spent in work not connected with the office; and whenever any traces of such unprofessional labour fell into his hands, he ruthlessly destroyed them. And Chatterton, though he knew that few situations would have given him better opportunities for pursuing his own tastes, was perpetually galled by Lambert's harsh treatment; through which, says Mrs. Edkins, he got to hate the profession, though he had before liked it, and had in fact chosen it himself. The thought that he was not his own master, but tied to an occupation which was distasteful and a ser-

---

[1] See Dix's Life of Chatterton, p. 57.
[2] See Dix's App. p. 316.

vitude which was degrading to him, was almost insupportable; and at home he avowed his intention of running away if he should not be dismissed.

It was probably the result of this position of affairs that about the end of the year 1769 he definitely formed the idea of leaving Bristol and trying his fortune as a writer in London, a scheme in which he considered that he had good hopes of success. For a year past Felix Farley's Journal, to which it had been his custom to send his smaller compositions, had been discarded; and he had established himself as a constant contributor to one of the most popular London periodicals, Hamilton's "Town and Country Magazine."

Amongst the contributions were "Ethelgar," "Kenrick," and other similar papers on Saxon heroes, obviously written in imitation of Ossian. There were also notes in Saxon heraldry, and in the number for May, 1769, the fine eclogue "Elinoure and Juga," which as we have seen was probably the first of the Rowley poems. Altogether during this year he contributed sixteen pieces to the same periodical all of purely literary interest. But now other interests had begun to engross his attention and give employment to his ready pen.

Towards the end of that year the state of public affairs in the metropolis was becoming somewhat serious. Popular feeling had been strongly aroused in opposition to the Earl of Bute, the favourite of George III., who had then been nine years on the throne. Severe press prosecutions had taken place on account of the publication of seditious matter; the demagogue Wilkes had been expelled the House of Commons, fined and imprisoned, and the term of his imprisonment was drawing to a close. The political ferment had no doubt infected the youths of Bristol and other large provincial towns, and Chatterton with his usual confidence was ready to rival Churchill as the popular political satirist. It was just at this period that the mysterious Junius was publishing his bold attacks on the government, and in the December number of the Public Advertizer appeared his famous "Address to the King." This Chatterton doubtless saw and admired; with his usual aptitude he imitated it, and in due course there appeared in the *Middlesex Journal* a letter signed "Decimus" in a style obviously copied from that of Junius, "To the Duke of Grafton on his resignation," an event which happened on Jan. 28, 1770.[1] This was followed by still higher flights, and for the time political writing completely occupied him. The satires Resignation, Kew Gardens, The Whore of Babylon, The Exhibition, of which the last three have many lines in common, all belong to this exciting period.

It is plain then, that by the early part of the year 1770, he had established tolerably intimate relations with more than one of the representatives of the London press; and as Thistlethwaite says, in his letter to Dean Milles, "The printers, finding him of advantage in their publications, were by no means sparing of their praises and compliments; adding thereto the most liberal promises of assistance and employment, should he choose to make London the place of his residence."

[1] See Political Letters, vol. i. p. 285, *et seq.*

To his following their advice the only obstacle were the indentures which bound him to Lambert. His object was therefore to induce the attorney to release him, and it was doubtless with this end in view that he gave way without restraint to fits of sullen humour amongst the servants, and even hinted at self-destruction.

In dealing with a mind so complex as Chatterton's, it is difficult to say how far his conduct was dictated by genuine impulse, and how far by the desire of producing an effect on others. The idea of suicide would naturally lose its horror when the old landmarks of religious faith were obliterated; and on Chatterton and many of his associates the sceptical tendency of the last century had already produced its effect. The poems written about this period plainly shew a freedom of opinion on religious questions which the dogmatism of the Temple vicar was calculated rather to increase than modify.

We may infer from a passage in the "Epistle" that this rationalizing spirit received further encouragement from a friendship which he made probably in the autumn of 1769; that of Mr. Michael Clayfield, a distiller.[1] He was apparently in good circumstances, and Chatterton was indebted to him both pecuniarily and for the loan of books. According to Mrs. Newton, her brother borrowed from him several books on astronomy; of his studies on which subject, we may suppose that the poem on the Copernican

---

[1] See vol. i. p. 71, lines 12-15.

system, written a few days after the Epistle to Mr. Catcott, was the result.[1]

He seems to have brought himself under Clayfield's notice by addressing to him his Elegy on the death of Thomas Phillips, which occurred about this time; for there still exists a MS. copy of the lines to Mr. Clayfield,[2] and on the same paper a part of the Elegy; the whole being evidently an unfinished draught of the copy really sent. However he made his acquaintance, he found in him a kind friend, and it is noticeable that in that strange composition which Chatterton called his "Last Will and Testament," Clayfield is the only friend he mentions with unreserved goodwill. Amongst satirical bequests to Catcott, Burgum, and other Bristol notables, he leaves to Mr. Clayfield 'the sincerest thanks his gratitude can give.'

Whatever influence this friendship may be supposed to have had on his religious opinions, for the future his creed became professedly that of the deist. In the British Museum there is a curious document[3] in Chatterton's handwriting which, with the title written on the back, runs as follows:—

The Articles of the Belief of me, Thomas Chatterton.

That God being incomprehensible: it is not re-

---

[1] See vol. i. p. 77 and *note*. Bryant says that the only books he borrowed were Martin's Philosophical Grammar, and one vol. of Martin's Philosophy. See Bryant's "Observations," &c. p. 533.

[2] See vol. i. p. 57 and *note*.

[3] It is written on a fragment of paper about eight inches square, much soiled and worn, apparently from having been long carried in the pocket.

quired of us to know the mysterys of the Trinity, &c., &c., &c., &c.

That it matters not whether a Man is a Pagan, Turk, Jew, or Christian, if he acts according to the Religion he professes.

That if a man leads a good moral Life, he is a Christian.

That the Stage is the best School of Morality: and

That The Church of Rome (some Tricks of Priest-craft excepted) is certainly the true Church.

T. CHATTERTON.

Such a confession of faith is by no means incompatible with a serious intention of terminating his difficulties by self-destruction. The idea at any rate was familiar to him. It is related, that one evening as he was sitting with a party of friends the conversation turned upon suicide, as to whether it implied bravery or cowardice. Chatterton, it is said, suddenly drew from his breast a pocket pistol and holding it to his head exclaimed: "Now! if one had but the courage to pull the trigger." The anecdote is not authenticated,[1] and it is not probable that he was in the habit of carrying firearms about. But it possibly has some foundation, and his tragic fate a few months later at least proves that such menaces may not have been absolutely without meaning. The few lines on Suicide[2] were probably written about this period.

But whatever may have been the amount of

[1] It is given in the Memoir prefixed to the Cambridge edition of Chatterton's works, 1842, but without authority.

[2] Vol. i. p. 82.

underlying seriousness, his present object was manifestly to impress his master with the necessity of dismissing him. Old Mrs. Lambert, who lived with her son, was terrified at the reports which reached her; but the attorney himself seems to have paid little attention to them, till one day he found amongst his apprentice's papers a letter to Mr. Clayfield, thanking him for his past kindness and telling him that on its receipt the writer "should be no more." Lambert immediately sent the letter to Barrett, who summoned Chatterton to him and, "questioned him closely upon the occasion in a tender and friendly manner, but forcibly urged to him the horrible crime of self-murder, however glossed over by our present libertines; blaming the bad company and principles he had adopted. This betrayed him into some compunction, and by his tears he seemed to feel it. At the same time he acknowledged he wanted for nothing, and denied any distress upon that account."[1] The next day he sent his adviser the following letter:[2]—

SIR,

Upon recollection, I don't know how Mr. Clayfield could come by his Letter, as I intended to have given him a Letter but did not. In regard to my Motives for the supposed rashness, I shall observe that I keep no worse Company than *myself;* I never drink to Excess, and have, without Vanity, too much Sense to be attached to the

[1] See Barrett's History of Bristol, p. 646.

[2] The original is in the British Museum.

mercenary retailers of Iniquity. No; it is my PRIDE, my damn'd, native, unconquerable Pride, that plunges me into Distraction. You must know that the 19-20th of my Composition is Pride. I must either live a Slave, a Servant; to have no Will of my own, no Sentiments of my own which I may freely declare as such;—or DIE. Perplexing Alternative! but it distracts me to think of it: I will endeavor to learn Humility, but it cannot be here. What it may cost me in the trial Heaven knows!

I am, Y[r] much Obliged, unhappy,
hble Sert.

Thursday Fvening. T. C.

Whether the first letter to Clayfield was a genuine announcement of his intention to commit suicide, and whether the pedantic surgeon's admonitions really aroused any shortlived compunction in the boy, it is impossible to say. If, as is most likely, he had hoped to frighten Lambert into dismissing him, he was for the present unsuccessful; and for a few weeks affairs went on as before.

One morning in April, however, the attorney found on his apprentice's desk—left there, it may be assumed, on purpose,—a document, which, if it did not convince him of the sincerity of Chatterton's design, must at least have satisfied him of what he had probably suspected before, that his apprentice was out of his senses.

It commences with some verses on Burgum, Catcott, and Barrett, containing, to all appearance, his candid opinion of these worthies, and a sort of apology for his unceremonious treatment of them.

After abruptly terminating these, the author changed to prose, and beginning "This is the last Will and Testament of me, Thomas Chatterton, of the city of Bristol," he announces his death on the evening of the next day, "being the feast of the Resurrection," and proceeds for several pages with mock bequests to various friends and patrons, and minute directions as to his own tomb and epitaph, including inscriptions to sundry imaginary ancestors. The whole is a medley of jest and earnest—absurdity interspersed with passages of seeming seriousness. It is endorsed: "All this wrote between eleven and two o'clock, Saturday, in the utmost distress of mind, April 14, 1770."[1]

Whatever the real import of this extraordinary composition, it produced a due effect on Lambert, who apparently was no longer desirous of the responsibility of retaining Chatterton in his service. The indentures were cancelled forthwith,[2] and he made immediate preparations for starting for London. A small subscription was raised amongst his friends and patrons; what it amounted to is not known; but by its assistance, and with a fair balance, we may suppose, in his pocket, he found himself in little more than a week on the London coach.

---

[1] See vol. i. pp. 267-275.

[2] It seems doubtful whether all the formalities consequent on the termination of the engagement between Chatterton and his master were completed before his hurried departure. In three letters home he mentions a "clearance" due from him to Lambert. See letters III., VII., and IX.; pp. 343, 357, and 358.

He arrived in town on the 25th or 26th of April, 1770, at five in the evening.[1] From his first letter to his mother we gather that he had several relations in London, one of whom, Mrs. Ballance, lodged at the house of a Mr. Walmsley, a plasterer, in Shoreditch. Chatterton himself obtained a room in the same house. The family was composed of the plasterer and his wife, a niece of the latter, who was a girl of about seventeen, and her brother, who was about three years younger. From these people Sir Herbert Croft, on making inquiries about nine years later, obtained many interesting particulars of Chatterton's London life.[2]

The literary patrons on whom he chiefly relied for a start in his career were Hamilton the proprietor of the Town and Country Magazine, Edmunds, the editor of the Middlesex Journal,—to both of whom he was well known by name—Fell, the editor and printer of the Freeholder's Magazine, and Dodsley, the publisher in Pall Mall, with whom, it will be remembered, he had already had some correspondence about the publication of Ælla.

To these he lost no time in presenting himself, and from all, by his own account, he received great encouragement. Fell at once accepted articles for the Freeholder's Magazine, a political miscellany advocating popular views, while Edmunds, to whom Chatterton had lately forwarded the first part of his satire, Kew Gardens, continued to insert 'Deci-

---

[1] His first letter is dated April 26. It is doubtful whether it was written the day after he arrived or late the same night.

[2] See Love and Madness, pp. 189, *et seq.*

mus' letters and other papers. Hamilton readily accepted more miscellaneous articles for his Magazine, but with regard to the Annual Register, published by Dodsley, it does not appear that any arrangement was effected.

For the present matters seemed prosperous, and Chatterton indulged in the highest anticipations. Since he had first commenced political writing he had distinctly identified himself with what was then called the "patriotic" side, the side on which the demagogue Wilkes, backed up by the solid support of the City of London and the co-operation of its Lord Mayor, Beckford, was opposing the government of the day.

The editors of the patriotic newspapers were doubtless glad enough to avail themselves of the services of so ready and caustic a pen as Chatterton's, but their willingness or ability to pay him for them was more doubtful. Hitherto his contributions sent from Bristol had been made without any expectation of remuneration, or were only acknowledged by a few copies of the journal in which they appeared; but he was then maintained at the expense of his master, while now he was absolutely dependent for existence on the proceeds of his literary labour.

He had not been three weeks in town before the position of affairs began to change; the government, stung by the virulent attacks of the public journals, again had recourse to legal prosecution, and by the middle of May the printer of the Middlesex Journal had been tried by the House of Lords, fined, and committed to Newgate, while Fell, having offended "certain persons," was suddenly called to account by his creditors and deposited in the King's Bench.[1]

That Chatterton soon began to experience the hardships and vicissitudes incident on a literary life is clear from his letters home, notwithstanding the boastful and confident terms in which they are expressed. He exaggerates and expatiates on the more attractive features of his daily life; on projected literary schemes; on his introductions to great people, and on the places of amusement he frequents, which, as he says, and truly enough for one whose employment obliged him to be conversant with current topics, were as necessary to him as food.

Mrs. Ballance, when he had been in town two or three weeks, recommended him to get into some office, whereupon "he stormed about the room like a madman and frightened her not a little by telling her he hoped, with the blessing of God, very soon to be sent prisoner to the Tower, which would make his fortune . . . . . He frequently said he would settle the nation before he had done." He was, she says, "as proud as Lucifer." He very soon quarrelled with her for calling him "cousin Tommy," and asked if she ever heard of a poet's being called Tommy. "I might have had twenty places before now," he himself writes home, "could I humble myself to go into a comptor, but state matters suit me better than commercial."[2]

---

[1] See letter III. vol. i. p. 342.
[2] See letter IX. vol. i. p. 358.

Towards the end of May, Beckford in person presented to the King a remonstrance from the City of London;[1] with reference to which Chatterton addressed a letter to the Lord Mayor, and according to his own account received a personal introduction to him. On his patronage he relied for future success; "but the devil of the matter is," he writes, "there is no money to be got on this side of the question. Interest is on the other side. But he is a poor author who cannot write on both sides." And on this sentiment he did not hesitate to act, if we may believe Walpole's statement that he saw an unpublished letter to Lord North by Chatterton, signed MODERATOR, which he describes as "an encomium on the administration for rejecting the Lord Mayor Beckford's remonstrance." It bears the date May 26th, the very same as another letter, signed PROBUS, addressed to the Lord Mayor, and abusing the government on the same occasion.[2]

By this time, indeed, Chatterton must have been too well aware of the precarious nature of political writing, and, however abstemious in his habits, must have been brought face to face with absolute want. He took his meals with his relative and fellow-lodger, Mrs. Ballance; but his dinner consisted

---

[1] The remonstrance presented by Beckford, as well as his reply to the royal answer, were really written by John Horne, better known as Horne Tooke. See Rogers' Historical Gleanings (Life of Horne Tooke), p. 215. Both may be read in the "Town and Country Magazine" for 1770, p. 278.

[2] This statement rests on the authority of Walpole, who, as we have seen, is not to be implicitly trusted. It is however very likely to be true.

generally of only a tart and glass of water. Sometimes he was seen by the plasterer's nephew, who shared his bedroom, to pull out a sheep's-tongue from his pocket and eat it, and this, we may believe, was the only animal food he ate.[1] The small fund he had brought from Bristol had probably been exhausted, and as to his earnings for literary work, it is too certain that the men with whom he had to deal were taking advantage of the boy's inexperience and necessities.

The following list of receipts for the first month of his London life was discovered in his pocket-book after his death:

	£	s.	d.
Received to May 23, of Mr. Hamilton for Middlesex	1	11	6
" of B.[2]	1	2	3
" of Fell, for the Consuliad . . .	0	10	6
" of Mr. Hamilton, for Candidus and Foreign Journal	0	2	0
" of Mr. Fell	0	10	6
" Middlesex Journal	0	8	6
" Mr. Hamilton, for 16 Songs . . .	0	10	6
	4	15	9

Towards the end of June Chatterton's failing political prospects reached their crisis. He had probably counted much on the effect of the letter which he had addressed to the Lord Mayor on the rejection of the Remonstrance, and which was to appear in the "North Briton" at the end of that month; it was already in type when, on the 21st,

---

[1] See Love and Madness, p. 192.

[2] Perhaps Bingley, of the "North Briton."

Beckford suddenly died, and the essay was returned to its author, whose main hope was thus destroyed. "He was," says Mrs. Ballance, "perfectly frantic and out of his mind, and said he was ruined."

He soon, however, regained self-possession, and with his usual energy set about making the best of the occasion; that he was not altogether unsuccessful the following quaint endorsement, written on the back of the returned MS., shows:

Accepted by Bingley, set for, and thrown out of the North Briton, 21st June, on account of the Lord Mayor's death.

	£	s.	d.	£	s.	d.
Lost by his death on this Essay				1	11	6
Gained in Elegies	2	2	0			
" Essays	3	3	0			
				5	5	0
Am glad he is dead by				3	13	6

It was probably written for the information of his friend Thomas Cary, whose address it also bears.

Very shortly after this event he changed his lodgings,[1] having been with the Walmsleys nine weeks. He gave no reason for doing so, but it was

[1] There is some doubt about the time of this change. One of the African Eclogues, the Death of Nicou (see vol. i. p. 204), is dated Brooke Street, June 12th, when he had been in London less than seven weeks. But, on the other hand, Mrs. Walmsley stated that he stayed with her nine weeks in all; and Mrs. Ballance describes his conduct on the death of Beckford, which happened on June 21, as if he were still lodging in the same house with her. Moreover, the first letter home in which he intimates the change is dated July 8.

probably to conceal his increasing poverty from his relations. In the first letter home after this change dated July 8, he gave his new address as Mrs. Angel, sack-maker,[1] Brook Street, Holborn; the number has been ascertained to be 39.

Political writing, at any rate on the popular side, had now become almost impracticable. "The printers of the daily publications," he writes, "are all frightened out of their patriotism, and will take nothing unless 'tis moderate or ministerial. I have not had five patriotic essays this fortnight, all must be ministerial or entertaining."

His resources, however, were not as yet quite exhausted. In a letter to his mother, about three weeks after his arrival, he gives her an account of his having made acquaintance, in the pit of a theatre, with a music-seller, who, hearing he could write, desired him to write a few songs for him.[2] These his friend showed to a Doctor in Music, and Chatterton was invited to compose for the Ranelagh and the Marylebone Gardens.

About a year before, as we find from a MS. (dated Aug. 12, 1769), he had commenced a sort of musical extravaganza, entitled Amphitryon; but it is unfinished, and was probably put aside for other work.[3] His ear for music, as we may gather from his letters, was good, and, in addition to the dramatic power which he possessed in a high degree,

---

[1] Equivalent to the modern mantua-maker. The *sacque* hung down at the back from the shoulders to the ground.

[2] See letter III. vol. i. p. 342.

[3] See the List of Chatterton's MSS. in the British Museum, on pp. 375-378 of this volume.

his humour and readiness well adapted him for this sort of composition. He now probably thought of the unused MS., and, by altering the plot, largely reducing the number of characters, and retaining only a portion of the verse, he produced the very spirited musical extravaganza or burletta, The Revenge.

For this he was paid the sum of five guineas, as is known by the receipt still preserved. It was probably the only occasion on which he received a sum at all adequate to his labour, and though the hardly-earned coins scarcely did more than suffice for his own pressing wants, a portion of it was immediately spent in sending off a long-talked-of box of presents for the home circle.[1]

Another product of these weeks was probably the 'Balade of Charitie,' the latest but not the least beautiful of the Rowley poems. He had soon after his arrival in London meditated a resumption of his Rowley "transcriptions." Writing to his mother, on May 14, he says: "Had Rowley been a Londoner instead of a Bristowyan I could have lived by copying his works," and in two letters he asks particularly that the MS. Glossary may be sent to him. The 'Balade of Charitie' was sent to the editor of the Town and Country Magazine, in which two months previously 'Elinoure and Juga' had appeared, but it was rejected. It is dated Bristol, July 4, from which it may be inferred that its author still deemed it as important as ever to keep his secret.[2]

The amount of literary work that Chatterton per-

---

[1] See letter VII. vol. i. p. 356. [2] See vol. ii. p. 110.

formed in the few months during which he was in London is astonishing. He contributed to magazines and journals of every class. The publications mentioned by him are the Town and Country, Freeholder's, Court and City, London, Christian, and Gospel Magazines, The London Museum, Middlesex Journal, North Briton, and there were doubtless several others. In these appeared beside the African Eclogues and several sets of verses of less merit, political essays and letters, and numerous light and worthless prose pieces suited to the tastes of the fashionable readers of that day, such as The Adventures of a Star, Maria Friendless, The Unfortunate Fathers, and a series entitled the Hunter of Oddities, which ran through eleven numbers of the Town and Country Magazine.

It is true that some of these papers were not original. It was a too common practice in the last century for one writer to make unsparing use of the labours of another, and Chatterton, in such hack-writing as this, was not more scrupulous than others. The paper entitled "Maria Friendless" was, as Bryant first pointed out, almost a literal transcript of the story of "Misella" in Johnson's Rambler, and Maitland spent much unnecessary ingenuity in showing that two articles which appeared severally in Dodsley's Annual Register and the Freeholder's Magazine, were both copied from the same source.[1] But nearly all were undoubtedly original. Hamilton had apparently a large number of such

---

[1] See "Chatterton; an Essay," by S. R. Maitland, D.D., p. 55, *et seq.*

contributions from Chatterton, which he kept in reserve. The latter, in writing to his sister on July 20th, says: "Nearly all the next number of the Town and Country is mine;" but of course only a portion of these contributions appeared, and it is too likely that none of them were paid for. In the same pocket-book which contained the memorandum of receipts given above, is also a note that £11 was due to him for articles accepted.

Thus, with no further means of disposing of his work, and unable to obtain payment for what he had already done, his situation had, by the middle of August, become almost desperate. One forlorn hope still remained. It will be remembered that when younger he had solicited Barrett to give him some instruction in surgery, and though the doctor did not consent, Chatterton had probably gained from his books some little theoretical knowledge of the subject. At any rate, he considered it sufficient to enable him to give an opinion on medical subjects, and in one of his letters to his sister we find him giving some advice as to the treatment of a friend who was unwell, with all the confidence of a legitimate practitioner.[1]

To go out to sea as a surgeon, had no doubt early presented itself to his mind as a last resource, and in the letter just referred to, written little more than a month after his arrival in town, he says: "I might have a recommendation to Sir George Colebrook, an East India Director, as qualified for an office in no ways despicable; but I shall

[1] See letter IV. p. 349.

not take a step to the sea whilst I can continue on land." The time had now come when it seemed impossible to do so any longer, and his last remaining hope was that Mr. Barrett would give him a certificate testifying to his possessing the very scanty qualifications then required for a surgeon's mate. In the last letter preserved, which is addressed to George Catcott, after much affected and forced talk about Bristol and other general matters, his real object appears in the concluding paragraph. "Mr. Barrett has it in his power to assist me greatly, by his giving me a physical character. I hope he will."

This letter is dated August 12th. Barrett's refusal, which must have reached him in five or six days, left him without resource. For a few days longer he lingered on in gradually increasing destitution. Without any means of earning a subsistence, he was too proud to beg it, or even to accept it as an alms. Mr. Cross, an apothecary in Brook Street with whom he had formed acquaintance, several times, it is said, pressed him to take a meal with him, but he continually declined. Once only was he induced to join him at supper, and he was then observed to eat "voraciously." A day or two later Mrs. Angel his landlady noticed his evident want, and "as she knew he had not eaten anything for two or three days, she begged he would take some dinner with her on the 24th of August; but he was offended at her expressions, which seemed to hint he was in want, and assured her he was not hungry."[1]

---

[1] Love and Madness, p. 195.

This day was his last. During the night of Friday the 24th of August, by means of arsenic in water, he put an end to his life. His remains, distorted with the death struggle, were discovered when his door was broken open the next day. The floor of the room was strewn with the torn-up remnants of his latest work.[1]

So perished, in destitution, obscurity, and despair, one whose name might under different circumstances have ranked amongst the first of his own generation. Overwhelmed by the neglect of his fellow-men, hopeless of any future career, unconscious even of the fame, which slowly though it has been accorded, was already laid in store for him, he deliberately and stoically resigned his life. Some, appealing to evidence of very doubtful weight, have felt satisfaction in the hypothesis that Chatterton was insane;[2] but this supposition will hardly

---

[1] Barrett (p. 647) states that opium was the poison employed; but Croft, who saw the coroner and speaks on the authority of the few notes taken at the inquest says arsenic (Love and Madness, p. 196). In respect to the scraps of paper with which the floor was strewed, we may well suppose that the remains of the MS. glossary were amongst them. It is probable that several poems were also destroyed. Amongst these were, perhaps, the completion of "Goddwyn"; a tragedy called "The Apostate," of which Barrett received a portion (see Bryant's "Observations," p. 517); "The Justice of Peace," named in the Rowleian memoir of Canynge; as well as a drama ascribed to Stowe, mentioned in conjunction with some of Rowley's in one of Chatterton's notes (as yet unprinted) to the last of the fictitious MSS. in the British Museum (Add. MSS. 5766. C.) See Wilson's "Chatterton," p. 304.

[2] Southey especially; see Quarterly Review, vol. xvi. p. 539; also vol. iii. p. 219; Byron was of the same opinion. See Wilson's "Chatterton," pp. 218, 304.

commend itself to a deliberate judge. Far from showing any trace of insanity, his mind displayed a power of self-command and thought even above the average. It is true that in such records of the last few weeks of his life, as his letters and writings supply, there is an absence of any distinct foreshadowing of the tragic end, which seems to point to the last act as the result of an unpremeditated and ungovernable impulse; but unless his character has been misinterpreted, the apparent gaiety and humour are but too plainly the cloaks of a sterner mood and a deeper purpose, which his pride and reserve suffered no fellow creature to share. In one of his latest magazine papers there is, however, a passage which though in the midst of trivial surroundings, may be regarded as throwing some light on his end. "There is," he writes, "a principle in man (a shadow of the Divinity) which constitutes him the image of God; you may call it conscience, grace, inspiration, the spirit, or whatever name your education gives it. If a man acts according to this regulator he is right: if contrary to it, he is wrong. It is an approved truth that this principle varies in every rational being. As I can reconcile suicide to this principle, with me it is consequently no crime. Suicide is sometimes a noble insanity of the soul: and often the result of a mature and deliberate approbation of the soul. If ever a crime, it is only so to society: there indeed it always appears an irrational emotion, but when our being becomes unsocial, when we neither assist or are assisted by society, we do not injure it by laying down our load of life."[1] To such sophistry, too soon put into practice, his fate has given a pathetic significance; but it is surely incompatible with the idea of insanity.

Chatterton's latest biographer, Dr. Wilson, has well said that he "did not wear his heart upon his sleeve." As his writings exemplify a twofold life, so his character has a double aspect. The coarse satires, the trivial verses, and the worthless magazine contributions which he did not hesitate to avow as his own, are the fruits of that restless spirit of emulation which continually urged him since his infant days to take prëeminence amongst his compeers; while the more serious creations of his mind, themselves unacknowledged yet associated with all his nobler but unconfessed aspirations, are the sole exponents of the truer inspiration in possession of which he walked in mental solitude,

A phantom amongst men, companionless,

* * * * * *

While his own thoughts along that rugged way
Pursued like raging hounds their father and their prey.

And this habitual reserve, this constant concealment of the better part of his nature beneath an unworthy mask, must surely not be ignored in forming an opinion as to his personal character and habits. His career during the later months of his Bristol life as well as in London, has been too generally regarded as one about which it would be

---

[1] This passage occurs in a short story called "The Unfortunate Fathers," to be found in Southey and Cottle's edition of Chatterton's Works, vol. iii. p. 224.

charitable to be silent, or represented as a course of reckless profligacy, to support which he did not hesitate to employ his pen in the service of men who pandered to the popular taste for worthless and vile literature. But though it is true that his necessities allowed no scruples as to the disposal of his work or the manner of its execution, a very little research will shew that the greater number of the periodicals he contributed to were respectable representatives of the current literature, and that the style of his writings was not inferior to that sanctioned by the general taste of the period. And with regard to his personal habits, almost all the direct evidence we have, tends to prove that he was not the profligate generally supposed. That innocence and purity of thought were early lost, is plainly shewn by too many proofs in Chatterton's own hand-writing; and in the knowledge of good and evil in life, his prematurity of mind was as clearly evinced as in all other knowledge. But all that we know of the manner of his life as well as the testimony of his friends, tends to modify the opinion that might be formed from some of his own writings. The strict control which regulated his diet, the few hours given to rest, the constant pre-occupation of his mind on work, his partiality for the society of respectable women, and above all, the strength of his attachment to his relations, are altogether opposed to the idea of licentious indulgence. On this point Thistlethwaite, who while Chatterton was at Bristol, could scarcely fail to be well informed, wrote to Dean Milles as follows:

I admit that amongst Chatterton's papers may be found many passages not only immoral, but bordering upon a libertinism gross and unpardonable, which, for the regard I bear his memory, I wish he had never written; but which I nevertheless believe to have originated rather from a warmth of imagination, aided by a vain affectation of singularity, than from any natural depravity or from a heart vitiated by evil example. The opportunities a long acquaintance with him afforded me, justify me in saying, that whilst he lived in Bristol he was not the debauched character represented. Temperate in his living, moderate in his pleasures, and regular in his exercises, he was undeserving of the aspersion. What change London might have effected in him I know not, but from the strain of his letters to his mother and sister, and his conduct towards them after he quitted Bristol, and also from the testimony of those with whom he lodged, I have no doubt but the intemperances and irregularities laid to his charge, either did not exist at all, or at the worst, are considerably aggravated beyond what candour can approve.[1]

On this point therefore we may without hesitation give the preponderance to external evidence, rather than to that furnished by his own writings.[2] But the case is very different with regard to the more important question of the merit of those

---

[1] Dean Milles' edition of the Rowley Poems, page 461.

[2] That Chatterton wilfully exaggerated his own vices may be inferred from a passage in Kew Gardens. See vol. i. p. 173, last paragraph.

writings themselves, in which alone is involved the claims of their author to the remembrance of posterity. Chatterton's literary reputation has not yet been satisfactorily established; it has hitherto been affected by prejudices partly dependent on the ambiguity surrounding his works, and partly on the sentiments, whether of sympathy or contempt, which his history has never failed to excite. His real fame, depending on more discriminate judgments, has been one of hearsay rather than of independent opinion; and is founded less on the concurrent testimony of his countrymen, than on the private taste of the few individuals who have penetrated the veil of obscurity and falsification with which his writings are invested.

There is only one practical method of meeting this difficulty. This plan, first indicated by Warton, and lately exemplified more fully by Dr. Wilson, is now applied for the first time to a complete edition of the Rowley poems; and the result, it is hoped, will be the establishment of his reputation on a wider and surer basis.

A distinguishing characteristic of Chatterton's mind, which the student of his life cannot fail to observe, is his ready perception of the forms and channels in and through which human thought found expression during the more uncultured periods of English history. The century at the middle point of which Chatterton was born, has been well described as "a valley of dry bones,"[1]

---

[1] An Essay on the Revival of Ballad literature, by Mr. J. W. Hales, published with the second volume of the edition

and in no respect was it (during the earlier part at least,) more apparently lifeless than in its neglect of the inheritance received from preceding ages. The manifold glories of gothic architecture, in which we now recognise the genius and devotion of our ancestors shining through the mists of ignorance and superstition, were absolutely unheeded; whilst in respect to literature, nearly all but that which formally satisfied the critical requirements of contemporary taste was regarded with indiscriminate indifference. Chaucer and Spenser formed part of the furniture of good libraries, and were the study of perhaps a few enthusiasts; but not till the year 1765, when Bp. Percy diffidently made public his "Reliques of Ancient English Poetry," was there anything like a general knowledge of even the existence of a popular mediæval literature.

It was at this juncture that Chatterton was beginning to exert his extraordinary powers of mind; and though born in the humblest circumstances, and trained under the most meagre system, he seized at once on ideas which the labours and investigations of scholars, and a more extended and philosophical knowledge of history are only at this day making familiar to the public in general.

On this ground alone he might be judged to have earned the sympathy at least of antiquarians; but it is amongst these, perhaps, that he has found his most implacable enemies. It has been his fate

---

of the Percy Folio MS. (Ed. Hales and Furnivall) may be consulted with advantage on this subject.

to displease two opposing parties, both those who allowed themselves to be deceived by the Rowley fiction and those who were less credulous. The former, irritated by the general want of acceptance of a story on which they had staked their reputation, endeavoured to strengthen their own case by weakening that of their adversaries, and not only depreciated Chatterton's intellect, but with less apparent reason traduced his moral character; while the latter ignoring, or unable to discern whatever there is of real merit in the poems, regarded their author as simply an impostor.

That they possess real merit must be conceded by all who, having taken the trouble to penetrate their disguise, are in a position to form an independent opinion. In originality of thought (notwithstanding some evident plagiarism), Chatterton, if the early age at which he began to compose be taken into account, stands before any poet on record.[1] And even if the Rowley poems are to be judged with the production of more mature writers of his time, they stand out as unmistakeable tokens of that impending revival in European literature of which the present century has seen the fulfilment. Abjuring by instinct the taint of Gallicism simultaneously influencing both the life and literature of

---

[1] There is one man, a contemporary of Chatterton, in whose favour this statement should perhaps be qualified. That great and singular though hardly recognised genius, William Blake, is said to have composed original verse between the ages of eleven and twelve. He was born in 1757, five years after Chatterton, and in later years was an admirer of the poems of "Rowley."

Germany and England, and which had more or less subjected all our great writers, since the Restoration, to conventional and narrow critical limits, his genius led him to early models as a truer school of poetry; and if he has failed to exert that influence which must be attributed to Burns, Wordsworth, Keats, and the many other poets, who having

> Gazed on nature's naked loveliness,

and followed her in singleness of heart, have gradually restored the purity of English literature, it must be ascribed less to want of innate ability or true perception, than to the shortness of his life, and the superficially unattractive form in which his great but erratic genius was evinced.

As to the actual amount of guilt involved in his deception there will always be different opinions, but few will now deny that his fame has been hardly dealt with. Of late years, owing to a more accurate knowledge of the English language, the deception has increased in transparency, and consequently decreased in its supposed enormity. There are many who with no consciousness of disloyalty to the cause of truth, or the honour of English literature, can afford to overlook the absurd paraphernalia of sham-antique parchments and badly imitated orthography, and recognise with respect a certain bold originality in a genius which points forward rather than backwards amongst its contemporaries, and which may be looked on rather as a lender to the future than a borrower from the past. To these the "forgery" of the Rowley romance will appear of little moment. In his poorly-furnished garret-studio surrounded by old parchments, and with his imagination full of the forms of mediæval life, the child-poet no doubt early conceived a scheme for the production of various imitated writings to be ascribed to some favourite character in his fancies, who was in fact his ideal self. A reason for secresy would be obvious, but the idea would not necessarily be accompanied by a sense of guilt. The attempt to work out his conception even to the extent of obtaining its acknowledgment by his own friends was no doubt effected with much premeditation and careful concealment, and even elaborate deception; but it is reasonable as well as charitable to assume that in its origin at least, it involved no vicious intention, no avaricious end. The idea arose, we cannot doubt, in feelings of a purely subjective nature; resulting from a remarkable affiliation of his mind with the circumstances of a past age, as he had pictured it and dreamt over it. Such a sympathy with the unreal can be compared to nothing in literary history but that of Keats's mind with another period of antiquity, and the intensity with which he realised a mythical Hellenic life. The strength of Chatterton's imagination threw him back similarly into another ideal life, and so forcibly, that at times we may well believe the completeness of his self-identification with the poet-priest Rowley.

As soon however as he discovered that his imitated MSS. might be made a source, if not of pecuniary profit, at least of advancement, (which was not before the publication of the account of the opening of the old bridge,) and proceeded to act upon this discovery, it is impossible entirely to exonerate him. The only excuses which can be urged, are his youth and inexperience, and the blind credulity of those who allowed themselves to be deceived by him. That he should ever have ventured to submit the truth of his own imperfect conceptions to the test of a more general criticism, or attempted to force them on others by prevarications which naturally grew more unscrupulous and defiant at every iteration, was in the first instance the result of a want of experience and more extended knowledge of the world which the greatest and most precocious mind can attain only by the ordinary course. No candid person will pretend to doubt that such a system of deception, when once commenced, had its bad effect on his character and contributed to the fatal termination of his short career; and it is but just that such blame as is his due, should not be omitted from a review of his life; but to exaggerate it as has been too often done, to attribute antecedently, to a child of twelve years old, all the sentiments which may be supposed to animate a commercial forger or a thief, to assume that he deliberately and wantonly formed the design of deceiving the world for no other reasons than avarice coupled with an innate love of deception, indicate the malice of weak minds stung by disappointed curiosity and injured vanity rather than the fair and liberal spirit of enlightened criticism.

Now, more than a century since his death, there are few, if any, minds in which such sentiments will find a place. But there are doubtless still some to whom all that is attractive in the history of this gifted boy will not suffice to dispel its darker features. The dreamy, but affectionate child—such as we may picture him when, still untainted by the world, he wandered along the stately aisles of St. Mary's, calling up strange figures of forgotten times,—will be forgotten under the guise (too easily assumed) of irreverent satirist and moral delinquent: while the unwearying industry and strict self-denial, with which he secretly pressed forward towards the unattained goal of duly acknowledged merit, will in vain appeal against the violation of truth or the imputed crime of thoughtlessly falsified history. To such as these his fate at least may be an expiation; the bitterness of disappointed hope, of unrecognized genius, the neglect of fellow-men, the pangs of bodily hunger, and the last despairing agony of a self-inflicted death have surely atoned for errors of which the effect, if ever felt, has long since passed away.

What remains of his story may be told in few words. An inquest was held on his body, and on the 28th of August it was consigned to a pauper's grave in the burial-ground of Shoe-Lane workhouse in the parish of St. Andrew's, Holborn, in which Brook Street is situated. His name is wrongly entered in the parish register as William Chatterton, to which a later hand has added the words "the poet." But there is good reason to believe that he did not find his last resting-place here. It is said that by the interest of some friends in London his mother was enabled to have the body conveyed to Bristol, and that Chatterton's uncle, Richard Philips, the sexton of St. Mary's, who had always regarded his nephew with peculiar affection, buried it secretly in Redcliff churchyard. The story itself is by no means incredible, and is as well authenticated as many of the received facts of his life.[1] It is at any rate a pleasing uncertainty which will allow us to hope that his grave is not with the nameless; that his body lies in the consecrated ground which had been the care of many generations of his forefathers, and within the shadow of that church which will ever form the noblest and most fitting monument to Chatterton's genius.

[1] It was first given in one of the valuable appendices to Dix's "Life," p. 299; and was afterwards further corroborated. See Dr. Wilson's "Chatterton," p. 309, and Pryce's "Memorials of the Canynges' family," p. 293.

ACKNOWLEDGED POEMS.

ON THE LAST EPIPHANY, OR, CHRIST COMING TO JUDGMENT.[1]

BEHOLD! just coming from above,
The judge, with majesty and love!
The sky divides, and rolls away,
T'admit him through the realms of day!
The sun, astonished, hides its face,
The moon and stars with wonder gaze
At Jesu's bright superior rays!
Dread lightnings flash, and thunders roar,
And shake the earth and briny shore;
The trumpet sounds at heaven's command,
And pierceth through the sea and land;
The dead in each now hear the voice,

---

[1] Written by Chatterton when only just past ten years of age, and inserted in Felix Farley's Bristol Journal, January 8, 1763. See Dix's Life of Chatterton, p. 209.

The sinners fear and saints rejoice;
For now the awful hour is come,
When every tenant of the tomb
Must rise, and take his everlasting doom.

A HYMN FOR CHRISTMAS DAY.

[From a copy by Sir Herbert Croft, in the same volume as the next. Probably written in 1763.]

ALMIGHTY Framer of the skies!
O let our pure devotion rise,
Like incense in Thy sight!
Wrapt in impenetrable shade
The texture of our souls was made,[1]
Till Thy command gave light.

The sun of glory gleamed, the ray
Refined the darkness into day,
And bid the vapours fly:
Impelled by His eternal love,
He left His palaces above
To cheer our gloomy sky.

How shall we celebrate the day,
When God appeared in mortal clay,
The mark of worldly scorn;
When the archangel's heavenly lays
Attempted the Redeemer's praise,
And hailed salvation's morn!

---

[1] Orig.—" were made."

A humble form the Godhead wore,
The pains of poverty He bore,
  To gaudy pomp unknown:
Though in a human walk He trod,
Still was the man Almighty God,
  In glory all His own.

Despised, oppressed, the Godhead bears
The torments of this vale of tears,
  Nor bade His vengeance rise;
He saw the creatures He had made
Revile His power, His peace invade;
  He saw with Mercy's eyes.

How shall we celebrate His name,
Who groaned beneath a life of shame,
  In all afflictions tried!
The soul is raptured to conçeive
A truth, which Being must believe,
  The God Eternal died.

My soul, exert thy powers, adore,
Upon devotion's plumage soar
  To celebrate the day:
The God from whom creation sprung
Shall animate my grateful tongue;
  From Him I'll catch the lay!

X. Y.

SLY DICK.[1]

SHARP was the frost, the wind was high,
And sparkling stars bedecked the sky,
Sly Dick, in arts of cunning skilled,
Whose rapine all his pockets filled,
Had laid him down to take his rest
And soothe with sleep his anxious breast.
'Twas thus a dark infernal sprite,
A native of the blackest night,
Portending mischief to devise,
Upon Sly Dick he cast his eyes;
Then straight descends th' infernal sprite,
And in his chamber does alight:
In visions he before him stands,
And his attention he commands.
Thus spake the sprite: "Hearken, my friend,
And to my counsels now attend.
Within the garret's spacious dome
There lies a well stored wealthy room,
Well stored with cloth and stockings too,
Which I suppose will do for you;
First from the cloth take thou a purse,
For thee it will not be the worse,

---

[1] From a copy in the handwriting of Sir Herbert Croft, in the volume of Chatterton's works purchased by Mr. Waldron at the sale of Sir Herbert's Library. He says "this was written by Chatterton at about eleven: as well as the [preceding] Hymn." We may therefore date it 1763.

A noble purse rewards thy pains,
A purse to hold thy filching gains;
Then, for the stockings, let them reeve,
And not a scrap behind thee leave;
Five bundles for a penny sell,
And pence to thee will come pell-mell;
See it be done with speed and care."
Thus spake the sprite and sunk in air.

When in the morn, with thoughts erect,
Sly Dick did on his dream reflect,
Why faith, thinks he, "'tis something too,
It might—perhaps—it might—be true,
I'll go and see." Away he hies,
And to the garret quick he flies,
Enters the room, cuts up the clothes,
And after that reeves up the hose;
Then of the cloth he purses made,
Purses to hold his filching trade.

Cætera desunt.

THE CHURCHWARDEN AND THE APPARITION.

A FABLE.[1]

THE night was cold, the wind was high,
And stars bespangled all the sky;
Churchwarden Joe[2] had laid him down,
And slept secure on bed of down;
But still the pleasing hope of gain,
That never left his active brain,
Exposed the churchyard to his view,
That seat of treasure wholly new.
"Pull down that cross," he quickly cried,
The mason instantly complied:
When lo! behold, the golden prize
Appears—joy sparkles in his eyes.
The door now creaks, the window shakes,
With sudden fear he starts and wakes;[3]
Quaking and pale, in eager haste

---

[1] Written by Chatterton at the age of eleven, and printed in Felix Farley's Bristol Journal, January 7, 1764. See Dix's Life of Chatterton, p. 211.

[2] Printed J*E in the journal; the person meant was Joseph Thomas, then churchwarden of St. Mary, Redcliffe.

[3] "The wind was high, the window shakes,
With sudden start the miser wakes."
Gay's Fables; *The Miser and Plutus.*

This clear case of imitation is interesting, as showing one of Chatterton's sources of inspiration.

His haggard eyes around he cast;
A ghastly phantom, lean and wan,
That instant rose, and thus began:
"Weak wretch—to think to blind my eyes!
Hypocrisy's a thin disguise;
Your humble mien and fawning tongue
Have oft deceived the old and young.
On this side now, and now on that,
The very emblem of the bat:
Whatever part you take, we know
'Tis only interest makes it so,
And though with sacred zeal you burn,
Religion's only for your turn;
I'm Conscience called!" Joe greatly feared;
The lightning flashed—it disappeared.

APOSTATE WILL.[1]

IN days of old, when Wesley's power
Gathered new strength by every hour;
Apostate Will, just sunk in trade,
Resolved his bargain should be made;
Then straight to Wesley he repairs,
And puts on grave and solemn airs;

---

[1] This poem is transcribed, says Sir Herbert Croft, "from an old pocket-book in his mother's possession. It appears to be his first, perhaps his only copy of it; and is evidently his handwriting. By the date he was eleven years and almost five months old. It is not the most extraordinary performance in the world: but, from the circumstances of Chatterton's parentage and education, it is unlikely, if not

Then thus the pious man address'd:
"Good sir, I think your doctrine best;
Your servant will a Wesley be,
Therefore the principles teach me."
The preacher then instructions gave,
How he in this world should behave:
He hears, assents, and gives a nod,
Says every word's the word of God,
Then lifting his dissembling eyes,
"How blessèd is the sect!" he cries;
"Nor Bingham, Young, nor Stillingfleet,
Shall make me from this sect retreat."
He then his circumstance declared,
How hardly with him matters fared,
Begg'd him next morning for to make
A small collection for his sake.
The preacher said, "Do not repine,
The whole collection shall be thine."
With looks demure and cringing bows,
About his business straight he goes.
His outward acts were grave and prim,

---

impossible, that he should have met with any assistance or correction. Whereas, when we read the ode which Pope wrote at twelve, and another of Cowley at thirteen, we are apt to suspect a parent, friend, or tutor, of an amiable dishonesty, of which we feel, perhaps, that we should be guilty. Suspicions of this nature touch not Chatterton. He knew no tutor, no friend, no parent—at least no parent who could correct or assist him.

This poem appears to have been aimed at somebody, who had formerly been a Methodist, and was lately promoted (to the dignity, perhaps, of opening a pew or a grave; for Chatterton was the sexton's son [nephew]) in the established church."—*Love and Madness*; ed. 1780, p. 147.

The Methodist appeared in him.
But, be his outward what it will,
His heart was an apostate's still.
He'd oft profess an hallowed flame,
And every where preached Wesley's name;
He was a preacher, and what not,
As long as money could be got;
He'd oft profess, with holy fire,
"The labourer's worthy of his hire."

It happen'd once upon a time,
When all his works were in their prime,
A noble place appeared in view;
Then—to the Methodists, adieu!
A Methodist no more he'll be,
The Protestants serve best for *he*.
Then to the curate straight he ran,
And thus address'd the reverend man:
"I was a Methodist, 'tis true;
With penitence I turn to you.
O that it were your bounteous will
That I the vacant place might fill!
With justice I'd myself acquit,
Do every thing that's right and fit."
The curate straightway gave consent—
To take the place he quickly went.
Accordingly he took the place,
And keeps it with dissembled grace.

April 14th, 1764.

THE ROMANCE OF THE KNIGHT.

MODERNISED BY CHATTERTON,[1]

From "The Romaunte of the Knyghte, by John de Burgham."

THE pleasing sweets of spring and summer past,
The falling leaf flies in the sultry blast,
The fields resign their spangling orbs of gold,
The wrinkled grass its silver joys unfold,
Mantling the spreading moor in heavenly white,
Meeting from every hill the ravished sight.
The yellow flag uprears its spotted head,
Hanging regardant o'er its watery bed;
The worthy knight ascends his foaming steed,
Of size uncommon, and no common breed.
His sword of giant make hangs from his belt,
Whose piercing edge his daring foes had felt.
To seek for glory and renown he goes
To scatter death among his trembling foes;
Unnerved by fear, they trembled at his stroke;
So cutting blasts shake the tall mountain oak.

Down in a dark and solitary vale,
Where the curst screech-owl sings her fatal tale,
Where copse and brambles interwoven lie,
Where trees intwining arch the azure sky,

---

[1] See "Rowley Poems," vol. ii. p. 192, and the foot-note.

Thither the fate-marked champion bent his way,
By purling streams to lose the heat of day;
A sudden cry assaults his listening ear,
His soul's too noble to admit of fear.—
The cry re-echoes; with his bounding steed
He gropes the way from whence the cries proceed.
The arching trees above obscured the light,
Here 'twas all evening, there eternal night.
And now the rustling leaves and strengthened cry
Bespeaks the cause of the confusion nigh;
Through the thick brake th' astonished champion
sees
A weeping damsel bending on her knees:
A ruffian knight would force her to the ground,
But still some small resisting strength she found.
(Women and cats, if you compulsion use,
The pleasure which they die for will refuse.)
The champion thus: "Desist, discourteous knight,
Why dost thou shamefully misuse thy might?"
With eye contemptuous thus the knight replies,
"Begone! whoever dares my fury dies!"
Down to the ground the champion's gauntlet flew,
"I dare thy fury, and I'll prove it too."

Like two fierce mountain-boars enraged they fly,
The prancing steeds make Echo rend the sky,
Like a fierce tempest is the bloody fight,
Dead from his lofty steed falls the proud ruffian
knight.
The victor, sadly pleased, accosts the dame,
"I will convey you hence to whence you came."
With look of gratitude the fair replied—
"Content; I in your virtue may confide.

But," said the fair, as mournful she surveyed
The breathless corse upon the meadow laid,
"May all thy sins from heaven forgiveness find!
May not thy body's crimes affect thy mind!"

TO A FRIEND.[1]

March 6th, 1768.

Dear Friend,

I have received both your favours—The Muse alone must tell my joy.

O'ERWHELM'D with pleasure at the joyful news,
I strung the chorded shell, and woke the Muse.
Begin, O Servant of the Sacred Nine!
And echo joy through every nervous line;
Bring down th' ethereal choir to aid the song;
Let boundless raptures smoothly glide along.
My Baker's well! Oh words of sweet delight!
Now! now! my Muse, soar up th' Olympic height.
What wondrous numbers can the Goddess find
To paint th' ecstatic raptures of my mind?
I leave it to a Goddess more divine,
The beauteous Hoyland shall employ my line.

---

[1] Addressed, together with a Letter, to Mr. Baker, Charles-Town, South Carolina. Baker was an old school-fellow, who had gone to America. In the same letter were enclosed several of the poems on Miss Hoyland, first printed in the Supplement to Chatterton's Miscellanies, 1784.

TO THE BEAUTEOUS MISS HOYLAND.[1]

FAR distant from Britannia's lofty Isle,
What shall I find to make the Genius smile?
The bubbling fountains lose the power to please,
The rocky cataracts, the shady trees,
The juicy fruitage of enchanting hue,
Whose luscious virtues England never knew;
The variegated daughters of the land,
Whose numbers Flora strews with bounteous hand;
The verdant vesture of the smiling fields,
All the rich pleasures Nature's store-house yields,
Have all their powers tc wake the chorded string,—
But still they're subjects that the Muse can sing.
Hoyland, more beauteous than the God of Day,
Her name can quicken and awake the lay;
Rouse the soft Muse from indolence and ease,
To live, to love, and rouse her powers to please.
In vain would Phœbus, did not Hoyland, rise:
'Tis her bright eyes that gilds the Eastern skies;
'Tis she alone deprives us of the light;
And when she slumbers, then indeed 'tis night.
To tell the separate beauties of her face
Would stretch Eternity's remotest space,
And want a more than man to pen the line;
I rest—let this suffice, dear Hoyland's all divine.

---

[1] The *inamorata* of Chatterton's school-fellow, Baker. See the last poem. The "Acrostic" below shows that her Christian name was Eleanor. Chatterton writes in Baker's person, and therefore supposes himself to be far from England.

ODE TO MISS HOYLAND. (1768.)

AMIDST the wild and dreary dells,
The distant echo-giving bells,
The bending mountain's head;
Whilst Evening, moving through the sky,
Over the object and the eye,
Her pitchy robes doth spread;

There, gently moving through the vale,
Bending before the blustering gale,
Fell apparitions glide;
Whilst roaring rivers echo round,
The drear reverberating sound
Runs through the mountain side;

Then steal I softly to the grove,
And, singing of the nymph I love,
Sigh out my sad complaint;
To paint the tortures of my mind,
Where can the Muses numbers find?
Ah! numbers are too faint!

Ah! Hoyland, empress of my heart,
When will thy breast admit the dart,
And own a mutual flame?
When, wandering in the myrtle groves,
Shall mutual pleasures seal our loves,
Pleasures without a name?

Thou greatest beauty of the sex,
When will the little god perplex
  The mansions of thy breast?
When wilt thou own a flame as pure
As that seraphic souls endure,
  And make thy Baker[1] blest?

O! haste to give my passion ease,
And bid the perturbation cease
  That harrows up my soul!
The joy such happiness to find
Would make the functions of my mind
  In peace and love to roll.

ACROSTIC ON MISS ELEANOR HOYLAND.

(1768).

ENCHANTING is the mighty power of Love;
Life stript of amorous joys would irksome prove:
E'en Heaven's great Thunderer wore the easy chain,
And over all the world Love keeps his reign.
No human heart can bear the piercing blade,
Or I than others am more tender made.
Right through my heart a burning arrow drove,
Hoyland's bright eyes were made the bows of Love.
Oh! torture inexpressibly severe!
You are the pleasing author of my care.

---

[1] Chatterton is here writing in Baker's name. See p. 13, note 1.

Look down, fair angel, on a swain distrest,
A gracious smile from you would make me blest.
Nothing but that blest favour stills my grief—
Death, that denied, will quickly give relief.

ACROSTIC ON MISS SALLY CLARKE. (1768).

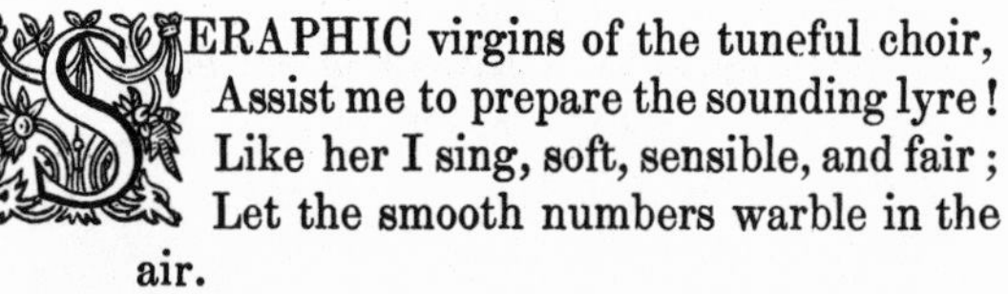

SERAPHIC virgins of the tuneful choir,
Assist me to prepare the sounding lyre!
Like her I sing, soft, sensible, and fair;
Let the smooth numbers warble in the air.
Ye prudes, coquets, and all the misled throng,
Can Beauty, Virtue, Sense, demand the song?
Look then on Clarke, and see them all unite:
A beauteous pattern to the always-right.
Rest here, my Muse, nor soar above thy sphere—
Kings might pay adoration to the fair,
Enchanting, full of joy, peerless in face and air.

TO MISS HOYLAND. (1768).

ONCE more the Muse to beauteous Hoyland sings;—
Her grateful tribute of harsh numbers brings
To Hoyland! Nature's richest, sweetest store,
She made an Hoyland, and can make no more.

Nor all the beauties of the world's vast round
United, will as sweet as her be found.
Description sickens to rehearse her praise—
Her worth alone will deify my days.
Enchanting creature! Charms so great as thine
May all the beauties of the day outshine.
Thy eyes to every gazer send a dart,
Thy taking graces captivate the heart.
O for a muse that shall ascend the skies,
And like the subject of the Epode rise;
To sing the sparkling eye, the portly grace,
The thousand beauties that adorn the face
Of my seraphic maid, whose beauteous charms
Might court the world to rush at once to arms;
Whilst the fair Goddess, native of the skies,
Shall sit above, and be the victor's prize.
O now, whilst yet I sound the tuneful lyre,
I feel the thrilling joy her hands inspire;
When the soft tender touch awakes my blood,
And rolls my passions with the purple flood.
My pulse beats high; my throbbing breast's on fire
In sad variety of wild desire.
O Hoyland! heavenly goddess! angel! saint!
Words are too weak thy mighty worth to paint;
Thou best, completest work that nature made,
Thou art my substance, and I am thy shade.
Possess'd of thee, I joyfully would go
Through the loud tempest, and the depth of woe.
From thee alone my being I derive—
One beauteous smile from thee makes all my hopes
alive.

TO MISS HOYLAND. (1768).

SINCE short the busy scene of life will prove,
Let us, my Hoyland, learn to live and love;
To love with passions pure as morning light,
Whose saffron beams, unsullied by the night,
With rosy mantles do the heavens streak,
Faint imitators of my Hoyland's cheek.
The joys of nature in her ruin'd state
Have little pleasure, though the pains are great:
Virtue and Love when sacred bands unite,
'Tis then that nature leads to true delight.
Oft as I wander through the myrtle grove,
Bearing the beauteous burden of my love,
A secret terror, lest I should offend
The charming maid on whom my joys depend,
Informs my soul, that virtuous minds alone
Can give a pleasure, to the vile unknown.
But when the body charming, and the mind
To every virtuous Christian act inclined,
Meet in one person, maid and angel join,
Who must it be, but Hoyland the divine?
What worth intrinsic will that man possess,
Whom the dear charmer condescends to bless?
Swift will the minutes roll, the flying hours,
And blessings overtake the pair by showers:
Each moment will improve upon the past,
And every day be better than the last.

Love means an unadulterated flame,
Though lust too oft usurps the sacred name;
Such passion as in Hoyland's breast can move,
'Tis that alone deserves the name of Love.
Oh, were my merit great enough to find
A favour'd station in my Hoyland's mind,
Then would my happiness be quite complete,
And all revolving joys as in a centre meet.

TO MISS HOYLAND. (1768).

ELL me, god of soft desires,
Little Cupid, wanton boy,
How thou kindlest up thy fires,
Giving pleasing pain and joy?

Hoyland's beauty is thy bow,
Striking glances are thy darts:
Making conquests never slow,
Ever gaining conquered hearts.

Heaven is seated in her smile,
Juno's in her portly air;
Not Britannia's favourite isle
Can produce a nymph so fair.

In a desert vast and drear,
Where disorder springs around,
If the lovely fair is there,
'Tis a pleasure-giving ground.

Oh my Hoyland! blest with thee,
I'd the raging storm defy,
In thy smiles I live, am free;
When thou frownest, I must die.

TO MISS HOYLAND. (1768).

WITH A PRESENT.

ACCEPT, fair Nymph, this token of my love,
Nor look disdainful on the prostrate swain:
By every sacred oath, I'll constant prove,
And act as worthy for to wear your chain.

Not with more constant ardour shall the sun
Chase the faint shadows of the night away;
Nor shall he on his course more constant run,
And cheer the universe with coming day,

Than I in pleasing chains of conquest bound,
Adore the charming author of my smart;—
For ever will I thy sweet charms resound,
And paint the fair possessor of my heart.

TO MISS HOYLAND. (1768).

COUNT all the flowers that deck the meadow's side,
When Flora flourishes in new-born pride;
Count all the sparkling orbits in the sky;

Count all the birds that through the æther fly;
Count all the foliage of the lofty trees,
That fly before the bleak autumnal breeze;
Count all the dewy blades of verdant grass;
Count all the drops of rain that softly pass
Through the blue æther, or tempestuous roar:
Count all the sands upon the breaking shore;
Count all the minutes since the world began;
Count all the troubles of the life of man;
Count all the torments of the d——d in hell;—
More are the beauteous charms that make my
nymph excel.

TO MISS CLARKE.[1] (1768).

O sing of Clarke my Muse aspires,
A theme by charms made quite divine.
Ye tuneful virgins, sound your lyres,
Apollo aid the feeble line.

If truth and virtue, wit and charms,
May for a fixed attention call,
The darts of Love and wounding arms—
The beauteous Clarke shall hold o'er all.

'Tis not the tincture of a skin,
The rosy lip, the charming eye;
No, 'tis a greater power within,
That bids the passion never die.

---

[1] See p. 16.

These Clarke possesses, and much more—
All beauty in her glances sport;
She is the goddess all adore
In country, city, and at court.

TO MISS HOYLAND.[1]

SWEET are thy charming smiles, my lovely maid,
Sweet as the flowers in bloom of spring arrayed;
Those charming smiles thy beauteous face adorn,
As May's white blossoms gaily deck the thorn.
Then why, when mild good-nature basking lies
'Midst the soft radiance of thy melting eyes;
When my fond tongue would strive thy heart to move,
And tune its tones to every note of love;
Why do those smiles their native soil disown,
And (changed their movements) kill me in a frown?

Yet is it true, or is it dark despair
That fears you're cruel whilst it owns you fair?
O speak, dear Hoyland! speak my certain fate,
Thy love enrapturing, or thy constant hate.
If death's dire sentence hangs upon thy tongue,
E'en death were better than suspense so long.

[1] From "Miscellanies in Prose and Verse," by Edward Gardner; Bristol, 1798.

TO MISS HOYLAND.

[First printed in 1803, from the original then in the possession of Mr. Gardner.]

O, gentle Muse, and to my fair one say,
My ardent passion mocks the feeble lay,
That love's pure flame my panting breast inspires,
And friendship warms me with her chaster fires.
Yes, more my fond esteem, my matchless love,
Than the soft turtle's, cooing in the grove;
More than the lark delights to mount the sky,
Then, sinking on the greensward, soft to lie;
More than the bird of eve, at close of day,
To pour in solemn solitude her lay;
More than grave Camplin[1] with his deep-toned note,
To mouth the sacred service got by rote;
More than sage Catcott[2] does his storm of rain,
Sprung from th' abyss of his eccentric brain,
Or than his wild-antique and sputtering brother
Loves in his ale-house chair to drink and pother;
More than soft Lewis,[3] that sweet pretty thing,
Loves in the pulpit to display his ring;
More than frail mortals love a brother sinner,
And more than Bristol aldermen their dinner,

---

[1] John Camplin, M.A. Precentor of Bristol.

[2] The Rev. Mr. Catcott wrote a book on the Deluge.

[3] Mr. Lewis was a dissenting preacher of note, then in Bristol. Chatterton calls him, in a letter dated May 14, 1770, a "pulpit-fop."

When full four pounds of the well-fatten'd haunch
In twenty mouthfuls fill the greedy paunch.

If these true strains can thy dear bosom move,
Let thy soft blushes speak a mutual love:
But if thy purpose settles in disdain,
Speak my dread fate, and bless thy favourite swain.

D. B.

TO MISS C.[1]

ON HEARING HER PLAY ON THE HARPSICHORD.

[From "Miscellanies in Prose and Verse," by Edward Gardner; Bristol, 1798.]

AD Israel's Monarch, when misfortune's dart
Pierced to its deepest core his heaving breast,
Heard but thy dulcet tones, his sorrowing heart,
At such soft tones, had soothed itself to rest.

Yes, sweeter far than Jesse's son's thy strains—
Yet what avail if sorrow they disarm?
Love's sharper sting within the soul remains,
The melting movements wound us as they charm.

---

[1] I guess Miss C. to be Miss Clarke, of whom he says, "*Like her* I sing," &c. See above, p. 16..

ELEGY

ON THE DEATH OF MR. JOHN TANDEY, SEN.

A sincere Christian Friend. He died 5th January, 1769, aged 76.[1]

I.

YE virgins of the sacred choir,
Awake the soul-dissolving lyre,
Begin the mournful strain;
To deck the much-loved *Tandey's* urn,
Let the poetic genius burn,
And all Parnassus drain.

II.

Ye ghosts! that leave the silent tomb
To wander in the midnight gloom,
Unseen by mortal eye;
Garlands of yew and cypress bring,
Adorn his tomb, his praises sing,
And swell the general sigh.

---

[1] The above-mentioned gentleman was a man of unblemished character; and father-in-law to Mr. William Barrett, author of the History of Bristol; and lies interred in *Redcliff church*, in the same vault with Mr. Barrett's wife.—The Elegy would have been inserted in one of the Bristol journals, but was suppressed at the particular request of Mr. Tandey's eldest son.—*Note by* CHATTERTON. It was first printed in 1803.

III.

Ye wretches, who could scarcely save
Your starving offspring from the grave,
By God afflicted sore,
Vent the big tear, the soul-felt sigh,
And swell your meagre infants' cry,
For *Tandey* is no more.

IV.

To you his charity he dealt,
His melting soul your miseries felt,
And made your woes his own:
A common friend to all mankind,
His face the index of his mind,
Where all the saint was shown.

V.

In him the social virtues joined,
His judgment sound, his sense refined,
His actions ever just.
Who can suppress the rising sigh,
To think such saint-like men must die,
And mix with common dust?

VI.

Had virtue power from death to save,
The good man ne'er would see the grave,
But live immortal here:
Hawksworth and *Tandey* are no more;
Lament, ye virtuous and ye poor,
And drop the unfeigned tear.

ON MR. ALCOCK, OF BRISTOL,

AN EXCELLENT MINIATURE PAINTER.[1]

YE Nine, awake the chorded shell,
Whilst I the praise of Alcock tell
In truth-dictated lays:
On wings of genius take thy flight,
O Muse! above the Olympic height,
Make echo sing his praise.

Nature, in all her glory drest,
Her flowery crown, her verdant vest,
Her zone ethereal blue,
Receives new charms from Alcock's hand;
The eye surveys, at his command,
Whole kingdoms at a view.

His beauties seem to roll the eye,
And bid the rëal arrows fly,
To wound the gazer's mind;
So taking are his men displayed,
That oft th' unguarded wounded maid
Hath wished the painter blind.

---

[1] This piece was published in the Town and Country Magazine [Feb. 1769], under the signature of Asaphides; after Chatterton's death, a linen-draper of Bristol laid claim to it as his production. But as Chatterton mentions it as his own, in the letter to his relation, Mr. Stephens of Salisbury, his right to it (such as it is) has been considered established.—Ed. (1842).

His pictures like to nature shew,
The silver fountains seem to flow,
    The hoary woods to nod;
The curling hair, the flowing dress,
The speaking àttitude, confess
    The fancy-forming god.

Ye classic Roman-loving fools,
Say, could the painters of the schools
    With Alcock's pencil vie?
He paints the passions of mankind,
And in the face displays the mind,
    Charming the heart and eye.

Thrice happy artist, rouse thy powers,
And send, in wonder-giving showers,
    Thy beauteous works to view:
Envy shall sicken at thy name,
Italians leave the chair of Fame,
    And own the seat thy due.

Bristol, Jan. 29, 1769. ASAPHIDES.

TO MR. HOLLAND.[1]

WHAT numbers, Holland, can the muses find,
To sing thy merit in each varied part,
When action, eloquence, and ease combined,
Make nature but a copy of thy art?

Majestic as the eagle on the wing,
Or the young sky-helm'd, mountain-rooted tree;
Pleasing as meadows blushing with the spring,
Loud as the surges of the Severn sea.

In terror's strain, as clanging armies drear;
In love, as Jove, too great for mortal praise;
In pity, gentle as the falling tear;
In all, superior to my feeble lays.

Black Anger's sudden rise, ecstatic Pain;
Tormenting Jealousy's self-cank'ring sting;
Consuming Envy, with her yelling train;
Fraud, closely shrouded with the turtle's wing:

Whatever passions gall the human breast,
Play in thy features, and await thy nod.
In thee, by art, the demon stands confest,
But nature on thy soul has stamped the god.

---

[1] This person was an actor of some provincial celebrity, whose performance of various characters at Bristol was for some time the engrossing subject of conversation among the friends of Chatterton.—Ed. (1842). The poem was first printed in the Town and Country Magazine, July, 1769.

So just thy action with thy part agrees,
Each feature does the office of a tongue;
Such is thy native elegance and ease,
Bv thee the harsh line smoothly glides along.

At thy feigned woe, we're rëally distrest,
At thy feigned tears, we let the rëal fall;
By every judge of nature 'tis confest,
No single part is thine, thou'rt all in all.

D. B.

Bristol, July 21 [1769].

TO MR. POWEL.[1]

WHAT language, Powel! can thy merits tell,
By nature formed in every path t' excel;
To strike the feeling soul with magic skill,
When every passion bends beneath thy will?
Loud as the howlings of the northern wind,
Thy scenes of anger harrow up the mind;
But most thy softer tones our bosoms move,
When Juliet listens to her Romeo's love.
How sweet thy gentle movements then to see—
Each melting heart must sympathize with thee.

---

[1] From "Miscellanies in Prose and Verse," by Edward Gardner; Bristol, 1798. Mr. Powel's death is lamented by Chatterton in the poem called "Clifton," which see.

Yet, though design'd in every walk to shine,
Thine is the furious, and the tender thine;
Though thy strong feelings and thy native fire
Still force the willing gazers to admire,
Though great thy praises for thy scenic art,
We love thee for the virtues of thy heart.

TO MRS. HAYWOOD, THE NOVELIST.[1]

I.

ET Sappho's name be heard no more,
Or Dido's fate by bards be sung,
When on the billow-beaten shore
The echo of Æneas rung.

[1] These lines are taken from a volume of Mrs. Haywood's novels, formerly belonging to the circulating library of a Bristol stationer, and now in the possession of the Earl of Limerick. They appeared a few years since in one of the monthly magazines, but now for the first time [1842] make part of Chatterton's collected works. The authoress to whom they are addressed was not distinguished for the morality of her earlier works. She produced "The Court of Carimania," "The New Utopia," with others of a like kind. Pope branded her for them in the Dunciad :—

"See in the circle next, Eliza placed,
Two babes of love close clinging to her waist," &c.

She afterwards appeared as a moralist, and produced "The Female Spectator," four vols., and numerous other works. She is represented as a woman of strict decorum and delicacy in her private character. She died in 1756. During the whole of Chatterton's life her works continued their great popularity. They are now entirely forgotten.—EDITOR (1842).

II.

Love, the great ruler of the breast,
  Proud and impatient to control,
In every novel stands confest,
  Waking to nature's scenes the soul.

III.

Haywood! thy genius was divine;
  The softer passions owned thy sway;
Thy easy prose, the flowing line,
  Accomplishments supreme display.

IV.

Pope, son of envy and of fame,
  Penned the invidious line in vain;
To blast thy literary name,
  Exceeds the power of human strain.

V.

Ye gay, ye sensible, ye fair,
  To what her genius wrote, attend;
You'll find engaging morals there
  To help the lover and the friend.

TO HORACE WALPOLE.

[From Dix's Life of Chatterton, p. 80; probably written in August, 1769.]

WALPOLE, I thought not I should ever see
So mean a heart as thine has proved to be.
Thou who, in luxury nurst, behold'st with scorn

The boy, who friendless, fatherless, forlorn,
Asks thy high favour—thou mayst call me cheat.
Say, didst thou never practise such deceit?
Who wrote Otranto? but I will not chide:
Scorn I'll repay with scorn, and pride with pride.
Still, Walpole, still thy prosy chapters write,
And twaddling letters to some fair indite;
Laud all above thee, fawn and cringe to those
Who, for thy fame, were better friends than foes;
Still spurn th' incautious fool who dares—

* * * * *

Had I the gifts of wealth and luxury shared,
Not poor and mean, Walpole! thou hadst not dared
Thus to insult. But I shall live and stand
By Rowley's side, when thou art dead and damned.

T. C.

JOURNAL SIXTH.[1]

'TIS mystery all, in every sect
You find this palpable defect,
The axis of the dark machine
Is enigmatic and unseen.
Opinion is the only guide
By which our senses are supplied;
Mere grief's conjecture, fancy's whim,
Can make our reason side with him.

---

[1] Copied from a poem in Chatterton's handwriting in the British Museum, and printed in 1803.

But this discourse perhaps will be
As little liked by you as me;
I'll change the subject for a better,
And leave the Doctor, and his letter.
A Priest, whose sanctimonious face
Became a sermon, or a grace,
Could take an orthodox repast,
And left the knighted loin the last;
To fasting very little bent,
He'd pray indeed till breath was spent.
Shrill was his treble as a cat,
His organs being choked with fat;
In college quite as graceful seen
As Camplin or the lazy Dean,
(Who sold the ancient cross to Hoare
For one church-dinner, nothing more;[1]
The Dean who, sleeping on the book,
Dreams he is swearing at his cook;)
This animated hill of oil
Was to another dean the foil.
They seemed two beasts of different kind,
Contra in politics and mind;
The only sympathy they knew,
They both loved turtle a-la-stew.
The Dean was empty, thin and long,
As Fowler's[2] back or head or song.
He met the Rector in the street,
Sinking a cánal with his feet.
"Sir," quoth the Dean, with solemn nod,
"You are a minister of God;

---

[1] Cf. note 1, p. 23, and Wilson's Life of Chatterton, p. 18.
[2] Jack Fowler, a Bristol poetaster, cf. p. 38.

And, as I apprehend, should be
About such holy works as me.
But, cry your mercy, at a feast
You only shew yourself a priest.
No sermon politic you preach,
No doctrine damnable you teach.
Did not we few maintain the fight,
Mystery might sink, and all be light.
From house to house your appetite
In daily sojourn paints ye right.
Nor lies, true-orthodox, you carry,
You hardly ever hang or marry.
Good Mr. Rector, let me tell ye
You've too much tallow in this belly.
Fast, and repent of every sin,
And grow like me, upright and thin;
Be active, and assist your mother,
And then I'll own ye for a brother."

"Sir," quoth the Rector in a huff,
"True, you're diminutive enough,
And let me tell ye, Mr. Dean,
You are as worthless too as lean;
This mountain, strutting to my face,
Is an undoubted sign of grace.
Grace, though you ne'er on turtle sup,
Will like a bladder blow you up,
A tun of claret swells your case
Less than a single ounce of grace."

"You're wrong," the bursting Dean replied,
"Your logic's on the rough-cast side,
The minor's right, the major falls,

Weak as his modern honour's walls.
A spreading trunk, with rotten skin,
Shews very little's kept within;
But when the casket's neat, not large,
We guess th' importance of the charge."

"Sir," quoth the Rector, "I've a story
Quite apropos to lay before ye.
A sage philosopher, to try
What pupil saw with reason's eye,
Prepared three boxes, gold, lead, stone,
And bid three youngsters claim each one.
The first, a Bristol merchant's heir,
Loved pelf above the charming fair;
So 'tis not difficult to say,
Which box the dolthead took away.
The next, as sensible as me,
Desired the pebbled one, d'ye see.
The other having scratch'd his head,
Considered, though the third was lead,
'Twas metal still surpassing stone,
So claimed the leaden box his own.
Now to unclose they all prepare,
And hope alternate laughs at fear.
The golden case does ashes hold,
The leaden shines with sparkling gold,
But in the outcast stone they see
A jewel,—such pray fancy me."[1]

"Sir," quoth the Dean, "I truly say
You tell a tale a pretty way;

---

[1] This story, told by Shakespeare and Gower, is in the Gesta Romanorum. See Warton, Hist. Eng. Poetry, i. cxcvii.; ed. 1840.

But the conclusion to allow—
'Fore-gad, I scarcely can tell how.
A jewel! Fancy must be strong
To think you keep your water long.
I preach, thank gracious heaven! as clear
As any pulpit-stander here,
But may the devil claw my face
If e'er I prayed for puffing grace,
To be a mountain, and to carry
Such a vile heap—I'd rather marry!
Each day to sweat three gallons full
And span a furlong on my skull.
Lost to the melting joys of love—
Not to be borne—like justice move."

And here the Dean was running on,
Through half a couplet having gone:
Quoth Rector peevish, "I sha'nt stay
To throw my precious time away.
The generous Burgum having sent
A ticket as a compliment,
I think myself in duty bound
Six pounds of turtle to confound."

"That man you mention," answers Dean,
"Creates in priests of sense the spleen,
His soul's as open as his hand,
Virtue distrest may both command;
That ragged virtue is a w——e,
I always beat her from my door.
But Burgum gives, and giving shews
His honour leads him by the nose.
Ah! how unlike the church divine,

Whose feeble lights on mountains shine,
And being placed so near the sky,
Are lost to every human eye.
His luminaries shine around
Like stars in the Cimmerian ground."

"Invidious slanderer!" quoth priest,
"O may I never scent a feast,
If thy curst conscience is as pure
As underlings in Whitefield's cure!
The church, as thy display has shewn,
Is turned a bawd to lustful town;
But what against the church you've said,
Shall soon fall heavy on your head.
Is Burgum's virtue then a fault?
Ven'son and heaven forbid the thought!
He gives, and never eyes return,
O may paste altars to him burn!
But whilst I talk with worthless you,
Perhaps the dinner waits—adieu."

This said, the Rector trudged along,
As heavy as Fowlerian song.
The hollow Dean, with fairy feet,
Stept lightly through the dirty street.
At last, arrived at destined place,
The bulky Doctor squeaks the grace:
"Lord bless the many-flavour'd meat,
And grant us strength enough to eat!
May all and every mother's son
Be drunk before the dinner's done.
When we give thanks for dining well, oh!
May each grunt out in Ritornello."

Amen! resounds to distant tide,
And weapons clang on every side,
The oily rivers burn around,
And gnashing teeth make doleful sound.
Now is the busy President
In his own fated element,
In every look and action great,
His presence doubly fills the plate.
Nobly invited to the feast,
They all contribute gold at least.
The Duke and President collected,
Alike beloved, alike respected.

AY, Baker, if experience hoar[1]
Has yet unbolted wisdom's door,
What is this phantom of the mind,
This love, when sifted and refined?
When the poor lover, fancy-frighted,
Is with [his] shadowy joys delighted,
A frown shall throw him in despair;
A smile shall brighten up his air.
Jealous without a seeming cause,
From flatt'ring smiles he misery draws;
Again, without his reason's aid,
His bosom's still, the devil's laid.
If this is love, my callous heart
Has never felt the rankling dart.

---

[1] This poem immediately follows the other. It has no title, and is written upon the same paper, a whole sheet, folded into four columns. See note 1, p. 12.

Oft have I seen the wounded swain
Upon the rack of pleasing pain,
Full of his flame, upon his tongue
The quivering declaration hung,
When lost to courage, sense, and reason,
He talked of weather and the season.
Such tremors never cowered me,
I'm flattering, impudent, and free,
Unmoved by frowns and lowering eyes,
'Tis smiles I only ask and prize;
And when the smile is freely given,
You're in the highway-road to heaven.
These coward lovers seldom find
That whining makes the ladies kind.
They laugh at silly silent swains
Who're fit for nothing but their chains.
'Tis an effrontery and tongue
On very oily hinges hung
Must win the blooming, melting fair,
And shew the joys of heaven here.
 A rake, I take it, is a creature
Who winds through all the folds of nature;
Who sees the passions, and can tell
How the soft beating heart shall swell;
Who, when he ravishes the joy,
Defies the torments of the boy.
Who with the soul the body gains,
And shares love's pleasures, not his pains.
Who holds his charmer's reputation
Above a tavern veneration;
And when a love-repast he makes,
Not even prying fame partakes.
Who looks above a prostitute, he

Thinks love the only price of beauty,
And she that can be basely sold
Is much beneath or love or gold.
Who thinks the almost dearest part
In all the body is the heart:
Without it, rapture cannot rise,
Nor pleasures wanton in the eyes;
The sacred joy of love is dead,
Witness the sleeping marriage bed.
This is the picture of a rake,
Shew it the ladies—won't it take?
A buck's a beast of th' other side,
And rëal but in hoofs and hide:
To nature and the passions dead,
A brothel is his house and bed;
To fan the flame of warm desire,
And after wanton in the fire,
He thinks a labour; and his parts
Were not designed to conquer hearts.[1]
The girls of virtue when he views,
Dead to all converse but the stews,
Silent as death, he's nought to say,
But sheepish steals himself away.
This is a buck to life display'd,
A character to charm each maid.
Now, prithee, friend, a choice to make,
Wouldst choose the buck before the rake?
The buck, as brutal as the name,
Invenoms every charmer's fame,
And though he never touched her hand,
Protests he had her at command.

---

[1] Two lines following omitted.

The rake, in gratitude for pleasure,
Keeps reputation dear as treasure.

* * * * *

[*After these asterisks follows, without title:*]

But Hudibrastics may be found
To tire ye with repeated sound;
So, changing for a Shandeyan style,
I ask your favour and your smile.

ODE.

Recitative.

In his wooden palace jumping,
Tearing, sweating, bawling, thumping,
"Repent, repent, repent,"
The mighty Whitefield cries,
Oblique light'ning in his eyes,
"Or die and be damn'd!" all around
The long-eared rabble grunt in dismal sound,
"Repent, repent, repent,"
Each concave mouth replies.
The comet of gospel, the lanthorn of light,
Is rising and shining
Like candles at night.
He shakes his ears,
He jumps, he stares;
Hark, he's whining!
The short-hand saints prepare to write,
And high they mount their ears.

Air.

"Now the devil take ye all,
Saints or no saints, all in a lump;

Here must I labour and bawl,
And thump, and thump, and thump;
And never a souse[1] to be got.
Unless—I swear by jingo,
A greater profit's made,
I'll forswear my trade,
My gown and market-lingo,
And leave ye all to pot."

Recitative.

Now he raves like brindled cat,
Now 'tis thunder,
Rowling,
Growling,
Rumbling,
Grumbling,
Noise and nonsense, jest and blunder.
Now he chats of this and that,
No more the soul-jobber,
No more the sly robber,
He's now an old woman who talks to her cat.
Again he starts, he beats his breast,
He rolls his eyes, erects his crest;
Hark! hark! the sound begins,
'Tis a bargain and sale for remission of sins.

Air.

" Say, beloved congregation,
In the hour of tribulation,
Did the power of man affray me?

---

[1] He means a *sou.* He was misled by Bailey, who gives " *Sous*, a French penny." At p. 46 it is rightly used.

Say, ye wives, and say, ye daughters,
Ha'n't I staunched your running waters?
I have laboured—pay me—pay me!

I have given absolution,
Don't withhold your contribution;
Men and angels should obey me—
Give but freely, you've remission
For all sins without condition;
You're my debtors, pay me, pay me!"

Recitative.

Again he's lost, again he chatters
Of lace and bobbin and such matters.
A thickening vapour swells—
Of Adam's fall he tells;
Dark as twice ten thousand hells
Is the gibberish which he spatters.
Now a most dismal elegy he sings,
Groans, doleful groans are heard about;
The Issacharian rout
Swell the sharp howl, and loud the sorrow rings.

He sung a modern buck, whose end
Was blinded prejudice and zeal;
In life, to every vice a friend,
Unfixed as fortune on her wheel.
He lived a buck, he died a fool,
So let him to oblivion fall,
Who thought a wretched body all,
Untaught in nature's or the passion's school.
Now he takes another theme,
Thus he tells his waking dream.

Air.

"After fasting and praying and grunting and
weeping,
My guardian angel beheld me fast sleeping;
And instantly capering into my brain,
Relieved me from prison of bodily chain.
The soul can be every thing as you all know,
And mine was transformed to the shape of a crow."
(The preacher or metre has surely mistook,
For all must confess that a parson's a rook.)

"Having wings, as I think I informed ye before,
I shot through a cavern and knocked at hell's door.
Out comes Mr. Porter Devil,
And, I'll assure ye, very civil.
"Dear sir," quoth he, "pray step within,
The company is drinking tea;
We have a stranger just come in,
A brother from the triple tree."

Well, in I walked, and what d'ye think?
Instead of sulphur, fire, and stink,
'Twas like a masquerade,
All grandeur, all parade.
Here stood an amphitheatre,
There stood the small Haymarket-house,
With devil-actors very clever, .
Who without blacking did Othello.
And truly, a huge horned fellow
Told me, he hoped I would endeavour
To learn a part, and get a souse;[1]
For pleasure was the business there.

---

[1] See note 1, p. 43.

A lawyer asked me for a fee,
To plead my right to drinking tea:
I begged his pardon; to my thinking,
I'd rather have a cheering cup,
For tea was but insipid drinking,
And brandy raised the spirits up.
So having seen each place in hell,
I straight awoke, and found all well."

Recitative.

Now again his cornet's sounding,
Sense and harmony confounding,
Reason tortured, scripture twisted,
Into every form of fancy;
Forms which never yet existed,
And but his óblique optics cán see.
He swears,
He tears,
With sputtered nonsense now he breaks the ears;
At last the sermon and the paper ends;
He whines, and hopes his well-beloved friends
Will contribute their sous
To pay the arrears for building a house;
With spiritual doctors, and doctors for poxes,
Who all must be satisfied out of the boxes.
Hark! hark!—his cry resounds,
"Fire and thunder, blood and wounds,
Contribute, contribute,
And pay me my tribute,
Or the devil, I swear,
hall hunt ye as sportsmen would hunt a poor hare.
Whoever gives, unto the Lord he lends."
The saint is melted, pays his fee, and wends;
And here the tedious length'ning Journal ends.

Ended Sat. evening, 30th Sept. 1769.

FRAGMENT.

[Printed in 1803, from a MS. in Chatterton's handwriting.]

FAR from the reach of critics and reviews,
Brush up thy pinions and ascend, my Muse!
Of conversation sing an ample theme,
And drink the tea of Heliconian stream.
Hail, matchless linguist! prating Delia, hail!
When scandal's best materials, hacknied, fail,
Thy quick invention lends a quick supply,
And all thy talk is one continued lie.
Know, thou eternal babbler, that my song
Could shew a line as venom'd as thy tongue.
In pity to thy sex, I cease to write
Of London journeys and the marriage-night.
The conversation which in taverns ring
Descends below my satire's soaring sting.
Upon his elbow-throne great Maro sits,
Revered at Forster's by the would-be wits;
Deliberately the studied jest he breaks,
And long and loud the polished table shakes;
Retailed in every brothel-house in town,
Each dancing booby vends it as his own.
Upon the emptied jelly-glass reclined,
The laughing Maro gathers up his wind;
The tail-bud 'prentice rubs his hands and grins,

Ready to laugh before the tale begins:
" To talk of freedom, politics, and Bute,
And knotty arguments in law confute,
I leave to blockheads, for such things designed,
Be it my task divine to ease the mind."

" To-morrow," says a Church of England priest,
" Is of good St. Epiphany the feast"—
" It nothing matters whether he or she,
But be all servants from their labour free."
The laugh begins with Maro, and goes round,
And the dry jest is very witty found:
In every corner of the room are seen
Round altars covered with eternal green,
Piled high with offerings to the Goddess Fame,
Which mortals chronicles and journals name;
Where in strange jumble flesh and spirit lie,
And illustration sees a jest-book nigh:
Anti-venereal med'cine cheek by jowl
With Whitfield's famous physic for the soul;
The patriot Wilkes's ever-famed essay,
With Bute and justice in the self-same lay:
Which of the two deserved (ye casuists tell)
The conflagrations of a hangman's hell?

The clock strikes eight; the taper dully shines;
Farewell, my muse, nor think of further lines:
Nine leaves, and in two hours, or something odd,
Shut up the book,—it is enough, by G-d!

28th Oct. [1769].

Sage Gloster's bishop sits supine between
His fiery floggers, and a cure for spleen:

The son of flame, enthusiastic Law,
Displays his bigot blade and thunders draw,
Unconscious of his neighbours, some vile plays,
Directing-posts to Beelzebub's highways;
Fools are philosophers in Jones's line,
And, bound in gold and scarlet, Dodsleys shine;
These are the various offerings Fame requires,
For ever rising to her shrines in spires;
Hence all Avaro's politics are drained,
And Evelina's general scandal's gained.

Where Satan's temple rears its lofty head,
And muddy torrents wash their shrinking bed;
Where the stupendous sons of commerce meet,
Sometimes to scold indeed, but oft to eat;
Where frugal Cambria all her poultry gives,
And where th' insatiate Messalina lives,
A mighty fabric opens to the sight:
With four large columns, five large windows dight;
With four small portals,—'tis with much ado
A common-council lady can pass through:
Here Hare first teaches supple limbs to bend,
And faults of nature never fails to mend.

Here conversation takes a nobler flight,
For nature leads the theme, and all is right;
The little god of love improves discourse,
And sage discretion finds his thunder hoarse;
About the flame the gilded trifles play,
Till, lost in forge unknown, they melt away;
And, cherishing the passion in the mind,
Their each idea's brightened and refined.

Ye painted guardians of the lovely fair,

Who spread the saffron bloom, and tinge the hair:
Whose deep invention first found out the art
Of making rapture glow in every part;
Of wounding by each varied attitude—
Sure 'twas a thought divinity endued.

* * * *

ELEGY

ON THE DEATH OF MR. PHILLIPS, OF FAIRFORD.[1]

[Thomas Phillips had been an usher in Colston's Hospital, and Chatterton had been his pupil. The poem may have been first written about October, 1769, and was first printed in the "Supplement to the Town and Country Magazine," 1769. Additions were made to it afterwards; see the foot-note.]

SSIST me, powers of Heaven! what do I hear?
Surprise and horror check the burning tear.
Is Phillips dead, and is my friend no more?

---

[1] "This Elegy on the death of Thomas Phillips seems to have cost Chatterton some labour. Not satisfied with a first attempt, he set to work two or three months after his original effusion, and coined his grief afresh. Southey was not aware of this till after the ruder draught was printed. The second copy had found its way by some means into the hands of the late eccentric Thomas Hill, the friend and companion of all the present, and too many of the departed race of literary men. Through his medium it reached the Laureate, who printed it in the same volume with the older copy, with the following explanatory note:—'As this latter Elegy contained seven or eight new stanzas, besides many verbal alterations, instead of cancelling the old, it was deemed proper

Gone like the sand divested from the shore?
And is he gone?—Can then the Nine refuse
To sing with gratitude a favour'd Muse?

ELEGY.

No more I hail the morning's golden gleam,
No more the wonders of the view I sing;
Friendship requires a melancholy theme,
At her command the awful lyre I string!

Now as I wander through this leafless grove,
Where tempests howl, and blasts eternal rise,[1]
How shall I teach the chorded shell to move,
Or stay the gushing torrent from my eyes?

Phillips! great master of the boundless lyre,
Thee would my soul-rack'd muse attempt to paint;[2]
Give me a double portion of thy fire,
Or all the powers of language are too faint.

Say, soul unsullied by the filth of vice,[3]

---

to let it remain, and to print the corrected copy also, by which the reader will be pleased in tracing Chatterton's various emendations.' In the present edition the corrected copy only is retained: the emendations referred to may be noted from the variations subjoined."—*Editor of the Edition of* 1842. The additions include the first six lines, and the stanzas marked with an asterisk.

[1] In the original copy:—
"Where the dark vapours of the ev'ning rise."

[2] Better expressed in the former version:—
"Thee would the *grateful* muse," &c.

[3] This stanza stood thus in the first copy:—
"Say what bold number, what immortal line
The image of thy genius can reflect?
Oh, lend my pen what animated thine,
To shew thee in thy native glories deck'd!"

Say, meek-eyed spirit, where's thy tuneful shell,
Which when the silver stream was locked with ice,
Was wont to cheer the tempest-ravaged dell?

*Oft as the filmy veil of evening drew
The thickening shade upon the vivid green,
Thou, lost in transport at the dying view,
Bid'st the ascending Muse display the scene.

When golden Autumn, wreathed in ripened corn,
From purple clusters prest the foamy wine,
Thy genius did his sallow brows adorn,
And made the beauties of the season thine.

With rustling sound the yellow foliage flies,
And wantons with the wind in rapid whirls;
The gurgling rivulet to the valley hies,
Whilst on its bank the spangled serpent curls.[1]

The joyous charms of Spring delighted saw
Their beauties doubly glaring in thy lay;
Nothing was Spring which Phillips did not draw,
And every image of his Muse was May.

So rose the regal hyacinthal star,
So shone the verdure of the daisied bed,
So seemed the forest glimmering from afar;
You saw the rëal prospect as you read.

Majestic Summer's blooming flowery pride
Next claimed the honour of his nervous song;
He taught the stream in hollow trills to glide,
And led the glories of the year along.

---

[1] More appropriately in the first copy:—
"And lost to sight, in dying murmurs curls."

Pale rugged Winter bending o'er his tread,
His grizzled hair bedropt with icy dew;
His eyes, a dusky light congealed and dead,
His robe, a tinge of bright ethereal blue.

His train a motleyed, sanguine, sable cloud,
He limps along the russet, dreary moor,
Whilst rising whirlwinds, blasting, keen, and loud,
Roll the white surges to the sounding shore.

Nor were his pleasures unimproved by thee;
Pleasures he has, though horridly deformed;
The polished lake, the silvered hill we see,
Is by thy genius fired,[1] preserved, and warmed.

The rough October[2] has his pleasures too;
But I'm insensible to every joy:
Farewell the laurel! now I grasp the yew,
And all my little powers in grief employ.

*Immortal shadow of my much-loved friend!
Clothed in thy native virtue meet my soul,
When on the fatal bed, my passions bend,
And curb my floods of anguish as they roll.

In thee each virtue found a pleasing cell,
Thy mind was honour, and thy soul divine;
With thee did every god[3] of genius dwell,
Thou wast the Helicon of all the Nine.

Fancy, whose various figure-tinctured vest
Was ever changing to a different hue;

---

[1] First copy—"fix'd."
[2] First copy—"November."
[3] First copy—"power."

Her head, with varied bays and flowerets drest,
Her eyes, two spangles of the morning dew.

With dancing attitude she swept thy string;
And now she soars, and now again descends;
And now, reclining on the zephyr's wing,
Unto the velvet-vested mead she bends.

Peace, decked in all the softness of the dove,
Over thy passions spread her silver plume;
The rosy veil of harmony and love
Hung on thy soul in one eternal bloom.

Peace, gentlest, softest of the virtues, spread
Her silver pinions, wet with dewy tears,
Upon her best distinguished poet's head,
And taught his lyre the music of the spheres.

Temp'rance, with health and beauty in her train,
And massy-muscled strength in graceful pride,
Pointed at scarlet luxury and pain,
And did at every frugal[1] feast preside.

*Black Melancholy, stealing to the shade,
With raging Madness, frantic, loud, and dire,
Whose bloody hand displays the reeking blade,
Were strangers to thy heaven-directed lyre.

Content, who smiles in every frown of fate,
Wreathed thy pacific brow and soothed thy ill:[2]
In thy own virtues and thy genius great,
The happy Muse laid every trouble still.

---

[1] In the first copy—"cheerful."
[2] "Content, who smiles at all the frowns of fate,
Fann'd from idea ev'ry seeming ill;"—first copy.

But see! the sickening lamp of day retires,[1]
And the meek evening shades the dusky grey;
The west faint glimmers with the saffron fires,
And like thy life, O Phillips! dies[2] away.

Here, stretched upon this heaven-ascending hill,
I'll wait the horrors of the coming night,
I'll imitate the gently-plaintive rill,
And by the glare of lambent vapours write.

Wet with the dew the yellow hawthorns bow;[3]
The rustic whistles through the echoing cave;[4]
Far o'er the lea the breathing cattle low,
And the full Avon lifts the darken'd wave.

Now, as the mantle of the evening swells
Upon my mind, I feel a thickening gloom!
Ah! could I charm by necromantic spells[5]
The soul of Phillips from the deathy tomb!

Then would we wander through this darkened vale,
In converse such as heavenly spirits use,
And, borne upon the pinions[6] of the gale,
Hymn the Creator, and exert[7] the Muse.

But, horror to reflection! now no more
Will Phillips sing, the wonder of the plain!

---

[1] "The sicken'd glare of day retires"—first copy.

[2] So at first; later copy, "flies."

[3] Note on this verse by Chatterton, "Expunged as too flowery for grief."

[4] In the first copy—
"The loud winds whistle through the echoing dell!
Far o'er the lea the breathing cattle low,
And the shrill shriekings of the screech-owl swell."

[5] "By friendship's potent spells"—first copy.

[6] First copy—"plumage." [7] First copy—"exhort."

When, doubting whether they might not adore,
Admiring mortals heard his nervous strain.

See! see! the pitchy vapour hides the lawn,
Nought but a doleful bell of death is heard,
Save where into a blasted oak withdrawn
The scream proclaims the curst nocturnal bird.[1]

Now rest, my Muse, but only rest to weep
A friend made dear by every sacred tie;
Unknown to me be comfort, peace, or sleep:
Phillips is dead—'tis pleasure then to die.

*Few are the pleasures Chatterton e'er knew,
Short were the moments of his transient peace;
But Melancholy robbed him of those few,
And this hath bid all future comfort cease.

*And can the Muse be silent, Phillips gone?
And am I still alive? My soul, arise!
The robe of immortality put on,
And meet thy Phillips in his native skies.

TO THE READER.

*Observe, in favour of a hobbling strain,
Neat as exported from the parent brain,
And each and every couplet I have penned,
But little laboured, and I never mend.

T. C.

---

[1] In the first copy, thus:—
"A mad'ning darkness reigns through all the lawn,
Nought but a doleful bell of death is heard,
Save where, into a hoary oak withdrawn," &c.

ON THOMAS PHILLIPS' DEATH.[1]

[See the note at the head of the preceding poem.]

TO Clayfield, long renowned the Muses' friend,
Presuming on his goodness, this I send;
Unknown to you, Tranquillity, and Fame,
In this address perhaps I am to blame.
This rudeness let necessity excuse,
And anxious friendship for a much-loved Muse.[2]
Twice have the circling hours unveil'd the east,
Since horror found me, and all pleasures ceased;
Since every number tended to deplore;
Since fame asserted Phillips was no more.

[3]Say, is he mansioned in his native spheres?
Or is't a vapour that exhales in tears?
Swift as idea, rid me of my pain,
And let my dubious wretchedness be plain.
It is too true: the awful lyre is strung,
His elegy the sister Muses sung.
O may he live, and useless be the strain!
Fly, generous Clayfield, rid me of my pain.[3]

---

[1] A copy of this poem in Chatterton's handwriting is in the British Museum. The variations of the autograph from the copy here printed are given below, the readings of the autograph being marked MS.

[2] A grateful tribute to a shadow'd muse.—MS.

[3] The weeping muse her pensive lyre displays,
And sung his fate in well-intended lays.
For your superior judgment here they stand,
To take a polish from your nobler hand.
My dross, in your imperial gold arrayed,
To be unto his mourning friends conveyed.—MS.

Forgive my boldness, think the urgent cause;
And who can bind necessity with laws?
I wait,[1] th' admirer of your noble parts,
You, friend to genius, sciences, and arts.

Bristol, Monday Evng.,
Oct. 30, —69. THOS. CHATTERTON.

ELEGY.

[AFTER GRAY.]

JOYLESS I seek the solitary shade,
Where dusky Contemplation veils the scene,
The dark retreat, of leafless branches made,
Where sickening sorrow wets the yellowed green.

The darksome ruins of some sacred cell,
Where erst the sons of Superstition trod,
Tottering upon the mossy meadow, tell
We better know, but less adore, our God.

Now, as I mournful tread the gloomy nave,[2]
Through the wide window, once with mysteries dight,
The distant forest, and the darkened wave
Of the swoln Avon ravishes my sight.

---

[1] End.—MS.

[2] The editions have *cave;* the reading *nave* is suggested in Wilson's Life of Chatterton, p. 227. The poem appears in the "Miscellanies," 1778, but was first printed in the "Town and Country Magazine," Nov. 1769.

But see the thickening veil of evening's drawn,
The azure changes to a sabled blue;
The rapturing prospects fly the lessening lawn,
And Nature seems to mourn the dying view.

Self-frighted Fear creeps silent through the gloom,
Starts at the rustling leaf, and rolls his eyes;
Aghast with horror, when he views the tomb,
With every torment of a hell, he flies.

The bubbling brooks in plaintive murmurs roll,
The bird of omen, with incessant scream,
To melancholy thoughts awakes the soul,
And lulls the mind to contemplation's dream.

A dreary stillness broods o'er all the vale,
The clouded moon emits a feeble glare;
Joyless I seek the darkling[1] hill and dale,
Where'er I wander, sorrow still is there.

Bristol, Nov. 17, 1769.

---

[1] The word *darkling* (like *flatling*) is an adverb, meaning *in the dark*. It is a common error to regard it as an adjective.

ELEGY, WRITTEN AT STANTON-DREW.[1]

[Transcribed from a MS. in Chatterton's handwriting, and printed in 1803.]

JOYLESS I hail the solemn gloom,
Joyless I view the pillars vast and rude
Where erst the fool of Superstition trod,
In smoking blood imbrued
And rising from the tomb—
Mistaken homage to an unknown God.
Fancy, whither dost thou stray,
Whither dost thou wing thy way?
Check the rising wild delight—
Ah! what avails this awful sight?
MARIA is no more!
Why, curst remembrance, wilt thou haunt my mind?
The blessings past are misery now;
Upon her lovely brow
Her lovelier soul she wore.
Soft as the evening gale
When breathing perfumes through the rose-hedged vale,
She was my joy, my happiness refined.
All hail, ye solemn horrors of this scene,
The blasted oak, the dusky green.
Ye dreary altars, by whose side
The druid-priest, in crimson dyed,

[1] Stanton-Drew is some seven miles to the S. of Bristol, and close to Norton Malreward, *the alleged place of Rowley's birth.*

The solemn dirges sung,
And drove the golden knife
Into the palpitating seat of life,
When, rent with horrid shouts, the distant valleys
rung.
The bleeding body bends,
The glowing purple stream ascends,
Whilst the troubled spirit near
Hovers in the steamy air;
Again the sacred dirge they sing,
Again the distant hill and coppice-valley ring.
Soul of my dear Maria, haste,
Whilst my languid spirits waste;
When from this my prison free,
Catch my soul, it flies to thee;
Death had doubly armed his dart,
In piercing thee, it pierced my heart.

CLIFTON.

[Cottle professed to print this from a copy in Chatterton's handwriting in the British Museum. There seems to be no such MS. It must have been taken from Gardner's "Miscellanies," 1798, where it first appeared.]

LIFTON, sweet village! now demands
the lay,
The loved retreat of all the rich and gay;
The darling spot which pining maidens
seek,
To give health's roses to the pallid cheek.
Warm from its font the holy water pours,
And lures the sick to Clifton's neighbouring bowers.

Let bright Hygeia her glad reign resume,
And o'er each sickly form renew her bloom.
Me, whom no fell disease this hour compels
To visit Bristol's celebrated wells,
Far other motives prompt my eager view;
My heart can here its favourite bent pursue;
Here can I gaze, and pause, and muse between,
And draw some moral truth from every scene.
Yon dusky rocks that from the stream arise,
In rude rough grandeur threat the distant skies,
Seem as if nature, in a painful throe,
With dire convulsions labouring to and fro,
(To give the boiling waves a ready vent)
At one dread stroke the solid mountain rent;
The huge cleft rocks transmit to distant fame
The sacred gilding of a good saint's name.[1]
Now round the varied scene attention turns
Her ready eye—my soul with ardour burns;
For on that spot my glowing fancy dwells,
Where cenotaph its mournful story tells—[2]
How Britain's heroes, true to honour's laws,
Fell, bravely fighting in their country's cause.
But though in distant fields your limbs are laid,
In fame's long list your glories ne'er will fade;
But, blooming still beyond the gripe of death,
Fear not the blast of time's inclouding breath.
Your generous leader raised this stone to say,
You followed still where honour led the way:

---

[1] They are called St. Vincent's Rocks.

[2] Alluding to the cenotaph erected by Sir W. Draper to the memory of the soldiers of the 79th Regiment who fell at the siege of Pondicherry, the capture of Manilla, &c. See Chilcott's Hist. of Bristol, p. 357.

And by this tribute, which his pity pays,
Twines his own virtues with his soldiers' praise.
Now Brandon's cliffs my wandering gazes meet,
Whose craggy surface mocks the lingering feet;
Queen Bess's gift, (so ancient legends say)
To Bristol's fair; where to the sun's warm ray
On the rough bush the linen white they spread,
Or deck with russet leaves the mossy bed.

Here as I musing take my pensive stand,
Whilst evening shadows lengthen o'er the land,
O'er the wide landscape cast the circling eye,
How ardent memory prompts the fervid sigh!
O'er the historic page my fancy runs,
Of Britain's fortunes—of her valiant sons.
Yon castle, erst of Saxon standards proud,
Its neighbouring meadows dyed with Danish blood.
Then of its later fate a view I take:
Here the sad monarch lost his hope's last stake;
When Rupert bold, of well-achieved renown,
Stained all the fame his former prowess won.[1]
But for its ancient use no more employed,
Its walls all mouldered and its gates destroyed;
In history's roll it still a shade retains,
Though of the fortress scarce a stone remains.
Eager at length I strain each aching limb,
And breathless now the mountain's summit climb.
Here does attention her fixed gaze renew,
And of the city takes a nearer view.

---

[1] Prince Rupert surrendered Bristol Castle to Fairfax and Cromwell, 10th Sept. 1645, soon after the defeat at Naseby, 14th June. The castle was destroyed by Cromwell, 1655. See Chilcott, p. 67.

The yellow Avon, creeping at my side,
In sullen billows rolls a muddy tide;
No sportive Naiads on her streams are seen,
No cheerful pastimes deck the gloomy scene;
Fixed in a stupor by the cheerless plain,
For fairy flights the fancy toils in vain:
For though her waves, by commerce richly blest,
Roll to her shores the treasures of the west,
Though her broad banks trade's busy aspect wears,
She seems unconscious of the wealth she bears.
Near to her banks, and under Brandon's hill,
There wanders Jacob's ever-murmuring rill,[1]
That, pouring forth a never-failing stream,
To the dim eye restores the steady beam.
Here too (alas! though tottering now with age)
Stands our deserted, solitary stage,
Where oft our Powel, Nature's genuine son,[2]
With tragic tones the fixed attention won:
Fierce from his lips his angry accents fly,
Fierce as the blast that tears the northern sky;
Like snows that trickle down hot Ætna's steep,
His passion melts the soul, and makes us weep:
But oh! how soft his tender accents move—
Soft as the cooings of the turtle's love—
Soft as the breath of morn in bloom of spring,
Dropping a lucid tear on zephyr's wing!
O'er Shakespeare's varied scenes he wandered wide,
In Macbeth's form all human power defied;
In shapeless Richard's dark and fierce disguise,
In dreams he saw the murdered train arise;

---

[1] Jacob's Wells, beneath Brandon Hill.
[2] See the poem printed at p. 30.

Then what convulsions shook his trembling breast,
And strewed with pointed thorns his bed of rest!
But fate has snatched thee—early was thy doom,
How soon enclosed within the silent tomb!
No more our raptured eyes shall meet thy form,
No more thy melting tones our bosoms warm.
Without thy powerful aid, the languid stage
No more can please at once and mend the age.
Yes, thou art gone! and thy beloved remains
Yon sacred old cathedral wall contains;
There does the muffled bell our grief reveal,
And solemn organs swell the mournful peal;
Whilst hallowed dirges fill the holy shrine,
Deservèd tribute to such worth as thine.
No more at Clifton's scenes my strains o'erflow,
For the Muse, drooping at this tale of woe,
Slackens the strings of her enamoured lyre,
The flood of gushing grief puts out her fire:
Else would she sing the deeds of other times,
Of saints and heroes sung in monkish rhymes;
Else would her soaring fancy burn to stray,
And through the cloistered aisle would take her way,
Where sleep, (ah! mingling with the common dust)
The sacred bodies of the brave and just.
But vain the attempt to scan that holy lore,
These softening sighs forbid the Muse to soar.
So treading back the steps I just now trod,
Mournful and sad I seek my lone abode.

O F

EPISTLE

TO THE REVEREND MR. CATCOTT.[1]

[Printed in the Supplement to the Miscellanies, 1784.]

December 6th, 1769.

WHAT strange infatuations rule mankind!
How narrow are our prospects, how confined!
With universal vanity possessed,
We fondly think our own ideas best;
Our tottering arguments are ever strong;
We're always self-sufficient in the wrong.

What philosophic sage of pride austere
Can lend conviction an attentive ear?
What pattern of humility and truth
Can bear the jeering ridicule of youth?
What blushing author ever ranked his muse
With Fowler's, poet-laureate of the stews?
Dull Penny, nodding o'er his wooden lyre,
Conceits the vapours of Geneva fire.
All in the language of Apostles cry,
If angels contradict me, angels lie.

---

[1] This Epistle is unintelligible unless it be remembered that it refers constantly to "A Treatise on the Deluge," by A. Catcott, A.M., first published in 1761, and revised in 1768. Chatterton freely satirizes Mr. Catcott's "system."

As all have intervals of ease and pain,
So all have intervals of being vain:
But some of folly never shift the scene,
Or let one lucid moment intervene;
Dull single acts of many-footed prose
Their tragi-comedies of life compose;
Incessant madding for a system toy,
The greatest of Creation's blessings cloy;
Their senses dozing a continual dream,
They hang enraptured o'er the hideous scheme:
So virgins, tottering into ripe three-score,
Their greatest likeness in baboons adore.

When you advance new systems, first unfold
The various imperfections of the old;
Prove nature hitherto a gloomy night,
You the first focus of primæval light.
'Tis not enough you think your system true,
The busy world would have you prove it too:
Then, rising on the ruins of the rest,
Plainly demonstrate your ideas best.
Many are best; one only can be right,
Though all had inspiration to indite.

Some this unwelcome truth perhaps would tell,
Where Clogher stumbled, Catcott fairly fell.[1]
Writers on rolls of science long renowned
In one fell page are tumbled to the ground.
We see their systems unconfuted still;
But Catcott can confute them—if he will.

---

[1] Catcott criticizes an Account of the Deluge, by the Bishop of Clogher.

Would you the honour of a priest mistrust,
An excommunication proves him just.

Could Catcott from his better sense be drawn
To bow the knee to Baal's sacred lawn?
A mitred rascal to his long-eared flocks
Gives ill example, * * * *
Yet we must reverence sacerdotal black,
And saddle all his faults on nature's back;
But hold, there's solid reason to revere—
His lordship has six thousand pounds a year:
In gaming solitude he spends the nights,
He fasts at Arthur's, and he prays at White's;
Rolls o'er the pavement with his Swiss-tailed six,
At White's, the Athanasian creed for tricks;
Whilst the poor curate in his rusty gown
Trudges unnoticed through the dirty town.

If God made order, order never made
These nice distinctions in the preaching trade.
The servants of the devil are revered,
And bishops pull the fathers by the beard.
Yet in these horrid forms salvation lives,
These are religion's representatives;
Yet to these idols must we bow the knee—
Excuse me, Broughton, when I bow to thee.
But sure religion can produce at least
One minister of God—one honest priest.

Search nature o'er, procure me, if you can,
The fancied character, an honest man;
(A man of sense, not honest by constraint,
For fools are canvass, living but in paint).
To Mammon or to Superstition slaves,

All orders of mankind are fools, or knaves;
In the first attribute by none surpassed,
Taylor endeavours to obtain the last.

Imagination may be too confined;
Few see too far; how many are half blind!
How are your feeble arguments perplexed
To find out meaning in a senseless text!
You rack each metaphor upon the wheel,
And words can philosophic truths conceal.
What Paracelsus humoured as a jest,
You realize, to prove your system best.
Might we not, Catcott, then infer from hence,
Your zeal for Scripture hath devoured your sense?
Apply the glass of reason to your sight,
See nature marshal oozy atoms right;
Think for yourself, for all mankind are free:
We need not inspiration how to see.
If Scripture contradictory you find,
Be orthodox, and own your senses blind.

How blinded are their optics, who aver,
What inspiration dictates cannot err.
Whence is this boasted inspiration sent,
Which makes us utter truths we never meant?
Which couches systems in a single word,
At once depraved, abstruse, sublime, absurd?
What Moses tells us might perhaps be true,
As he was learn'd in all the Egyptians knew.
But to assert that inspiration's given,
The copy of philosophy in heaven,
Strikes at religion's root, and fairly fells
The awful terrors of ten thousand hells.
Attentive search the Scriptures, and you'll find

What vulgar errors are with truths combined.
Your tortured truths, which Moses seemed to know,
He could not unto inspiration owe;
But if from God one error you admit,
How dubious is the rest of Holy Writ!

What knotty difficulties fancy solves!
The heavens irradiate, and the earth revolves;
But here imagination is allowed
To clear this voucher from its mantling cloud:
From the same word we different meanings quote,
As David[1] wears a many-coloured coat.
O Inspiration, ever hid in night,
Reflecting various each adjacent light!
If Moses caught thee in the parted flood;
If David found thee in a sea of blood;
If Mahomet with slaughter drenched thy soil,
On loaded asses bearing off thy spoil;
If thou hast favoured Pagan, Turk, or Jew,
Say, had not Broughton inspiration too?
Such rank absurdities debase his line,
I almost could have sworn he copied thine.

Confute with candour, where you can confute,
Reason and arrogance but poorly suit.
Yourself may fall before some abler pen,
Infallibility is not for men.
With modest diffidence new schemes indite,
Be not too positive, though in the right.
What man of sense would value vulgar praise,
Or rise on Penny's prose, or duller lays?
Though pointed fingers mark the man of fame,

---

[1] Meaning *Joseph*.

And literary grocers chaunt your name;
Though in each tailor's bookcase Catcott shines,
With ornamental flowers and gilded lines;
Though youthful ladies, who by instinct scan
The Natural Philosophy of Man,
Can every reason of your work repeat,
As sands in Africa retain the heat:
Yet check your flowing pride: will all allow
To wreathe the laboured laurel round your brow?
Some may with seeming arguments dispense,
Tickling your vanity to wound your sense:
But Clayfield censures, and demonstrates too,
Your theory is certainly untrue;
On reason and Newtonian rules he proves
How distant your machine from either moves.
But my objections may be reckoned weak,
As nothing but my mother-tongue I speak;
Else would I ask, by what immortal Power
All Nature was dissolved as in an hour?
How, when the earth acquired a solid state,
And rising mountains saw the waves abate,
Each particle of matter sought its kind,
All in a strata[1] regular combined?
When instantaneously the liquid heap
Hardened to rocks, the barriers of the deep,
Why did not earth unite a stony mass,
Since stony filaments through all must pass?
If on the wings of air the planets run,
Why are they not impelled into the sun?
Philosophy, nay, common sense, will prove
All passives with their active agents move.

---

[1] Put for *stratum*; cf. "stratas," p. 74.

If the diurnal motion of the air
Revolves the planets in their destined sphere,
How are the secondary orbs impelled?
How are the moons from falling headlong held?

'Twas the Eternal's fiat, you reply;
And who will give Eternity the lie?
I own the awful truth, that God made all,
And by His fiat worlds and systems fall;
But study nature; not an atom there
Will unassisted by her powers appear.

The fiat, without agents, is, at best,
For priestcraft or for ignorance a vest.
Some fancy God is what we nature call,
Being itself material, all in all;
The fragments of the Deity we own,
Is vulgarly as various matter known.
No agents could assist creation's birth:
We trample on our God, for God is earth.
'Tis past the power of language to confute
This latitudinary attribute.

How lofty must imagination soar,
To reach absurdities unknown before!
Thanks to thy pinions, Broughton,[1] thou hast brought
From the moon's orb a novelty of thought!
Restrain, O Muse, thy unaccomplished lines,
Fling not thy saucy satire at divines;
This single truth thy brother bards must tell—
Thou hast one excellence, of railing well;

---

[1] Rev. T. Broughton; see Wilson's Life of Chatterton, p. 67.

But disputations are befitting those
Who settle Hebrew points, and scold in prose.

O Learning! where are all thy fancied joys,
Thy empty pleasures and thy solemn toys?
Proud of thy own importance, though we see
We've little reason to be proud of thee:
Thou putrid fœtus of a barren brain,
Thou offspring illegitimate of Pain.

Tell me, sententious mortals, tell me whence
You claim the preference to men of sense?
[Burgum] wants learning: see the lettered throng [1]
Banter his English in a Latin song.
Oxonian sages hesitate to speak
Their native language, but declaim in Greek.
If in his jests a discord should appear,
A dull lampoon is innocently clear.
Ye classic dunces, self-sufficient fools,
Is this the boasted justice of your schools?
[Burgum] has parts—parts which would set aside
The laboured acquisitions of your pride;
Uncultivated now his genius lies,
Instruction sees his latent beauties rise;
His gold is bullion, yours debased with brass,
Impressed with folly's head to make it pass.

But [Burgum] swears so loud, so indiscreet,
His thunders rattle through the listening street!—
Ye rigid Christians, formally severe,
Blind to his charities, his oaths you hear;
Observe his virtues: calumny must own

---

[1] Cf. "Kew Gardens," which supplies the name *Burgum*.

A noble soul is in his actions shown:
Though dark this bright original you paint,
I'd rather be a [Burgum] than a saint.
Excuse me, Catcott, if from you I stray,
The Muse will go where merit leads the way:
The owls of learning may admire the night,
But [Burgum] shines with reason's glowing light.

Still admonition presses to my pen,
The infant Muse would give advice to men.
But what avails it, since the man I blame
Owns no superior in the paths of fame?
In springs, in mountains, stratas, mines, and rocks,
Catcott is every notion orthodox.
If to think otherwise you claim pretence,
You're a detested heretic in sense.[1]
But oh! how lofty your ideas soar,[2]
In showing wondering cits the fossil store!
The ladies are quite ravished, as he tells
The short adventures of the pretty shells;
Miss Biddy sickens to indulge her touch,
Madam more prudent thinks 'twould seem too much.
The doors fly open, instantly he draws
The sparry load, and—wonders of applause;
The full-dressed lady sees with envying eye
The sparkle of her diamond pendants die;
Sage natural philosophers adore
The fossil whimsies of the numerous store.

---

[1] *Renounce* is written over the two first words of this line: which is the true meaning is uncertain, both being in his own handwriting, and uncancelled.—SOUTHEY'S *Edition.* But *renounce* makes no sense.

[2] Printed "roar" in the editions.

But see! the purple stream begins to play;
To shew how fountains climb the hilly way:
Hark what a murmur echoes through the throng—
Gods! that the pretty trifle should be wrong!
Experience in the voice of reason tells,
Above its surface water never swells.
Where is the priestly soul of Catcott now?
See what a triumph sits upon his brow!
And can the poor applause of things like these,
Whose souls and sentiments are all disease,
Raise little triumphs in a man like you,
Catcott, the foremost of the judging few?
So at Llewellin's your great brother[1] sits,
The laughter of his tributary wits,
Ruling the noisy multitude with ease,
Empties his pint, and sputters his decrees.

Dec. 20th, 1769.

Mr. Catcott will be pleased to observe that I admire many things in his learned Remarks. This poem is an innocent effort of poetical vengeance, as Mr. Catcott has done me the honour to criticise my trifles. I have taken great poetical liberties, and what I dislike in verse possibly deserves my approbation in the plain prose of truth.—The many admirers of Mr. Catcott may, on perusal of this, rank me as an enemy: but I am indifferent in all things; I value neither the praise nor the censure of the multitude.

---

[1] Mr. George Catcott; see the next poem.

A NEW SONG.[1]

TO MR. G. CATCOTT; 1769.

AH blame me not, Catcott, if from the right way
My notions and actions run far;
How can my ideas do other but stray,
Deprived of their ruling north-star?

Ah blame me not, Broderip, if, mounted aloft,
I chatter, and spoil the dull air;[2]
How can I imagine thy foppery soft,
When discord's the voice of my fair?

If Turner remitted my bluster and rhymes,
If Harding was girlish and cold,
If never an ogle was got from Miss Grimes,
If Flavia was blasted and old;

I chose without liking, and left without pain,
Nor welcomed the frown with a sigh;
I scorned like a monkey to dangle my chain,
And paint them new charms with a lie.

Once Cotton was handsome; I flamed and I burned,
I died to obtain the bright queen:

---

[1] Printed from the original in the British Museum.

[2] Alluding to Broderip the organist, who turned Chatterton out of the organ-loft, apparently for talking too much.

But when I beheld my epistle returned,
By Jesu, it altered the scene.

" She's damnable ugly," my vanity cried,
" You lie," says my conscience, " you lie "
Resolving to follow the dictates of pride,
I drew her a hag to my eye.

But would she regain her bright lustre again,
And shine in her natural charms,
'Tis but to accept of the works of my pen,
And permit me to use my own arms.

THE COPERNICAN SYSTEM.[1]

THE sun revolving on his axis turns,
And with creative fire intensely burns;
Impelled the forcive air, our earth supreme
Rolls with the planets round the solar gleam.
First Mercury completes his transient year,

---

[1] "Mr. Corser, of Totterdown, has favoured me with the following anecdote of Chatterton.—Mr. C. was intimately acquainted with him, and well remembers that he once met him on a Sunday morning, at the gate of Temple church, when the bells were chiming for service: there being yet some time to spare before the prayers commenced, Chatterton proposed their taking a walk together, in the churchyard, which was then open to the public, and laid out like a garden. 'Come,' said he, 'I want to read to you something I have just written;' and when arrived at a secluded spot, he read to Mr. Corser a treatise on Astronomy, and

Glowing, refulgent, with reflected glare;
Bright Venus occupies a wider way,
The early harbinger of night and day;
More distant still, our globe terraqueous turns,
Nor chills intense, nor fiercely heated burns;
Around her rolls the lunar orb of light,
Trailing her silver glories through the night.
On the earth's orbit see the various signs,
Mark where the sun, our year completing, shines;
First the bright Ram his languid ray improves;
Next glaring watery, through the Bull he moves;
The amorous Twins admit his genial ray;
Now burning, through the Crab he takes his way;
The Lion flaming, bears the solar power;
The Virgin faints beneath the sultry shower.
Now the just Balance weighs his equal force,
The slimy Serpent swelters in his course;
The sabled Archer clouds his languid face:
The Goat, with tempests, urges on his race;
Now in the Waterer his faint beams appear,
And the cold Fishes end the circling year.
Beyond our globe, the sanguine Mars displays
A strong reflection of primæval rays;
Next belted Jupiter far distant gleams,
Scarcely enlightened with the solar beams:
With four unfixed receptacles of light,
He tours majestic through the spacious height:
But farther yet the tardy Saturn lags,

---

stated that he had not yet finished it, but that he intended to make it the subject of a poem. Not long afterwards there appeared the following poem in the Town and Country Magazine" [Dec. 1769].—Dix's *Life of Chatterton*; p. 53.

And five attendant luminaries drags;
Investing with a double ring his pace,
He circles through immensity of space.

These are Thy wondrous works, first Source of good![1]
Now more admired in being understood.

D.

Bristol, Dec. 23 [1769].

THE DEFENCE.

[Printed in the Supplement to the Miscellanies, 1784.]

Dec. 25th, 1769.

NO more, dear Smith,[2] the hacknied tale renew;
I own their censure, I approve it too.
For how can idiots, destitute of thought,
Conceive or estimate, but as they're taught?
Say, can the satirizing pen of Shears
Exalt his name, or mutilate his ears?
None but a Lawrence can adorn his lays,
Who in a quart of claret drinks his praise.
Taylor repeats what Catcott told before,
But lying Taylor is believed no more.
If in myself I think my notion just,
The church and all her arguments are dust.

---

[1] "These are Thy glorious works, Parent of good."—Milton, P. L. v. 153.

[2] William Smith; see the "Elegy on Mr. W. Smith."

Religion's but Opinion's bastard son,
A perfect mystery, more than three in one.
'Tis fancy all, distempers of the mind;
As education taught us, we're inclined.
Happy the man, whose reason bids him see
Mankind are by the state of nature free;
Who, thinking for himself, despises those
That would upon his better sense impose;
Is to himself the minister of God,
Nor treads[1] the path where Athanasius trod.
Happy (if mortals can be) is the man,
Who, not by priest but Reason, rules his span:
Reason, to its possessor a sure guide,
Reason, a thorn in Revelation's side.
If Reason fails, incapable to tread
Through gloomy Revelation's thickening bed,
On what authority the Church we own?
How shall we worship deities unknown?
Can the Eternal Justice pleased receive
The prayers of those who, ignorant, believe?
Search the thick multitudes of every sect,
The Church supreme, with Whitfield's new elect;
No individual can their God define,
No, not great Penny, in his nervous line.
But why must Chatterton selected sit
The butt of every critic's little wit?
Am I alone for ever in a crime,
Nonsense in prose, or blasphemy in rhyme?
All monosyllables a line appears:
Is it not very often so in Shears?

---

[1] Formerly misprinted *dreads;* see Notes and Queries, 2nd S. vi. 182.

See generous Eccas lengthening out my praise,
Enraptured with the music of my lays;
In all the arts of panegyric graced,
The cream of modern literary taste.

"Why, to be sure, the metaphoric line
Has something sentimental, tender, fine;
But then how hobbling are the other two—
There are some beauties, but they're very few.
Besides the author, 'faith 'tis something odd,
Commends a reverential awe of God.
Read but another fancy of his brain,
He's atheistical in every strain."
Fallacious is the charge—'tis all a lie,
As to my reason I can testify,
I own a God, immortal, boundless, wise,
Who bid our glories of creation rise;
Who formed His varied likeness in mankind,
Centring His many wonders in the mind;
Who saw religion a fantastic night,
But gave us reason to obtain the light.
Indulgent Whitfield scruples not to say,
He only can direct to heaven's high-way;
While bishops with as much vehémence tell,
All sects[1] heterodox are food for hell.
Why then, dear Smith, since doctors disagree,
Their notions are not oracles to me:
What I think right I ever will pursue,
And leave you liberty to do so too.

---

[1] "Sorts" is written under "sects;" both in the author's hand-writing, and uncancelled.

SENTIMENT. 1769.

[Printed in the Supplement to the Miscellanies, 1784.]

SINCE we can die but once, what matters it,
If rope or garter, poison, pistol, sword,
Slow-wasting sickness, or the sudden burst
Of valve arterial in the noble parts,
Curtail the miseries of human life?
Though varied is the cause, the effect's the same:
All to one common dissolution tends.

THE ADVICE.

ADDRESSED TO MISS M[ARIA] R[UMSEY], OF BRISTOL.

[First printed in the Supplement to the Town and Country Magazine for 1769.]

REVOLVING in their destined sphere,
The hours begin another year,
As rapidly to fly;
Ah! think, Maria, (ere in grey
Those auburn tresses fade away,)
So youth and beauty die.

Though now the captivated throng
Adore with flattery and song,
And all before you bow;
Whilst, unattentive to the strain,
You hear the humble Muse complain,
Or wreath your frowning brow:

Though poor Pitholeon's feeble line,
In opposition to the nine,
Still violates your name:
Though tales of passion, meanly told,
As dull as Cumberland, as cold,
Strive to confess a flame:

Yet, when that bloom and dancing fire
In silvered reverence shall expire,
Aged, wrinkled, and defaced;
To keep one lover's flame alive
Requires the genius of a Clive,
With Walpole's mental taste.[1]

Though rapture wantons in your air,
Though beyond simile you're fair,
Free, affable, serene;
Yet still one attribute divine
Should in your composition shine—
Sincerity, I mean.

Though numerous swains before you fall,
'Tis empty admiration all,
'Tis all that you require;
How momentary are their chains!
Like you, how unsincere the strains
Of those who but admire!

---

[1] This stanza has been brought forward by the friends of Walpole, as a proof that Chatterton altered his opinion with respect to Walpole's treatment of him. Most probably it is only satire in disguise.—Dix's *Life of Chatterton*. Certainly it is, for the "Clive" here mentioned is not *Lord* Clive, as has been supposed, but Kitty Clive the actress, who bade farewell to the stage in an epilogue written for her by Walpole, spoken April 24, 1769, and printed in both the Town and Country and Universal Magazines for that month

Accept, for once, advice from me,
And let the eye of censure see
Maria can be true:
No more for fools or empty beaux
Heaven's representatives disclose,
Or butterflies pursue;

Fly to your worthiest lover's arms,
To him resign your swelling charms,
And meet his generous breast:
Or, if Pitholeon suits your taste,
His muse, with tattered fragments graced,
Shall read your cares to rest!

D. B.

Jan. 1, 1770.

VERSES

WRITTEN BY CHATTERTON, TO A LADY IN BRISTOL.[1]

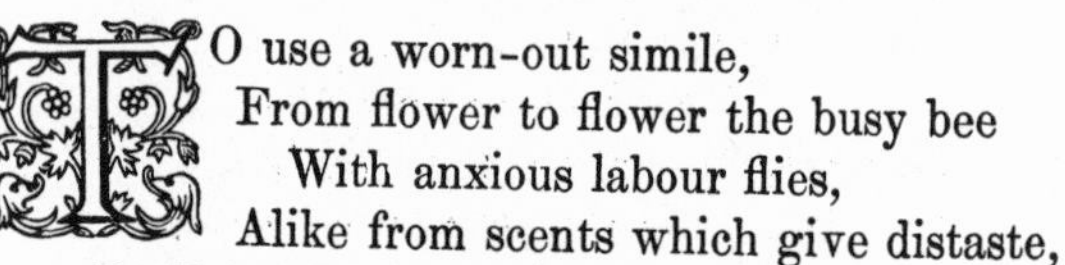

TO use a worn-out simile,
From flower to flower the busy bee
With anxious labour flies,
Alike from scents which give distaste,
By Fancy as disgusting placed,
Repletes his useful thighs.

---

[1] From a copy given by Chatterton to Mr. Henry Kator, a sugarbaker of Bristol; printed in 1803. This piece is in the same strain and metre as the "Advice," addressed to Miss Rumsey, and probably belongs to the same period. A MS. copy of it still exists, from which it appears to have been addressed to Miss C., probably Miss Clarke. For this information I am indebted to Professor Wilson.

Nor does his vicious taste prefer
The fopling of some gay parterre,
The mimicry of art,
But round the meadow-violet dwells;
Nature, replenishing his cells,
Does ampler stores impart.

So I, a humble-dumble drone,
Anxious and restless when alone,
Seek comfort in the fair;
And featured up in tenfold brass,
A rhyming, staring, amorous ass,
To you address my prayer.

But ever in my love-lorn flights
Nature untouch'd by art delights—
Art ever gives disgust.
"Why?" says some priest of mystic thought;
The bard alone by nature taught
Is to that nature just.

But ask your orthodox divine,
If he[1] perchance should read the[2] line
Which fancy now inspires:
Will all his sermons, preaching, prayers,
His hell, his heaven, his solemn airs,
Quench nature's rising fires?

In natural religion free,
I to no other bow the knee,
Nature's the God I own:

---

[1] The old reading "ye" seems wrong.
[2] So in MS. copy; the editions have *this*.

Let priests of future torments tell,
Your anger is the only hell,
No other hell is known.

I steeled by destiny was born,
Well fenced against a woman's scorn,
Regardless of that hell;
I fired by burning planets came
From flaming hearts to catch a flame,
And bid the bosom swell.

Then catch the shadow of a heart,
I will not with the substance part,
Although that substance burn,
Till as a hostage you remit
Your heart, your sentiment, your wit,
To make a safe return.

A reverend cully-mully puff
May call this letter odious stuff,
With no Greek motto graced,
Whilst you, despising the poor strain,
" The dog's insufferably vain
To think to please my taste!"

This vanity, this impudence[1]
Is all the merit, all the sense
Through which to fame I trod;
These (by the Trinity 'tis true)
Procure me friends and notice too,
And shall gain you, by G—d.

---

[1] So in MS. copy; the editions have—'Tis vanity, 'tis impudence.

HECCAR AND GAIRA.

AN AFRICAN ECLOGUE.

[Printed in the Supplement to the Miscellanies, 1784.]

Jan. 3, 1770.

WHERE the rough Caigra rolls the surgy wave,
Urging his thunders through the echoing[1] cave;
Where the sharp rocks, in distant horror seen,
Drive the white currents through the spreading green;
Where the loud tiger, pawing in his rage,
Bids the black archers of the wilds engage;
Stretched on the sand, two panting warriors lay,
In all the burning torments of the day.
Their bloody javelins reeked one living steam,
Their bows were broken at the roaring stream;
Heccar, the chief of Jarra's fruitful hill,
Where the dark vapours nightly dews distil,
Saw Gaira, the companion of his soul,
Extended where loud Caigra's billows roll;
Gaira, the king of warring archers found,
Where daily lightnings plough the sandy ground,

---

[1] *Distant* is written under *echoing* in the MS.

Where brooding tempests howl along the sky,
Where rising deserts whirled in circles fly.

HECCAR.

Gaira, 'tis useless to attempt the chace,
Swifter than hunted wolves they urge the race;
Their lessening forms elude the straining eye,
Upon the plumage of macaws they fly.
Let us return, and strip the reeking slain,
Leaving the bodies on the burning plain.

GAIRA.

Heccar, my vengeance still exclaims for blood,
'Twould drink a wider stream than Caigra's flood.
This javelin, oft in nobler quarrels tried,
Put the loud thunder of their arms aside.
Fast as the streaming rain, I poured the dart,
Hurling a whirlwind through the trembling heart:
But now my lingering feet revenge denies,
O could I throw my javelin from my eyes!

HECCAR.

When Gaira the united armies broke,
Death winged the arrow, Death impelled the stroke.
See, piled in mountains on the sanguine sand,
The blasted of the lightnings of thy hand.
Search the brown desert and the glossy green,
There are the trophies of thy valour seen.
The scattered bones mantled in silver white,
Once animated, dared the force[1] in fight.
The children of the wave, whose pallid race

---

[1] Query, whether not intended for *foes?*—SOUTHEY'S *Edition.*

Views the faint sun display a languid face,
From the red fury of thy justice fled
Swifter than torrents from their rocky bed.
Fear with a sickened silver tinged their hue:
The guilty fear, when vengeance is their due.

GAIRA.

Rouse not Remembrance from her shadowy cell,
Nor of those bloody sons of mischief tell.
Cawna, O Cawna! decked in sable charms,
What distant region holds thee from my arms?
Cawna, the pride of Afric's sultry vales,
Soft as the cooling murmur of the gales,
Majestic as the many-coloured snake,
Trailing his glories through the blossomed brake:
Black as the glossy rocks, where Eascal roars,
Foaming through sandy wastes to Jaghir's shores;
Swift as the arrow, hasting to the breast,
Was Cawna, the companion of my rest.

The sun sat lowering in the western sky,
The swelling tempest spread around the eye;
Upon my Cawna's bosom I reclined,
Catching the breathing whispers of the wind.
Swift from the wood a prowling tiger came,
Dreadful his voice, his eyes a glowing flame;
I bent the bow, the never-erring dart
Pierced his rough armour, but escaped his heart;
He fled, though wounded, to a distant waste,
I urged the furious flight with fatal haste;
He fell, he died—spent in the fiery toil,
I stripped his carcase of the furry spoil,
And, as the varied spangles met my eye,

"On this," I cried, "shall my loved Cawna lie."
The dusky midnight hung the skies in grey;
Impelled by love, I winged the airy way;
In the deep valley and the mossy plain,
I sought my Cawna, but I sought in vain.
The pallid shadows of the azure waves
Had made my Cawna, and my children, slaves!
Reflection maddens to recal the hour;
The gods had given me to the demon's power.
The dusk slow vanished from the hated lawn,
I gained a mountain glaring with the dawn.
There the full sails, expanded to the wind,
Struck horror and distraction in my mind;
There Cawna, mingled with a worthless train,
In common slavery drags the hated chain.
Now judge, my Heccar, have I cause for rage?
Should aught the thunder of my arm assuage?
In ever-reeking blood this javelin dyed
With vengeance shall be never satisfied;
I'll strew the beaches with the mighty dead
And tinge the lily of their features red!

HECCAR.

When the loud shriekings of the hostile cry
Roughly salute my ear, enraged I'll fly;
Send the sharp arrow quivering through the heart,
Chill the hot vitals with the venomed dart;
Nor heed the shining steel or noisy smoke,
Gaira and Vengeance shall inspire the stroke.

THE CONSULIAD.[1]

AN HEROIC POEM.

OF warring senators, and battles dire,
Of quails uneaten, Muse, awake the lyre!
Where Campbell's chimneys overlook
the square,
And Newton's future prospects hang in air;
Where counsellors dispute, and cockers match,
And Caledonian earls in concert scratch;
A group of heroes occupied the round,
Long in the rolls of infamy renown'd.
Circling the table all in silence sat,
Now tearing bloody lean, now champing fat;
Now picking ortolans and chicken slain
To form the whimsies of an *à-la-reine;*
Now storming castles of the newest taste,
And granting articles to forts of paste;
Now swallowing bitter draughts of Prussian beer;

---

[1] The Consuliad, a political piece, written at Bristol, is in the highest strain of party scurrility.—DR. GREGORY. It is printed in the "Miscellanies," 1778; but probably first appeared in the Freeholder's Magazine, as the poet received 10*s.* 6*d.* for it from Mr. Fell, the editor.

The first draught of this poem is preserved in the British Museum. It is there called the "Constabiliad," and commences—

"Of roaring constables, and battles dire,
Of geese uneaten," &c.

There are frequent variations from the printed copy throughout the whole of the poem.

Now sucking tallow of salubrious deer.
The god of cabinets and senates saw
His sons, like asses, to one centre draw.

Inflated Discord heard, and left her cell,
With all the horrors of her native hell;
She on the soaring wings of genius fled,
And waved the pen of Junius round her head.
Beneath the table, veiled from sight, she sprung,
And sat astride on noisy Twitcher's tongue:
Twitcher, superior to the venal pack
Of Bloomsbury's notorious monarch, Jack;
Twitcher, a rotten branch of mighty stock,
Whose interest winds his conscience as his clock;
Whose attributes detestable have long
Been evident and infamous in song.
A toast's demanded! Madoc swift arose,
Pactolian gravy trickling down his clothes:
His sanguine fork a murdered pigeon prest,
His knife with deep incision sought the breast.
Upon his lips the quivering accents hung,
And too much expedition chained his tongue.
When thus he sputtered: "All the glasses fill,
And toast the great Pendragon of the hill,
Mab-Uther Owein, a long train of kings,
From whom the royal blood of Madoc springs:
Madoc, undoubtedly of Arthur's race,
You see the mighty monarch in his face:
Madoc, in bagnios and in courts adored,
Demands this proper homage of the board."

"Monarchs!" said Twitcher, setting down his beer,
His muscles wreathing a contemptuous sneer;
"Monarchs—of mole-hills, oyster-beds, a rock—

These are the grafters of your royal stock:
My pony Scrub can sires more valiant trace—"
The mangled pigeon thunders on his face;
His opening mouth the melted butter fills,
And dropping from his nose and chin distils.
Furious he started, rage his bosom warms;
Loud as his lordship's morning dun he storms.
"Thou vulgar imitator of the great,
Grown wanton with the excrements of state,
This to thy head notorious Twitcher sends—"
His shadow body to the table bends,
His straining arm uprears a loin of veal,
In these degenerate days for three a meal;
In ancient times, as various writers say,
An alderman or priest eat three a day.
With godlike strength the grinning Twitcher plies
His stretching muscles, and the mountain flies!
Swift as a cloud that shadows o'er the plain,
It flew, and scatter'd drops of oily rain.
In opposition to extended knives,
On royal Madoc's spreading chest it drives;
Senseless he falls upon the sandy ground,
Pressed with the steamy load that oozed around.
And now Confusion spread her ghastly plume,
And Faction separates the noisy room.
Balluntun, exercised in every vice
That opens to a courtier's paradise,
With Dyson trammelled, scruples not to draw
Injustice up the rocky hill of law:
From whose humanity the laurels sprung,
Which will in George's-Fields be ever young—
The vile Balluntun, starting from his chair,
To Fortune thus addressed his private prayer:

"Goddess of Fate's rotundity, assist
With thought-winged victory my untried fist:
If I the grinning Twitcher overturn,
Six Russian frigates at thy shrine shall burn;
Nine rioters shall bleed beneath thy feet;
And hanging cutters decorate each street."
The goddess smiled, or rather smoothed her frown,
And shook the triple feathers of her crown;
Instilled a private pension in his soul.
With rage inspired, he seized a Gallic roll;
His bursting arm the missive weapon threw,
High o'er his rival's head it whistling flew;
Curraras, for his Jewish soul renowned,
Received it on his ear, and kissed the ground—
Curraras, versed in every little art,
To play the minister's or felon's part,
Grown hoary in the villanies of state,
A title made him infamously great;
A slave to venal slaves, a tool to tools,
The representative to knaves and fools.
But see commercial Bristol's genius sit,
Her shield a turtle-shell, her lance a spit:
See, whilst her nodding aldermen are spread,
In all the branching honours of the head;
Curraras, ever faithful to the cause,
With beef and venison their attention draws:
They drink, they eat, then sign the mean address;
Say, could their humble gratitude do less?
By disappointment vexed, Balluntun flies,
Red lightnings flashing in his dancing eyes.
Firm as his virtue, mighty Twitcher stands,
And elevates for furious fight his hands:
One pointed fist his shadowed corps defends,

The other on Balluntun's eyes descends:
A darkling, shaking light his optics view,
Circled with livid tinges red and blue.
Now fired with anguish and inflamed by pride,
He thunders on his adversary's side:
With pattering blows prolongs the unequal fight;
Twitcher retreats before the man of might.
But Fortune, (or some higher power or god),
Oblique extended forth a sable rod:
As Twitcher retrograde maintained the fray,
The hardened serpent intercepts his way:
He fell, and falling with a lordly air,
Crushed into atoms the judicial chair.
Curraras, for his Jewish soul renowned,
Arose: but deafened with a singing sound.
A cloud of discontent o'erspread his brows;
Revenge in every bloody feature glows.
Around his head a roasted gander whirls,
Dropping Manilla sauces on his curls;
Swift to the vile Balluntun's face it flies,
The burning pepper sparkles in his eyes:
His India waistcoat, reeking with the oil,
Glows brighter red, the glory of the spoil.

The fight is general; fowl repulses fowl;
The victors thunder, and the vanquished howl.
Stars, garters, all the implements of show,
That decked the powers above, disgraced below.
Nor swords, nor mightier weapons did they draw,
For all were well acquainted with the law.
Let Drap—r to improve his diction fight;
Our heroes, like Lord George, could scold and write.
Gogmagog, early of the jockey club,

Empty as C—br—ke's oratorial tub,
A rusty link of ministerial chain,
A living glory of the present reign,
Versed in the arts of ammunition-bread,
He waved a red-wheat manchet round his head:
David-ap-Howel, furious, wild, and young,
From the same line as royal Madoc sprung,
Occurred, the object of his bursting ire,
And on his nose received the weapon dire:
A double river of congealing blood
O'erflows his garter with a purple flood.
Mad as a bull by daring mastiffs tore,
When ladies scream and greasy butchers roar;
Mad as B—rg—e when, groping through the park,
He kissed his own dear lady in the dark;
The lineal representative of kings
A carving weapon seized, and up he springs:
A weapon long in cruel murders stained,
For mangling captive carcases ordained.
But Fortune, Providence, or what you will,
To lay the rising scenes of horror still,
In Fero's person seized a shining pot,
Where bubbled scrips and contracts, flaming hot,
In the fierce Cambrian's breeches drains it dry:
The chapel totters with the shrieking cry,
Loud as the mob's reiterated yell,
When Sawny rose, and mighty Chatham fell.

Flaccus, the glory of a masquerade,
Whose every action is of trifles made,
At Grafton's well-stored table ever found;
Like Grafton too for every vice renowned:
Grafton, to whose immortal sense we owe

The blood which will from civil discord flow;
Who swells each grievance, lengthens every tax,
Blind to the ripening vengeance of the axe:
Flaccus, the youthful, degagée, and gay,
With eye of pity saw the dreary fray:
Amidst the greasy horrors of the fight,
He trembled for his suit of virgin white.
Fond of his eloquence and easy flow
Of talk verbose, whose meaning none can know:
He mounts the table, but through eager haste
His foot upon a smoking court-pie placed:
The burning liquid penetrates his shoe,
Swift from the rostrum the declaimer flew;
But, learnedly heroic, he disdains
To spoil his pretty countenance with strains.
Remounted on the table now he stands,
Waves his high-powdered head and ruffled hands.
" Friends! Let this clang of hostile fury cease,
Ill it becomes the plenipos of peace;
Shall olios, for internal battle drest,
Like bullets outward perforate the breast?
Shall javelin bottles blood ethereal spill?
Shall luscious turtle without surfeit kill?"
More had he said: when, from Doglostock flung,
A custard pudding trembled on his tongue:
And, ah! misfortunes seldom come alone,
Great Twitcher rising seized a polished bone;
Upon his breast the oily weapon clangs;
Headlong he falls, propelled by thickening bangs.
The prince of trimmers, for his magic famed,
Quarlendorgongos by infernals named,
By mortals Alavat in common styled—
Nursed in a furnace, Nox and Neptune's child—

Bursting with rage, a weighty bottle caught,
With crimson blood and weighty spirits fraught;
To Doxo's head the gurgling woe he sends,
Doxo, made mighty in his mighty friends.
Upon his front the stubborn vessel sounds,
Back from his harder front the bottle bounds:
He fell. The royal Madoc rising up,
Reposed him weary on his painful crup:
The head of Doxo, first projecting down,
Thunders upon the kingly Cambrian's crown:
The sanguine tumour swells; again he falls;
On his broad chest the bulky Doxo sprawls.
Tyro the sage, the sensible, the strong,
As yet unnoticed in the muse-taught song,
Tyro, for necromancy far renowned,
A greater adept than Agrippa found;
Oft as his phantom-reasons intervened,
De Vir is pensioned, the defaulter screened;
Another C[ar]t[ere]t remains in Clare;
In Fletcher, fifty Jefferies appear;
Tyro stood neuter, till the champions tired
In languid attitudes a truce desired.
Long was the bloody fight; confusion dire
Has hid some circumstances from the lyre:
Suffice it, that each hero kissed the ground,
Tyro excepted, for old laws renowned;
Who stretching his authoritative hand,
Loudly thus issued forth his dread command.
"Peace, wrangling senators, and placemen, peace,
In the King's name, let hostile vengeance cease!"
Aghast the champions hear the furious sound,
The fallen unmolested leave the ground.
"What fury, nobles, occupies your breast?

What, patriot spirits, has your minds possessed?
Nor honorary gifts nor pensions please,
Say, are you Covent-Garden patentees!
How? wist you not what ancient sages said,
'The council quarrels, and the poor have bread.'
See this court-pie with twenty-thousand drest;
Be every thought of enmity at rest:
Divide it, and be friends again," he said:
The council-god returned; and discord fled.

C.

Bristol, Jan. 4, 1770.

RESIGNATION. A POEM.[1]

[The Duke of Grafton resigned the premiership, Jan. 28, 1770. See Political Letters; Letter I.]

HAIL, Resignation! hail, ambiguous dame,
Thou Parthian archer in the fight of fame!
When thou hast drawn the mystic veil between,
'Tis the poor Minister's concluding scene;
Sheltered beneath thy pinions he withdraws,
And tells us his integrity's the cause.
Sneaking to solitude, he rails at state,
And rather would be virtuous than be great;
Laments the impotence of those who guide,

---

[1] Copied from a poem in Chatterton's handwriting in the British Museum, and printed in 1803.

And wishes public clamours may subside.
But while such rogues as North or Sandwich steer,
Our grievances will never disappear.

Hail, Resignation! 'tis from thee we trace
The various villanies of power and place;
When rascals, once but infamy and rags,
Rich with a nation's ruin, swell their bags,
Purchase a title and a royal smile,
And pay to be distinguishably vile;
When big with self-importance thus[1] they shine,
Contented with their gleanings, they resign!
When ministers, unable to preside,
The tottering vehicle no longer guide,
The powerful Thane prepares to kick his Grace
From all his glorious dignities of place;
But still the honour of the action's thine,
And Grafton's tender conscience can resign.
Lament not, Grafton, that thy hasty fall
Turns out a public happiness to all;
Still by your emptiness of look appear
The ruins of a man who used to steer;
Still wear that insignificance of face,
Which dignifies you more than power or place.

Whilst now the Constitution tottering stands,
And needs the firm support of able hands,
Your Grace stood foremost in the glorious cause
To shake the very basis of our laws;
But, thanks to Camden and a noble few,
They stemmed Oppression's tide, and conquered you.

---

[1] A pen has been drawn through this and the preceding word in the MS. but no others substituted.

How can your prudence be completely praised
In flying from the storm yourself had raised?
When the black clouds of discord veiled the sky,
'Twas more than prudence in your Grace to fly;
For had the thunders burst upon your head,
Soon had you mingled with the headless dead;
Not Bute, though here the deputy of fate,
Could save so vile a minister of state.

Oft has the Carlton Sibyl[1] prophesied
How long each minister of state should guide,
And from the dark recesses of her cell,
When Bute was absent, would to Stuart tell
The secret fates of senators and peers,
What lord's exalted but to lose his ears,
What future plans the Junto have design'd,
What writers[2] are with Rockingham combined,
Who should accept a privy seal or rod,
Who's lord-lieutenant of the land of Nod,
What pensioned nobleman should hold his post,
What poor dependant scored without his host,
What patriot big with popular applause
Should join the ministry and prop the cause;
With many secrets of a like import,
The daily tittle-tattle of a court,
By common fame retail'd as office news
In coffee-houses, taverns, cellars, stews.
Oft from her secret casket would she draw
A knotty plan to undermine the law;

---

[1] The Princess Dowager of Wales, mother of George III.

[2] The word is obscure in the MS. The Marquis of Rockingham's first administration lasted from July, 1765 to July, 1766.

But though the council sat upon the scheme,
Time has discovered that 'tis all a dream;
Long had she known the date of Grafton's power,
And in her tablet mark'd his flying hour;
Rumour reports, a message from her cell
Arrived but just three hours before he fell.
Well knew the subtle minister of state
Her knowledge in the mysteries of fate,
And catching every pension he could find,
Obeyed the fatal summons—and resigned!

Far in the north, amidst whose dreary hills
None hear the pleasant murmuring sound of rills,
Where no soft gale in dying raptures blows,
Or aught which bears the look of verdure grows,
Save where the north wind cuts the solemn yew,
And russet rushes drink the noxious dew—
Dank exhalations drawn from stagnant moors,
The morning dress of Caledonia's shores—
Upon a bleak and solitary plain,
Exposed to every storm of wind and rain,
A humble cottage reared its lowly head,
Its roof with matted reeds and rushes spread.
The walls were osiers daubed with slimy clay,
One narrow entrance opened to the day.
Here lived a Laird,[1] the ruler of his clan,
Whose fame through every northern mountain ran;
Great was his learning, for he long had been
A student at the town of Aberdeen,
Professor of all languages at once;

---

[1] John Stuart, third Earl of Bute; first lord of the treasury from May, 1762 to April, 1763.

To him, some reckoned Chappelow[1] a dunce.
With happy fluency he learned to speak
Syriac or Latin, Arabic or Greek.
Not any tongue in which Oxonians sing
When they rejoice or blubber with the king,
To him appeared unknown: with sapient look
He taught the highland meaning of each crook.
But often when to pastimes he inclined,
To give some relaxation to his mind,
He laid his books aside, forgot to read,
To hunt wild goslings down the river Tweed,
To chase a starving weasel from her bed,
And wear the spoil triumphant on his head.
'Tis true his rent-roll just maintained his state,
But some, in spite of poverty, are great.
Though famine sunk her impress on his face,
Still you might there his haughty temper trace,
Descended from a catalogue of kings
Whose warlike arts Mac Pherson sweetly sings,
He bore the majesty of monarchs past,
Like a tall pine rent with the winter's blast,
Whose spreading trunk and withered branches show
How glorious once the lordly tree might grow.

Of all the warring passions in his breast,
Ambition still presided o'er the rest;
This is the spur which actuates us all,
The visionary height whence thousands fall,
The author's hobby-horse, the soldier's steed
Which aids him in each military deed,

---

[1] Professor of Arabic in the University of Cambridge from 1720 to 1768; eminent for his intimate acquaintance with the Oriental languages.

The lady's dresser, looking-glass, and paint,
The warm devotion of the seeming saint.

Sawney, the noble ruler of the clan,
Had numbered o'er the riper years of man,
Graceful in stature, ravishing his mien,
To make a conquest was but to be seen.
Fired by ambition, he resolved to roam
Far from the famine of his native home,
To seek the warmer climate of the south,
And at one banquet feast his eyes and mouth.
In vain the amorous highland lass complained,
The son of monarchs would not be restrained;
Clad in his native many-coloured suit,
Forth struts the walking majesty of Bute.
His spacious sword to a large wallet strung,
Across his broad capacious shoulders hung:
As from the hills the land of promise rose,
A secret transport in his bosom glows:
A joy prophetic, until then unknown,
Assured him all he viewed would be his own.
New scenes of pleasure recreate his sight,
He views the fertile meadows with delight;
Still in soliloquy he praised the view,
Nor was more pleased with future scenes at Kew.
His wonder broke in murmurs from his tongue,
No more the praise of highland hills he sung,
Till now a stranger to the cheerful green
Where springing flowers diversify the scene;
The lofty elm, the oak of lordly look,
The willow shadowing the bubbling brook,
The hedges blooming with the sweets of May
With double pleasure marked his gladsome way.

Having through varying rural prospects past,
He reached the great metropolis at last.
Here Fate beheld him as he trudged the street,
Bare was his buttocks and unshod his feet;
A lengthening train of boys displayed him great,
He seemed already minister of state.
The Carlton Sibyl saw his graceful mien,
And straight forgot her hopes of being Queen.[1]
She sighed, she wished; swift virtuous Chudleigh flew
To bring the Caledonian swain to Kew;
Then introduced him to her secret cell,—
What further can the modest numbers tell?
Suffice it that, among the youths of fire
Whom widows strong and amorous dames admire,[2]
None rode the broomstaff with so good a grace,
Or pleased her with such majesty of face;
Enraptured with her incubus, she sought
How to reward his merit as she ought.
Resolved to make him greatest of the great,
She led him to her hidden cave of state;
There spurs and coronets were placed around,
And privy seals were scattered on the ground;
Here piles of honorary truncheons lay,
And gleaming stars made artificial day;
With mystic rods, whose magic power is such
They metamorphose parties with a touch.
Here hung the princely prize[3] of gartered blue,
With flags of all varieties of hue.

---

[1] Two following lines omitted.
[2] Two following lines omitted.
[3] Obscure in MS. Lord Bute was made a Knight of the Garter, Sept. 22, 1762.

"These," said the Sibyl, "from this present hour
Are thine with every dignity of power.
No statesman shall be titularly great,
None shall obtain an office in the state
But such whose principles and manners suit
The virtuous temper of the Earl of Bute;
All shall pursue thy interest, none shall guide
But such as you repute are qualified.
No more on Scotland's melancholy plain
Your starving countrymen shall drink the rain,
But hither hasting on their naked feet,
Procure a place, forget themselves, and eat.
No southern patriot shall oppose my will,
If not my look, my Treasurer can kill;
His pistol never fails in time of need,
And who dares contradict my power shall bleed.
A future Barrington will also rise
With blood and death to entertain my eyes.
But this forestalls futurity and fate,
I'll choose the present hour to make thee great."
He bowed submission, and with eager view
Gazed on the withered oracle of Kew.
She seized a pendant garter, and began
To elevate the ruler of the clan;
Girt round his leg the honoured trifle shone,
And gathered double lustre from the throne;
With native dignity he filled the stall,
The wonder, jest, and enmity of all.
Not yet content with honorary grace,
The Sibyl, busy for the sweets of place,
Kicked out a minister, the people's pride,
And lifted Sawney in his place to guide.
The Leader of the Treasury he rose,

Whilst fate marked down the nation's future
woes.
Mad with ambition, his imperious hand
Scattered oppression through a groaning land;
Still taxes followed taxes, grants supplies,
With every ill resulting from excise.
Not satisfied with this unjust increase,
He struck a bolder stroke, and sold the peace;
The Gallic millions so convinced his mind,
On honourable terms the treaty's signed.

But who his private character can blame,
Or brand his titles with a villain's name?
Upon an estimation of the gains,
He stooped beneath himself to take the reins;
A good economist, he served the crown,
And made his master's interest his own.
His starving friends and countrymen applied
To share the ministry, assist to guide;
Nor asked in vain:—his charitable hand
Made Plenty smile in Scotland's barren land;
Her wandering sons, for poverty renowned,
Places and pensions, bribes or titles found.
Far from the south was humble merit fled,
And on the northern mountains reared her head;
And genius, having ranged beyond the Tweed,
Sat brooding upon bards who could not read;
Whilst courage, boasting of his highland might,
Mentions not Culloden's inglorious flight,
But whilst his lordship fills the honoured stall,
Ample provision satisfies them all.
The genius sings his praise, the soldier swears
To mutilate each murmuring caitiff's ears;

The father of his country they adore,
And live in elegance unknown before.

Nor yet unthankful he for power and place,
He praised the Sibyl with distinguished grace.
And oft repairing to [the] cell of hate,
He laid aside the dignity of state;—[1]
And had not virtuous Chudleigh held the door,
She to this moment might have been a whore.
Around this mystic sun of liquid gold
A swarm of planetary statesmen rolled;
Though some have since as ministers been known,
They shone with borrowed lustre not their own:
In every revolution, day and night,
From Bute they caught each particle of light;
He destined out the circles they fulfil,
Hung on the bulky nothing of his will.

How shall I brand with infamy a name
Which bids defiance to all sense of shame?
How shall I touch his iron soul with pain,
Who hears unmoved a multitude complain?
A multitude made wretched by his hand,
The common curse and nuisance of the land.
Holland,[2] of thee I sing—infernal wretch!
Say, can thy power of mischief further stretch?
Is there no other army to be sold,
No town to be destroyed for bribes and gold?
Or wilt thou rather sit contented down,
And starve the subject to enrich the crown?

---

[1] Six lines following omitted.
[2] Lord Holland, born 1705; died July 1, 1774.

That when the treasury can boast supplies,
Thy pilfering genius may have exercise;
Whilst unaccounted millions pay thy toil,
Thou art secure if Bute divides the spoil;
Catching his influence from the best of kings,
Vice broods beneath the shadow of his wings;
The vengeance of a nation is defied,
And liberty and justice set aside.
Distinguished robber of the public, say,
What urged thy timid spirit's hasty way?
She lived[1] in the protection of a king.
Did recollection paint the fate of Byng?
Did conscience hold that mirror to thy sight,
Or Aylyffe's ghost accompany thy flight?
Is Bute more powerful than the sceptred hand,
Or art thou safer in a foreign land?
In vain, the scene relinquished, now you grieve,
Cursing the moment you were forced to leave
The ruins on the Isle of Thanet built,
The fruits of plunder, villany, and guilt.
When you presume on English ground to tread,
Justice will lift her weapon at your head.
Contented with the author of your state,
Maintain the conversation of the great.
Be busy in confederacy and plot,
And settle what shall be on what is not;
Display the statesman in some wild design,
Foretell when North will tumble and resign,
How long the busy Sandwich, mad for rule,
Will lose his labour and remain a fool.
But your accounts, the subject of debate,

---

[1] MS. obscure.

Are much beneath the notice of the great.
Let bribed exchequer-tellers find them just,
Which, on the penalty of place, they must;
Before they're seen your honesty is clear,
And all will evidently right appear.

When as a Minister you had your day,
And gather'd light from Bute's superior ray,
His striking representative you shone,
And seem'd to glimmer in yourself alone;
The lives of thousands barter'd for a bribe,
With villanies too shocking to describe.
Your system of oppression testified
None but the conscientious Fox could guide.
As Bute is fixed eternal in his sphere,
And Ministers revolve around in air,
Your infamy with such a lasting ray
Glowed through your orb in one continual day:
Still ablest politicians hold dispute,
Whether you gave or borrowed light from Bute.
Lost in the blaze of his superior parts,
We often have descried your little arts.
But at a proper distance from his sphere
We saw the little villain disappear;
When dressed in titles, the burlesque of place,
A more illustrious rascal shewed his face;
Your destined sphere of Ministry now run,
You dropt like others in the parent sun;
There as a spot you purpose to remain,
And seek protection in the Sibyl's swain.
Grafton his planetary life began,
Though foreign to the system of the clan;
Slowly he rolled around the fount of light,

Long was his day, but longer was his night.
Irregular, unequal in his course,
Now languid he revolves, now rolls with force;
His scarce-collected light obliquely hurled
Was scattered ere it reached his frozen world.
Through all his under offices of place,
All had conspired to represent his Grace;
Lifeless and dull the wheels of state were driven,
Slow as a courtier on his road to heaven.
If expedition urged the dull machine,
He knew so little of the golden mean,
Swift hurry and confusion wild began
To discompose the Thane's determined plan.
Error, his secretary, lent his aid
To undermine each plot his cunning laid;
He wrote despatches in his Grace's name,
And ruined every project North could frame:
Yet as he blundered through the lengthened night,
He seriously protested all was right.

Since dissipation is thy only joy,
Go, Grafton, join the dance, and act the boy;
'Tis not for fops in cabinets to shine,
And justice must confess that title's thine.
Dress to excess, and powder into fame,
In drums and hurricanes exalt your name.
There you may glitter, there your worth may rise
Above the little reach of vulgar eyes.
But in the high departments of the state
Your talents are too trifling to be great;
There all your imperfections rise to view,
Not Sandwich so contemptible as you.
Bute from the summit of his power descried

Your glaring inability to guide,
And mustering every rascal in his gang,
Who might for merit all together hang,
From the black catalogue and worthy crew,
The jesuitical and scheming few,
Selected by the leader of the clan,
Received instructions for their future plan;
And, after proper adoration paid,
Were to their destined sphere of state conveyed,
To shine the Minister's satéllites,
Collect his light, and give his lordship ease,
Reform his crooked politics, and draw
A more severe attack upon the law;
Settle his erring revolutions right,
And give in just proportion day and night.

Alas! the force of Scottish pride is such,
These mushrooms of a day presumed too much;
Conscious of cunning and superior arts,
They scorned the Minister's too trifling parts;
Grafton resents a treatment so unjust,
And damns the Carlton Sibyl's fiery lust,
By which a scoundrel Scot oppressed the realm,
And rogues, below contempt, disgraced the helm.
Swift scandal caught the accents as they fell,
And bore them to the Sibyl's secret cell.
Enraged, she winged a messenger to Bute,
Some minister more able to depute;
Her character and virtue was a jest,
Whilst Grafton was of useless power possessed.
This done, her just desire of vengeance warm,
She gave him notice of the bursting storm;
Timid and dubious, Grafton faced about,

And trembled at the thoughts of being out;
But as no laws the Sibyl's power confined,
He dropped his blushing honours, and resigned!

Step forward, North! and let the doubtful see
Wonders and miracles revived in thee.
Did not the living witness haunt the court,
What ear had given faith to my report?
Amidst the rout of ministerial slaves,
Rogues who want genius to refine to knaves,
Who could imagine that the wretch most base
Should fill the highest infamy of place?
That North, the vile domestic of a peer
Whose name an Englishman detests to hear,
Should leave his trivial share of Bedford's gains,
Become a minister, and take the reins;
And from the meanest of the gang ascend
Above his worthy governor and friend?
This wondrous metamorphose of an hour
Sufficiently evinced the Sibyl's power.
To ruin nations, little rogues to raise,
A virtue supernatural displays;
What but a power infernal or divine
Could honour North, or make his Grace resign?

Some superficial politicians tell,
When Grafton from his gilded turret fell,
The Sibyl substituted North, a blank,
A mustered faggot to complete the rank,[1]
Without a distant thought that such a tool
Would change its being and aspire to rule.

---

[1] Written first, "As faggots in a muster fill a rank."

But such the humble North's indulgent fate,
When striding in the saddle of the state,
He caught by inspiration statesmanship,
And drove the slow machine and smacked his whip;
Whilst Bedford, wondering at his sudden skill,
With reverence viewed the packhorse of his will.

His Majesty (the buttons thrown aside)
Declared his fixed intention to preside.
No longer sacrificed to every knave,
He'd show himself discreet as well as brave;
In every cabinet and council-cause
He'd be dictator and enforce the laws;
Whilst North should in his present office stand
As understrapper to direct his hand.

Now, Expectation, now extend thy wing!
Happy the land whose minister's a king;
Happy the king, who, ruling each debate,
Can peep through every roguery of state!
See Hope, arrayed in robes of virgin white,
Trailing an arched variety of light,
Comes showering blessings on a ruined realm,
And shews the crowned director of the helm!
Return, fair goddess, till some future day,
The king has seen the error of his way;
And by his smarting shoulders seems to feel
The wheel of state is not a Catharine wheel.
Wise by experience, general nurse of fools,
He leaves the ministry to venal tools;
And finds his happy talents better suit
The making buttons for his favourite Bute;
In countenancing the unlawful views
Which North, the delegate of Bute, pursues;

In glossing with authority a train
Whose names are infamy, and objects gain.

Hail, filial duty! great, if rightly used,
How little when mistaken and abused!
Viewed from one point, how glorious art thou seen,
From others, how degenerate and mean!
A seraph or an idiot's head we see:
Often the latter stands the type of thee,
And, bowing at his parent's knee, is drest
In a long hood and many-coloured vest.

The sceptred king, who dignifies a throne,
Should be in private life himself alone;
No friend or mother should his conscience scan,
Or with the nation's head confound the man.
Like juggling Melchi Zadok's priestish plea,
Collected in himself, a king should be.
But truths may be unwelcome, and the lay
Which shall to royal ears such truths convey
The conflagrations of the hangman's ire
May roast, and execute with foreign fire.
The Muse who values safety shall return,
And sing of subjects where she cannot burn.
Continue, North, thy vile burlesque of power,
And reap the harvest of the present hour;
Collect, and fill thy coffers with the spoil,
And let thy gatherings recompense thy toil.
Whilst the rogues out revile the rascals in,
Repeat the proverb, "Let those laugh that win:"
Fleeting and transitory is the date
Of sublunary ministers of state;
Then whilst thy summer lasts prepare thy hay,
Nor trust to autumn and a future day.

I leave thee now, but with intent to trace
The villains and the honest men of place.
The first are still assisting in thy train
To aid the pillage and divide the gain;
The last, of known integrity of mind,
Forsook a venal party, and resigned!

Come, Satire! aid me to display the first,
Of every honest Englishman accursed;
Come, Truth, assist me to prepare the lays,
Where worth demands, and give the latter praise.
Ingenious Sandwich, whither dost thou fly
To shun the censure of the public eye?
Dost thou want matter for another speech,
Or other works of genius to impeach?
Or would thy insignificance and pride
Presume above thyself and seek to guide?
Pursue thy ignis-fatuus of power,
And call to thy assistance virtuous Gower;
Set Rigby's happy countenance in play
To vindicate whatever you can say.
Then, when you totter into place and fame,
With double infamy you brand your name.
Say, Sandwich, in the winter of your date,
Can you ascend the hobby-horse of state?
Do titles echo grateful in your ear?
Or is it mockery to call you peer?
In fifty's silvered age to play the fool,
And [rest] with rascals infamous a tool,
Plainly denote your judgment is no more;
Your honour was extinguished long before.

Say, if reflection ever blest thy mind,

Hast thou one rëal friend among mankind?
Thou hadst one once, free, generous, and sincere,
Too good a senator for such a peer;
Him thou hadst offered as a sacrifice
To lewdness, immorality, and vice;
Your patronizing scoundrels set the gin,
And friendship was the bait to draw him in.
What honourable villain could they find
Of Sandwich's latitudinary mind?
Though intimacy seemed to stop the way,
You they employed to tempt him and betray.
Full well you executed their commands,
Well you deserved the pension at their hands.
For you, in hours of trifling, he compiled
A dissertation blasphemous and wild.
Be it recorded, 'twas at your desire
He called for demons to assist his lyre;
Relying on your friendship, soon he found
How dangerous the support of rotten ground.
In your infernal attributes arrayed,
You seized the wished-for poem, and betrayed.

Hail, mighty Twitcher! can my feeble line
Give due reward to merit such as thine?
Not Churchill's keenest satire ever reached
The conscience of the rascal who impeached.
My humble numbers and untutored lay
On such a hardened wretch are thrown away;
I leave thee to the impotent delight
Of visiting the harlots of the night;
Go, hear thy nightingale's enchanting strain,
My satire shall not dart a sting in vain.
There you may boast one sense is entertained,

Though age present your other senses pained:
Go, Sandwich, if thy fire of lust compel,
Regale at Harrington's religious cell,
[Resort] of impotence and dire disease;
Exert your poor endeavours as you please,
The jest and bubble of the harlot crew;
What entertained your youth, in age pursue.

When Grafton shook Oppression's iron rod,
Like Egypt's lice, the instrument of God;
When Camden, driven from his office, saw
The last weak efforts of expiring law;
When Bute, the regulator of the state,
Preferred the vicious, to supplant the great;
When rank corruption through all orders ran,
And infamy united Sawney's clan;
When every office was with rogues disgraced,
And the Scotch dialect became the taste,
Could Beaufort with such creatures stay behind?
No, Beaufort was a Briton, and resigned.
Thy resignation, Somerset, shall shine
When time hath buried the recording line,
And, proudly glaring in the rolls of fame,
With more than titles decorate thy name.
Amidst the gathered rascals of the age,
Who murder noble parts, the court their stage,
One nobleman of honesty remains,
Who scorns to draw in ministerial chains;
Who honours virtue and his country's peace,
And sees with pity grievances increase;
Who bravely left all sordid views of place,
And lives the honour of the Beaufort race.

Deep in the secret, Barrington and Gower,

Raised upon villany, aspire to power;
Big with importance, they presume to rise
Above a minister they must despise;
Whilst Barrington, as secretary, shows
How many pensions paid his blood and blows.
And Gower, the humbler creature of the two,
Has only future prospects in his view.
But North requires assistance from the great,
To work another button in the state,
That Weymouth may complete the birthday-suit,
Full-trimmed by Twitcher, and cut out by Bute:
So many worthy schemers must produce
A statesman's coat of universal use;
Some system of economy, to save
Another million for another knave;
Some plan to make a duty, large before,
Additionally great, to grind the poor:
For 'tis a maxim with the guiding wise,
Just as the commons sink, the rich arise.

If ministers and privy-council knaves
Would rest contented with their being slaves,
And not with anxious infamy pursue
Those measures which will fetter others too,
The swelling cry of liberty would rest,
Nor Englishmen complain, nor knaves protest.
But courtiers have a littleness of mind,
And, once enslaved, would fetter all mankind.
'Tis to this narrowness of soul we owe
What further ills our liberties shall know;
'Tis from this principle our feuds began,
Fomented by the Scots, ignoble clan:
Strange that such little creatures of a tool,

By lust and not by merit raised to rule,
Should sow contention in a noble land,
And scatter thunders from a venal hand.
Gods! that these fly-blows of a stallion's day,
Warmed into being by the Sibyl's ray,
Should shake the constitution, rights, and laws,
And prosecute the Man of Freedom's cause!
Whilst Wilkes to every Briton's right appealed,
With loss of liberty that right he sealed:
Imprisoned and oppressed he persevered,
Nor Sawney or his powerful Sibyl feared.
The hag, replete with malice, from above
Shot poison on the screech-owl of her love;
Unfortunately to his pen it fell,
And flowed in double rancour to her cell;
Madly she raved; to ease her tortured mind,
The object of her hatred is confined:
But he, supported by his country's laws,
Bid her defiance, for 'twas Freedom's cause.
Her Treasurer and Talbot fought in vain,
Though each attain'd his favourite object—gain.
She sat as usual when a project fails,
Damned Chudleigh's phiz, and dined upon her nails.

Unhappy land! whose governed Monarch sees
Through glasses and perspective[s] such as these;
When, juggling to deceive his untried sight,
He views the ministry all trammelled right;
Whilst, to his eye the other glass applied,
His subjects' failings are all magnified.
Unheeded the petitions are received,
Nor one report of grievances believed;
'Tis but the voice of faction in disguise

That blinds with liberty the people's eyes:
'Tis riot and licentiousness pursues
Some disappointed placeman's private [views].[1]
And shall such venal creatures steer the helm,
Waving Oppression's banners round the realm?
Shall Britons to the vile detested troop,
Forgetting ancient honour, meanly stoop?
Shall we our rights and liberties resign,
To lay those jewels at a woman's shrine?
No: let us still be Britons! Be it known,
The favours we solicit are our own.
Engage, ye Britons, in the glorious task,
And stronger still enforce the things you ask:
Assert your rights, remonstrate with the throne,
Insist on liberty, and that alone.

Alas! America, thy ruined cause
Displays the ministry's contempt of laws.
Unrepresented thou art taxed, excised,
By creatures much too vile to be despised;
The outcast of an ousted gang are sent,
To bless thy commerce with [a][1] government.
Whilst pity rises to behold thy fate,
We see thee in this worst of troubles great;
Whilst anxious for thy wavering dubious cause,
We give thy proper spirit due applause.
If virtuous Grafton's sentimental taste
Is in his measures or his mistress placed,
In either 'tis originally rare,
One shews the midnight cully, one the peer:
Review him, Britons, with a proper pride,

---

[1] Omitted in the MS.

Was this a statesman qualified to guide?
Was this the minister whose mighty hand
Has scattered civil discord through the land?
Since smallest trifles, when ordained by fate,
Rise into power and counteract the great,
What shall we call thee, Grafton? Fortune's whip?
Or rather the burlesque of statesmanship:
When, daring in thy insolence of place,
Bold in an empty majesty of face,
We saw thee exercise thy magic rod,
And form a titled villain with a nod;
Turn out the virtuous, airily advance
The members of the council in a dance,
And honouring Sandwich with a serious [air],[1]
Commend the fancy of his solitaire?
These were thy actions, worthy of record,
Worthy the bubbled wretch and venal lord.
Since villainy is meritorious grown,
Step forward, for thy merit's not unknown.
What Mansfield's conscience shuddered to receive,
Thy mercenary temper cannot leave.
Reversions, pensions, bribes and titled views,
What mortal scoundrel can such things refuse?
If Dunning's nice integrity of mind
Will not in pales of interest be confined,
Let his uncommon honesty resign,
And boast the empty pension of the nine:
A Thurlow, grasping every offered straw,
Shines his successor, and degrades the law.
How like the ministry who linked his chains!
His measures tend incessantly to gains.

---

[1] Omitted.

If Weymouth dresses to the height of taste,
At once with fifty [venal][1] places laced,
Can such a summer insect of the state
Be otherwise than in externals great?
Thou bustling marplot of each hidden plan,
How wilt thou answer to the Sibyl's man?
Did thy own shallow politics direct
To treat the Mayor with purposed disrespect;
Or did it come in orders from above,
From her who sacrificed her soul to love?

Rigby, whose conscience is a perfect dice,
A just epitome of every vice,
Replete with what accomplishments support
The empty admiration of a court,
Yet wants a barony to grace record,
And hopes to lose the rascal in the lord.
His wish is granted, and the King prepares
A title of renown, to brand his heirs.
When vice creates the patent for a peer,
What lord so nominally great as Clare?
Whilst Chatham from his coroneted oak
Unheeded shook the senate with his croak,
The minister, too powerful to be right,
Laughed at his prophecy and second sight,
Since Mother Shipton's oracle of state
Forestalled the future incidents of fate.
Grafton might shake his elbows, dance, and dream,
'Twere labour lost to strive against the stream.
If Grafton in his juggling statesman's game
Bubbled for interest, betted but for fame,

---

[1] A word omitted in the MS.

The leader of the treasury could pay
For every loss in politics and play.

Sir Fletcher's noisy eloquence of tongue
Is on such pliant oily hinges hung,
Turned to all points of politics and doubt,
But though for ever worsted, never out.
Can such a wretched creature take the chair
And exercise his new-made power with air?
This worthy speaker of a worthy crew
Can write long speeches and repeat them too;
A practised lawyer in the venal court,
From higher powers he borrows his report;
Above the scandalous aspersion "tool,"
He only squares his conscience by a rule.
Granby, too great to join the hated cause,
Throws down his useless truncheon and withdraws;
Whilst, unrenowned for military deeds,
A youthful branch of royalty succeeds.

Let Coventry, Yonge, Palmerston, and Brett,
With resignation pay the crown a debt;
If, in return for offices of trust,
The ministry expect you'll prove unjust,
What soul that values freedom could with ease
Stoop under obligations such as these?
If you're a Briton (every virtue dead)
That would upon your dying freedom tread,
List in the gang, and piously procure
To make your calling and election sure:
Go, flatter Sawney for his jockeyship,
Assist in each long shuffle, hedge, and slip;
Thus rising on the stilts of favour, see

What Grafton was, and future dukes will be:
How Rigby, Weymouth, Barrington began
To juggle into fame and play the man.

Amidst this general rage of turning out,
What officer will stand, remains a doubt.
If virtue's an objection at the board,
With what propriety the council's stored!
Where could the Caledonian minion find
Such striking copies of his venal mind?
Search through the winding labyrinths of place,
See all alike politically base.
If virtues, foreign to the office, shine,
How fast the prodigies of state resign!
Still as they drop, the rising race begin
To boast the infamy of being in;
And generous Bristol, constant to his friend,
Employs his lifted crutches to ascend.
Look round thee, North! see, what a glorious scene!
O let no thought of vengeance intervene:
Throw thy own insignificance aside,
And swell in self-importance, power, and pride.
See Holland easy with his pilfered store,
See Bute intriguing how to pilfer more,
See Grafton's coffers boast the wealth of place,
A providence reserve to hedge and race.
New to oppressions and the servile chain,
Hark how the wrong'd Americans complain;
Whilst unregarded the petitions lie,
And liberty unnoticed swells her cry.
Yet, yet reflect, thou despicable thing,
How wavering is the favour of a king;

Think, since that feeble fence and Bute is all,
How soon thy humbug farce of state may fall;
Then catch the present moment while 'tis thine,
Implore a noble pension, and resign!

FEBRUARY.

AN ELEGY.

[Printed in the Town and Country Magazine, Feb. 1770.]

BEGIN, my Muse, the imitative lay,
Aonian doxies sound the thrumming string;
Attempt no number of the plaintive Gay,
Let me like midnight cats, or Collins[1] sing.

If in the trammels of the doleful line
The bounding hail, or drilling rain descend;
Come, brooding Melancholy, power divine,
And every unformed mass of words amend.

Now the rough Goat[2] withdraws his curling horns,
And the cold Waterer twirls his circling mop:
Swift sudden anguish darts through altering corns,
And the spruce mercer trembles in his shop.

---

[1] Probably not the well-known poet, but Emanuel Collins, a poetaster of Bristol; see Notes and Queries, 2nd S. vi. 533.

[2] Capricorn; the 'Waterer' is Aquarius.

Now infant authors, maddening for renown,
Extend the plume, and hum about the stage,
Procure a benefit, amuse the town,
And proudly glitter in a title-page.

Now, wrapt in ninefold fur, his squeamish grace
Defies the fury of the howling storm;
And, whilst the tempest whistles round his face,
Exults to find his mantled carcase warm.

Now rumbling coaches furious drive along,
Full of the majesty of city dames,
Whose jewels, sparkling in the gaudy throng,
Raise strange emotions and invidious flames.

Now Merit, happy in the calm of place,
To mortals as a Highlander appears,
And, conscious of the excellence of lace,
With spreading frogs and gleaming spangles glares;

Whilst Envy, on a tripod seated nigh,
In form a shoe-boy, daubs the valued fruit,
And, darting lightnings from his vengeful eye,
Raves about Wilkes, and politics, and Bute.

Now Barry, taller than a grenadier,
Dwindles into a stripling of eighteen;
Or sabled in Othello breaks the ear,
Exerts his voice, and totters to the scene.

Now Foote, a looking-glass for all mankind,
Applies his wax to personal defects;
But leaves untouch'd the image of the mind,
His art no mental quality reflects.

Now Drury's potent king extorts applause,
And pit, box, gallery, echo "how divine!"
Whilst, versed in all the drama's mystic laws,
His graceful action saves the wooden line.

Now—but what further can the Muses sing?
Now dropping particles of water fall;
Now vapours, riding on the north wind's wing,
With transitory darkness shadow all.

Alas! how joyless the descriptive theme,
When sorrow on the writer's quiet preys;
And, like a mouse in Cheshire cheese supreme,
Devours the substance of the lessening bays.

Come, February, lend thy darkest sky.
There teach the wintered muse with clouds to soar;
Come, February, lift the number high;
Let the sharp strain like wind through alleys roar.

Ye channels, wandering through the spacious street,
In hollow murmurs roll the dirt along,
With inundations wet the sabled feet,
Whilst gouts, responsive, join th' elégiac song.

Ye damsels fair, whose silver voices shrill
Sound through meandering folds of echo's horn,
Let the sweet cry of liberty be still,
No more let smoking cakes awake the morn.

O, Winter! put away thy snowy pride;
O, Spring! neglect the cowslip and the bell;
O, Summer! throw thy pears and plums aside;
O, Autumn! bid the grape with poison swell.

The pensioned muse of Johnson is no more!
Drowned in a butt of wine his genius lies:
Earth! Ocean! Heaven! the wondrous loss deplore,
The dregs of nature with her glory dies.

What iron Stoic can suppress the tear?
What sour reviewer reads with vacant eye?
What bard but decks his literary bier?
Alas! I cannot sing—I howl—I cry—

D. B.

Bristol, Feb. 12, [1770].

ELEGY.

[Printed in the "Miscellanies," 1778.]

ASTE, haste! ye solemn messengers of night,
Spread the black mantle on the shrinking plain;
But, ah! my torments still survive the light,
The changing seasons alter not my pain.

Ye variegated children of the spring;
Ye blossoms blushing with the pearly dew;
Ye birds that sweetly in the hawthorn sing;
Ye flowery meadows, lawns of verdant hue;

Faint are your colours, harsh your love-notes thrill,
To me no pleasure Nature now can yield:
Alike the barren rock and woody hill,
The dark-brown blasted heath, and fruitful field.

Ye spouting cataracts, ye silver streams,
  Ye spacious rivers, whom the willow shrouds,
Ascend the bright-crowned sun's far-shining beams,
  To aid the mournful tear-distilling clouds.

Ye noxious vapours, fall upon my head;
  Ye writhing adders, round my feet entwine;
Ye toads, your venom in my foot-path spread;
  Ye blasting meteors, upon me shine.

Ye circling seasons, intercept the year,
  Forbid the beauties of the spring to rise;
Let not the life-preserving grain appear;
  Let howling tempests harrow up the skies.

Ye cloud-girt, moss-grown turrets, look no more
  Into the palace of the god of day;
Ye loud tempestuous billows, cease to roar,
  In plaintive numbers through the valleys stray.

Ye verdant-vested trees, forget to grow,
  Cast off the yellow foliage of your pride:
Ye softly tinkling rivulets, cease to flow,
  Or, swelled with certain death and poison, glide.

Ye solemn warblers of the gloomy night,
  That rest in lightning-blasted oaks the day,
Through the black mantles take your slow-paced
    flight,
  Rending the silent wood with shrieking lay.

Ye snow-crowned mountains, lost to mortal eyes,
  Down to the valleys bend your hoary head;
Ye livid comets, fire the peopled skies—
  For—lady Betty's tabby cat is dead!

THE EXHIBITION; A PERSONAL SATIRE.

[This poem is represented only by the extract given by Professor Wilson, in his Life of Chatterton, p. 201. The reason for not printing more of it may be gathered from Professor Wilson's account of it. "The Exhibition no doubt belongs to the latest months of Chatterton's Bristol career. It has never been published; and it would have been well had it perished, with its evidence that youthful purity had been sullied, and the precocious boy was only too conversant with forbidden things. The copy in the Bristol Library bears date May 1st, 1770—a few days after he reached London,—when we find him also copying his 'Kew Gardens,' in order to transmit it to his friend Cary. It is entitled 'The Exhibition; a personal satyr [*sic*];' and fully merits its claim to personality in its satirical sketches. Amongst others, the Temple Vicar is dealt with in terms still freer than in the Epistle addressed to himself."]

THIS truth, this mighty truth—if truth can shine
In the smooth polish of a laboured line—
Catcott by sad experience testifies;
And who shall tell a sabled priest he lies?
Bred to the juggling of the specious band
Predestinated to adorn the land,
The selfish Catcott ripened to a priest,
And wore the sable livery of the Beast.
By birth to prejudice and whim allied,
And heavy with hereditary pride,

He modelled pleasure by a fossil rule,
And spent his youth to prove himself a fool;
Buried existence in a lengthened cave,
And lost in dreams whatever Nature gave.

May 1, 1770.

FRAGMENT.

[Transcribed from a MS. in Chatterton's handwriting and printed in 1803.]

INTEREST, thou universal god of men,
Wait on the couplet and reprove the pen;
If aught unwelcome to thy ears shall rise,
Hold jails and famine to the poet's eyes,
Bid satire sheathe her sharp avenging steel,
And lose a number rather than a meal.
Nay, prithee, honour, do not make us mad,
When I am hungry something must be had:
Can honest consciousness of doing right
Provide a dinner or a bed at night?
What though Astrea decks my soul in gold,
My mortal lumber trembles with the cold;
Then, cursed tormentor of my peace, begone!
Flattery's a cloak, and I will put it on.
In a low cottage, shaking with the wind,
A door in front, a span of light behind,
Tervono's lungs their mystic play began,
And nature in the infant marked the man.
Six times the youth of morn, the golden sun,
Through the twelve stages of his course had run,

Tervono rose, the merchant of the plain,
His soul was traffic, his elysium gain;
The ragged chapman found his word a law,
And lost in barter every favourite taw.
Through various scenes Tervono still ascends,
And still is making, still forgetting friends;
Full of this maxim, often heard in trade,
Friendship with none but equals should be made.
His soul is all the merchant. None can find
The shadow of a virtue in his mind.
Nor are his vices reason misapplied;
Mean as his spirit, sneaking as his pride.
At city dinner or a turtle feast
As expeditious as a hungry priest:
No foe to Bacchanalian brutal rites,
In vile confusion dozing off the nights.

Tervono would be flattered; shall I then
In stigmatizing satire shake the pen?
Muse, for his brow the laurel wreath prepare,
Though soon 'twill wither when 'tis planted there.
Come, panegyric; adulation, haste,
And sing this wonder of mercántile taste;
And whilst his virtue rises in my lines,
The patron's happy, and the poet dines.
Some, philosophically cased in steel,
Can neither poverty or hunger feel;
But that is not my case; the Muses know
What water-gruel stuff from Phœbus flow;
Then if the rage of satire seize my brain,
May none but brother poets meet the strain.
May bulky aldermen nor vicars rise,
Hung in terrorem to their brothers' eyes;

When, lost in trance by gospel or by law,
In to their inward room the senses draw,
There as they snore in consultation deep,
Are by the vulgar reckoned fast asleep.[1]

SUNDAY. A FRAGMENT.

[First printed in 1803. Cf. "Kew Gardens;" p. 172.]

HERVENIS, harping on the hackneyed text,
By disquisitions is so sore perplexed,
He stammers,—instantaneously is drawn
A bordered piece of inspiration-lawn,
Which being thrice unto his nose applied,
Into his pineal gland the vapours glide;
And now again we hear the doctor roar
On subjects he dissected thrice before.
I own at church I very seldom pray,
For vicars, strangers to devotion, bray.
Sermons, though flowing from the sacred lawn,
Are flimsy wires from reason's ingot drawn;
And, to confess the truth, another cause
My every prayer and adoration draws:
In all the glaring tinctures of the bow,
The ladies front me in celestial row.
(Though, when black melancholy damps my joys,
I call them nature's trifles, airy toys;
Yet when the goddess Reason guides the strain,
I think them, what they are, a heavenly train.)

---

[1] See p. 152.

The amorous rolling, the black sparkling eye,
The gentle hazel, and the optic sly;
The easy shape, the panting semi-globes,
The frankness which each latent charm disrobes;
The melting passions, and the sweet severe,
The easy amble, the majestic air;
The tapering waist, the silver-mantled arms,
All is one vast variety of charms.
Say, who but sages stretched beyond their span,
Italian singers, or an unmanned man,
Can see Elysium spread upon their brow,
And to a drowsy curate's sermon bow?

If (but 'tis seldom) no fair female face
Attracts my notice by some glowing grace,
Around the monuments I cast my eyes,
And see absurdities and nonsense rise.
Here rueful-visaged angels seem to tell,
With weeping eyes, a soul is gone to hell;
There a child's head, supported by duck's wings,
With toothless mouth a hallelujah sings:
In funeral pile eternal marble burns,
And a good Christian seems to sleep in urns.
A self-drawn curtain bids the reader see
An honourable Welchman's pedigree;
A rock of porphyry darkens half the place,
And virtues blubber with no awkward grace;
Yet, strange to tell, in all the dreary gloom
That makes the sacred honours of the tomb,
No quartered coats above the base[1] appear,
No battered arms, or golden corsets there.

* * * * *

[1] Printed "bel" in Southey's edition, which is nonsense.

KEW GARDENS.[1]

HAIL Kew! thou darling of the tuneful nine,
Thou eating-house of verse, where poets dine;
The temple of the idol of the great,
Sacred to council-mysteries of state;
Sir Gilbert oft, in dangerous trials known,
To make the shame and felony his own,

---

[1] "Printed from a transcript in the hand-writing of the late Mr. Isaac Reed, contained in Mr. Haslewood's collection, [and now in the British Museum.]

The poem of 'Kew Gardens,' had never been published complete. In Southey and Cottle's edition of Chatterton's Works, a few of the concluding lines were published, and the following note was added, vol. i. p. 202:—

'Every effort has been made to obtain the remainder of this poem, but without success. The last possessor who can be traced was the late Dr. Lort. His executor, Dr. Halifax, has obligingly communicated the preceding fragment, but the remainder of the poem never came into his possession. Many lines in the 'Extract from Kew Gardens,' appear in the 'Whore of Babylon,' but differently arranged.'

Chatterton refers to this poem in his will. I have not been able to ascertain the precise time when it was written, but it is evident that it must have been produced before April, 1770, from the fact of his having named it in the document referred to. I have been fortunate enough to procure a copy of the whole poem, through Mr. Gutch, and it is here for the first time printed entire."—DIX's *Life of Chatterton,* 1837.

Burns incense on thy altars, and presents
The grateful sound of clamorous discontents:
In the bold favour of thy goddess vain,
He brandishes his sword and shakes his chain.
He knows her secret workings and desires,
Her hidden attributes and vestal fires;
Like an old oak has seen her godhead fall
Beneath the wild descendant of Fingal,
And happy in the view of promised store
Forgot his dignity and held the door.
* * * * happy genius, comes along,
Humming the music of a Highland song:
Rough and unpolished in the tricks of state,
He plots by instinct, is by nature great.
Who, not a mantled herald, can dispute
The native grandeur of the house of Bute?
Who, not a Caledonian, can deny
By instinct all its noble branches lie?
'Tis an entailed estate upon the name,
To plunder, plot, and pillage into fame,
To live in splendour, infamy, and pride,
The guiders of the tools who seem to guide;
Or starve on honesty, in state their own,
And marshal sheep unnoticed and unknown.
* * * * versed in juntos and intrigues,
The fool and statesman in close union leagues;
Sits at the council's head; esteemed at most
An useful kind of circulating post,
Through whose short stage each future measure's laid,
And all the orders of the Thane conveyed.
He gives the written text by fortune wrote,
Sir Gilbert adds his necessary note.

Dyson, a plodding animal of state,
Who's classically little, to be great;
An instrument, made use of to record
The future witty speeches of his lord:
To write epistles to his powerful dame,
And in the dark supply his loss of flame;
To sell preferment; grovel in the dust,
The slave of interest and the slave of lust;
To lick his lordship's shoes, and find a flaw
In every statute that opposed his law;
To carry orders to the guiding tool,
To flatter * * * * with the hopes of rule;
To send congratulations to the man,
Who stands so well affected to the clan—
(To * * * * whose conscientious mind
Does universal service to mankind,
When, red with justice and the royal cause,
His bloody musket shook with court-applause:
When monarchs, representatives of God,
Honoured the rascal with a gracious nod,
Three ghosts in George's sanguine field were seen,
And two struck horror into Bethnal Green;
Soft Pity's voice, unnoticed by the Crown,
Stole in a murmur through the weeping town;
And Freedom, wandering restless and alone,
Saw no redress expected from the throne,
Then bade remonstrance wear a bolder dress,
And loudly supplicate, and force success:
* * * * heard, and, resting on his mace,
" The usual fees, my lord, and state the case."
" Three thousand, and reversion to your son:"
" The seals, my lord, are mine, the matter's done."
" This house of foolish cits, and drunken boys,

Offends my ears, like Broderip's[1] horrid noise:
'Tis a flat riot by the statute made,
Destructive to our happiness and trade."
"Thy action, * * * * is just in law,
In the defence of ministry *I'll* draw;
Nor doubt I, when in solemn pomp arrayed,
To act as bravely, be as richly paid."
So * * * * spoke, and in his usual way
When giving out his syllables for pay,
With happy fluency he scattered round
His nicely culled varieties of sound,
Unmeaning, unconnected, false, unfair:
All he can boast is modulated air)—
To bribe the common council to protest;
To learn a witless alderman to jest;
The father of the city to deprave,
And add the hummed apostate to the knave,
Who wisely disinherits his first-born,
And doats upon the blossom of his horn;
To fill up places by preferment void,
Is Dyson by the quadruples employed;
He bears the message of the gartered Fate,[2]
The running footman to the favoured great:
When spent with labour, overgrown with spoil,
Some barony or earldom pays his toil.

Whilst two chief actors wisely keep away,
And two before the mystic curtain play;
The goddess, mourning for her absent god,
Approves the flying measures with a nod.
Her approbation, with her power combined,

---

[1] A Bristol organist, who offended Chatterton by turning him out of the organ-loft.
[2] Editions, "trate."

Exalts her tools above the common kind.
She turns the movements of the dark machine,
Nor is her management of state unseen;
Regardless of the world, she still turns round,
And tumbles * * * * to his native ground.
Great in possession of a mystic ring,
She leads the Lords and Commons in a string.
Where is the modest Muse of Jones retired,[1]
So bashful, so impatiently admired?
Ah! is that noble emulation dead,
Which bade the laurels blossom on his head,
When Kew's[2] enchanting heap of stones was sung
In strains superior to a mortal tongue,
And kitchen-gardens most luxurious glowed
With flowers which ne'er in Mayor's window blowed;
Where cabbages, exotic'ly divine,
Were tagged in feet, and measured with a line?
Ah! what invention graced the happy strain;
Well might the laureate bard of Kew be vain!
Thy Clifton[3] too! how justly is the theme
As much the poet's as his jingling dream.
Who but a Muse inventive, great, like thine,
Could honour Bristol with a nervous line?
What generous, honest genius would have sold
To knaves and catamites his praise for gold?

---

[1] Henry Jones, author of "The Earl of Essex," and other pieces. He had been a bricklayer, in Ireland, before he was taken under the protection of the late Earl of Chesterfield.—MS. note.

[2] See "Kew Garden," a poem, in two cantos. By Henry Jones, 4to. 1767.—MS. note.

[3] "Clifton, a poem, in two cantos, including Bristol and all its environs." By Henry Jones, 4to. 1766.—MS. note.

To leave alone the notions which disgrace
This hawking, peddling, catamitish place,
Did not thy iron conscience blush to write
This Tophet of the gentle arts polite?
Lost to all learning, elegance, and sense,
Long had the famous city told her pence;
Avarice sat brooding in her white-washed cell,
And pleasure had a hut at Jacob's Well.[1]
Poor Hickey, ruined by his fine survey,
Perpetuates Elton in the saving lay.
A mean assembly-room, absurdly built,
Boasted one gorgeous lamp of copper gilt;
With farthing candles, chandeliers of tin,
And services of water, rum, and gin.
There, in the dull solemnity of wigs,
The dancing bears of commerce murder jigs;
Here dance the dowdy belles of crooked trunk,
And often, very often, reel home drunk;
Here dance the bucks with infinite delight,
And club to pay the fiddlers for the night,
While Broderip's hum-drum symphonies of flats
Rival the harmony of midnight cats.
What charms has music, when great Broderip sweats
To torture sound to what his brother sets!
With scraps of ballad tunes, and *gude Scotch sangs*,
Which god-like Ramsay to his bagpipe twangs,
With tattered fragments of forgotten plays,
With Playford's melody to Sternhold's lays,
This pipe of science, mighty Broderip, comes,
And a strange, unconnected jumble thrums.
Roused to devotion in a sprightly air,

[1] Where the old theatre at Bristol stood.—MS. note.

Danced into piety, and jigged to prayer ;
A modern hornpipe's murder greets our ears,
The heavenly music of domestic spheres ;
The flying band in swift transition hops
Through all the tortured, vile burlesque of stops.
Sacred to sleep, in superstitious key
Dull, doleful diapasons die away ;
Sleep spreads his silken wings, and lulled by sound,
The vicar slumbers, and the snore goes round ;
Whilst Broderip at his passive organ groans
Through all his slow variety of tones.
How unlike Allen ! Allen[1] is divine !
His touch is sentimental, tender, fine ;
No little affectations e'er disgraced
His more refined, his sentimental taste :
He keeps the passions with the sound in play,
And the soul trembles with the trembling key.[2]

---

[1] Organist of Redcliff Church, and also of Temple.

[2] "It is a curious fact, that in the poem of Kew Gardens, there are consecutively fifty lines transplanted from a yet unpublished poem, [a copy of which is now in the Bristol Library,] called 'The Exhibition;' and, scattered here and there, are repeatedly three or four continuous lines borrowed from the same production, which is, by the bye, a most infamously satirical tirade against the Doctors, the Surgeons, and the Clergymen of the day. Perhaps it would be awkward, and no very easy matter, to fill up with the names the various hiatus—the initial and tail letters, together with the ——— and the * * * which occur in every line of the 'Kew Gardens,' but without it the poem is almost unintelligible and the wit lost, or nearly so, and this is not to be wondered at after the lapse of sixty years."—*Bristol Paper*.

"Chatterton wrote also an indecent satirical poem, called 'The Exhibition,' occasioned by the improper behaviour of a person in Bristol. The satire of this poem is local, and

The groves of Kew, however misapplied
To serve the purposes of lust and pride,
Were, by the greater monarch's care, designed
A place of conversation for the mind;
Where solitude and silence should remain,
And conscience keep her sessions and arraign.
But ah! how fallen from that better state!
'Tis now a heathen temple of the great,
Where sits the female pilot of the helm,
Who shakes oppression's fetters through the realm.
Her name is Tyranny, and in a string
She leads the shadow of an infant king;[1]
Dispenses favours with a royal hand,
And marks, like destiny, what lord shall stand;
Her four-fold representative displays
How future statesmen may their fortune raise;
While thronging multitudes their offerings bring,
And bards, like Jones, their panegyrics sing.
The loyal aldermen, a troop alone,
Protest their infamy, to serve the throne;
The merchant-tailor minister declares
He'll mutilate objections with his shears.
Sir Robert, in his own importance big,
Settles his potent, magisterial wig;

---

the characters of most of the surgeons in Bristol are delineated in it. Some descriptive passages in this poem have great merit. Thus, speaking of a favourite organist, probably Mr. Allen, he says:—

> He keeps the passions with the sound in play,
> And the soul trembles with the trembling key."

Dr. Gregory.

[1] See the impudent frontispiece to the third volume of the "New Foundling Hospital for Wit."—MS. note.

Having another legacy in view,
Accepts the measure and improves it too.
Before the altar all the suppliants bow,
And would repeat a speech if they knew how;
A gracious nod the speaking image gave,
And scattered honours upon every knave.
The loyal sons of Caledonia came,
And paid their secret homage to the dame,
Then swore, by all their hopes of future reign,
Each measure of the junto to maintain,
The orders of the ministry to take,
And honour * * * for his father's sake.
Well pleased, the goddess dignified his grace,
And scattered round the benefits of place;
With other pensions blessed his lordship's post,
And smiled on murdered * * * * injured ghost.
Through all the happy lovers' numerous clan
The inexhausted tides of favour ran:
* * *, * * *, happy in a name,
Emerged from poverty to wealth and fame;
And English taxes paid (and scarcely too)
The noble generosity of Kew.
Kew! happy subject for a lengthened lay,
Though thousands write, there's something still to say;
Thy garden's elegance, thy owner's state,
The highest in the present list of fate,
Are subjects where the muse may wildly range,
Unsatiate, in variety of change;
But hold, my dedication is forgot;
Now—shall I praise some late-ennobled Scot?
Exalt the motto of a Highland lord,

And prove him great, like Guthrie,[1] by record?
(Though were the truth to all the nobles known,
The vouchers he refers to are his own.)
Shall I trace * * * 's powerful pedigree,
Or show him an attorney's clerk, like me?
Or shall I rather give to * * * * its due,
And to a Burgum[2] recommend my Kew?
Why sneers the sapient Broughton[3] at the man?
Broughton can't boast the merit Burgum can.
How lofty must imagination soar,
To reach absurdities unknown before!
Thanks to thy pinions, Broughton, thou hast brought
From the moon's orb a novelty of thought.

Burgum wants learning—see the lettered throng
Banter his English in a Latin song.
If in his jests a discord should appear,
A dull lampoon is innocently dear:
Ye sage, Broughtonian, self-sufficient fools,
Is this the boasted justice of your schools?
Burgum has parts, parts which will set aside
The laboured acquisitions of your pride;
Uncultivated now his genius lies,
Instruction sees his latent talents rise;
His gold is bullion, yours debased with brass,
Impressed with folly's head to make it pass.
But Burgum swears so loud, so indiscreet,
His thunders echo through the listening street;

---

[1] William Guthrie, compiler of the "Complete History of the English Peerage," 4to. 1762.—MS. note.

[2] The Bristol pewterer.

[3] The Rev T. Broughton, Vicar of St. Mary, Redcliffe, author of "An Historical Dictionary of all Religions."

Ye rigid Christians, formally severe,
Blind to his charities, his oaths you hear;
Observe his actions—calumny must own
A noble soul is in these actions shown:
Though dark this bright original you paint,
I'd rather be a Burgum than a saint.

Hail, Inspiration! whose Cimmerian night
Gleams into day with every flying light:
If Moses caught thee at the parted flood;
If David found thee in a sea of blood;
If Mahomet with slaughter drenched thy soil,
On loaded asses bearing off the spoil;
If thou hast favoured Pagan, Turk, or Jew,
Say, had not Broughton inspiration too?
Such rank absurdities debase his line,
I almost could have sworn he copied thine.
Hail, Inspiration! whose auspicious ray
Immortalized great Armstrong[1] in a day:
Armstrong, whose Caledonian genius flies
Above the reach of humble judgment's ties;
Whose lines prosaic regularly creep,
Sacred to dulness and congenial sleep.
Hail, Inspiration! whose mysterious wings
Are strangers to what rigid [Johnson] sings;
By him thy airy voyages are curbed,
Nor moping wisdom's by thy flight disturbed;
To ancient lore and musty precepts bound,
Thou art forbid the range of fairy ground.
Irene[2] creeps so classical and dry,

[1] "Day, an Epistle to John Wilkes, Esq." 4to. 176—. This poem was written by Dr. Armstrong, but is not collected in his works.—MS. note.

[2] Dr. Johnson's tragedy.—MS. note.

None but a Greek philosopher can cry;
Through five long acts unlettered heroes sleep,
And critics by the square of learning weep.
Hark! what's the horrid bellowing from the stage?
Oh! 'tis the ancient chorus of the age;
Grown wise, the judgment of the town refines,
And in a philosophic habit shines;
Models each pleasure in scholastic taste,
And heavenly Greece is copied and disgraced.
The False Alarm,[1] in style and subject great,
The mighty Atlas of a falling state,
Which makes us happy, insolent, and free,
O god-like Inspiration! came from thee.
* * * * whose brazen countenance, like mine,
Scorns in the polish of a blush to shine,
Scrupled to vindicate his fallen Grace,
Or hint he acted right—till out of place.
Why will the lovers of the truth deplore
That miracles and wonders are no more?
Why will the deists, impudently free,
Assert what cannot now, could never be?
Why will religion suffer the reproach,
Since * * * * dresses well and keeps a coach?
Bristol and * * * * have bestowed their pence,
And * * * after * * * echoed sense.
Since * * * * once by providence, or chance,
Tumbled his lengthening quavers in a dance:
Since Catcott seemed to reason, and display
The meaning of the words he meant to say:
Since Warburton, his native pride forgot,
Bowed to the garment of the ruling Scot;

---

[1] By Dr. Johnson, published in 1770; see p. 149.

And offered * * * * ghost (a welcome gift)
And hoped, in gratitude, to have a lift;
An universal primacy, at least,
A fit reward for such a stirring priest:
Since Horne imprudently displayed his zeal,
And made his foe the powerful reasons feel:
Since * * * has meaning in his last discourse:
Since * * * * borrowed honesty by force,
And trembled at the measures of the friend
His infant conscience shuddered to defend:
Since * * * in his race of vice outrun,
Scrupled to do what * * * * since hath done.
Hail, Inspiration! Catcott learns to preach,
And classic Lee attempts by thee to teach;
By inspiration North directs his tools,
And [Bute] above by inspiration rules,
Distils the thistles of the gartered crew,
And drains the sacred reservoirs of Kew.
Inspired with hopes of rising in the kirk,
Here * * * * whines his Sunday's journey-work;
Soft * * * * undeniably a saint,
Whimpers in accent so extremely faint,
You see the substance of his empty prayer,
His nothing to the purpose in his air;
His sermons have no arguments, 'tis true,
Would you have sense and pretty figures too?
With what a swimming elegance and ease
He scatters out distorted similes!
It matters not how wretchedly applied,
Saints are permitted to set sense aside:
This oratorial novelty in town
Dies into fame, and ogles to renown;
The dowdy damsels of his chosen tribe

Are fee'd to heaven, his person is the bribe;
All who can superficial talk admire,
His vanity, not beauty, sets on fire:
Enough of * * * * let him ogle still,
Convince with nonsense, and with foppery kill,
Pray for the secret measures of the great,
And hope the Lord will regulate the state:
Florid as Klopstock,[1] and as quick as me
At double epithet or simile;
His despicable talents cannot harm
Those who defy a Johnson's "False Alarm."
Hail, Inspiration! piously I kneel,
And call upon thy sacred name with zeal;
Come, spread thy sooty pinions o'er my pen,
Teach me the secrets of the lords of men;
In visionary prospects let me see
How [Bute] employs his sense, derived from thee;
Display the mystic Sibyl of the isle,
And dress her wrinkled features in a smile;
Of past and secret measures let me tell,
How [Grafton] pilfered power, and Chatham fell:
Chatham, whose patriotic actions wear
One single brand of infamy—the peer;
Whose popularity again thinks fit
To lose the coronet, revive the Pitt;
And in the upper house (where leading peers
Practise a minuet step, or scratch their ears)
He warmly undertakes to plead the cause
Of injured liberty, and broken laws.

---

[1] A German writer, some of whose works have been translated into English. See particularly the "Messiah," and the "Death of Adam."—MS. note.

Hail, Inspiration! from whose fountain flow
The strains which circulate through all the Row,
With humblest reverence thy aid I ask,
For this laborious and herculean task.
How difficult to make a piece go down
With booksellers, reviewers, and the town;
None with a Christian, charitable love,
A kind and fixed intention to approve,
The wild excursions of the Muse will read.
Alas! I was not born beyond the Tweed!
To public favour I have no pretence,
If public favour is the child of sense:
To paraphrase on Home in Armstrong's rhymes,
To decorate Fingal in sounding chimes,
The self-sufficient Muse was never known,
But shines in trifling dulness all her own.
Where, rich with painted bricks and lifeless white,
Four dirty alleys in a cross unite,
Where avaricious sons of commerce meet
To do their public business in the street;
There stands a dome to dulness ever dear,
Where * * * * models justice by the square;
Where bulky aldermen display their sense,
And Bristol patriots wager out their pence:
Here, in the malice of my stars confin'd,
I call the Muses to divert my mind;
Come, Inspiration! mysticly instil
The spirit of a * * * * in my quill,
An equal terror to the small and great,
To lash an alderman or knave of state.

Here * * * thundering through the spacious court,
Grounds equity on Jeffries's report;

And oft, explaining to the lords of trade,
Proves himself right by statutes never made;
In * * * * able politicians see
Another * * * * in epitome.
If good Sir * * * * did not bawl so loud,
What has he else superior to the crowd?
His peruke boasts solemnity of law:
E'en there might counsellors detect a flaw.
But Providence is just, as doctors tell,
That triple mystery's a good sentinel;
Was * * * * not so noisy, and more wise,
The body corporate would close its eyes.
Useless the satire, stoically wise,
Bristol can literary rubs despise;
You'll wonder whence the wisdom may proceed,
'Tis doubtful if her aldermen can read;
This as a certainty the Muse may tell,
None of her common-councilmen can spell:
Why, busy * * * * wilt thou trouble * * *
Their worships hear, and understand like thee.

Few beings absolutely boast the man,
Few have the understanding of a Spanne;
Every idea of a city mind
Is to commercial incidents confined:
True! some exceptions to this general rule
Can show the merchant blended with the fool.
* * * * with magisterial air commits:
* * * * presides the chief of city wits;
In jigs and country-dances * * * * shines,
And * * * * slumbers over Mallet's lines:
His ample visage, oft on nothing bent,
Sleeps in vacuity of sentiment.

When in the venerable gothic hall,
Where fetters rattle, evidences bawl,
Puzzled in thought by equity or law,
Into their inner room his senses draw;
There, as they snore[1] in consultation deep,
The foolish vulgar deem him fast asleep.

If silent * * * * senatorial pride
Rose into being as his avarice died,
Scattering his hundreds, rattling in his coach,
What mortal wonders at the fair * * * *
Though royal horners burn in powdered flames,
When fell the pretty nymph of many names?
Still we behold her fiery virtue stand,
As firm as * * * * regulating band.
* * * * within whose sacerdotal face,
Add all the honorary signs of grace;
Great in his accent, greater in his size,
But mightier still in turtle and mince-pies:
Whose entertaining flows of eloquence,
In spite of affectation, will be sense.
Why, patriotic [Johnson], art thou still?
What pensioned lethargy has seized thy quill?
Hast thou forgot the murmurs of applause
Which buzzed about the leader of the cause;
When, dressed in metaphors, the fluent * * *
Rose from his chair, and slumbering drawled his
speech?
When * * * * fired with loyalty and place,
Forsook his breeding to defend his Grace:
And saving * * * * from a furious blow,
Insisted on his plan, a double row.

---

[1] MS. copy 'sneer;' but see p. 134.

Rise * * * * bid remonstrance tell the throne,
When freedom suffers, London's not alone:
Take off the load of infamy and shame
Which lies on Bristol's despicable name;
Revive thy ardour for thy country's cause,
And live again in honour and applause.
Alas! the patriot listens to his whore,
And popularity is heard no more;
The dying voice of liberty's forgot,
No more he drinks damnation to the Scot.
* * * * no longer in his quarrel fights;
No further dulness witty * * * * writes:
In organs and an organist renowned,
He rises into notice by a sound,
Commemorates his spirit in a tone,
By * * * * created, rival of a groan:
O be his taste immortal as the lays!
For * * * invents and tuneful [Broderip] plays;
And this harmonious jangling of the spheres,
To give the whole connexion, Bristol hears.

Hail, Kew! thy more important powers I sing,
Powers which direct the conscience of a king;
The English number daringly would soar
To thy first power, [the Babylonish whore.]
Come, Newton,[1] and assist me to explain
The hidden meanings of the present reign.
Newton, accept the tribute of a line[2]

[1] Bishop of Bristol, author of a work "On the Prophecies."

[2] The poem, from this line to the end, is an expansion of a shorter one, published with the title of "The Whore of Babylon." The latter differs from this very slightly, the collation being given in the footnotes. It also enables us to fill up some of the blanks, and complete the present poem.

From one whose humble genius honours thine;
Mysterious shall the mazy numbers seem,
To give thee matter for a future dream;
Thy happy talent, meanings to untie,
My vacancy of meaning may supply;
And where the Muse is witty in a dash,
Thy explanations may enforce the lash.
How shall the line, grown servile in respect,
To North or Sandwich infamy direct?
Unless a wise ellipsis intervene,
How shall I satirize the sleepy dean?[1]
Perhaps the Muse might fortunately strike
A highly finished picture, very like;
But deans are all so lazy, dull, and fat,
None could be certain worthy Barton sat.
Come then, my Newton, leave the musty lines
Where Revelation's farthing-candle shines;
In search of hidden truths let others go—
Be thou the fiddler to my puppet-show.
What are these hidden truths but secret lies,
Which from diseased imaginations rise?
What if our politicians should succeed
In fixing up the ministerial creed,
Who could such golden arguments refuse,
Which melts and proselytes the hardened Jews?
When universal reformation bribes
With words and wealthy metaphors, the tribes,
To empty pews the brawny chaplain swears,
Whilst none but trembling superstition hears.
When ministers, with sacerdotal hands,
Baptize the flock in streams of golden sands,

---

[1] Dr. Barton, Dean of Bristol.

Through every town conversion wings her way,
And conscience is a prostitute for pay.

Faith removes mountains ; like a modern dean,
Faith can see virtues which were never seen :
Our pious ministry this sentence quote,
To prove their instrument's superior vote ;
Whilst Luttrell, happy in his lordship's voice,
Bids faith persuade us 'tis the people's choice.
This mountain of objections to remove,
This knotty, rotten argument to prove,
Faith insufficient, Newton caught the pen,
And proved[1] by demonstration, one was ten :
What boots it if he reasoned right or no ?
'Twas orthodox—the Thane[2] would have it so.
Whoe'er shall doubts and false conclusions draw
Against the inquisition of the law,
With gaolers, chains, and pillories must plead,
And Mansfield's conscience settle right his creed.
" Is Mansfield's conscience then," will Freedom cry,
" A standard-block to dress our notions by ?
Why, what a blunder has the fool let fall !
That Mansfield has no conscience, none at all !"
Pardon me, Freedom, this and something more
The knowing writer might have known before ;
But, bred in Bristol's mercenary cell,
Compelled in scenes of avarice to dwell,
What generous passion can my dross refine ?
What besides interest can direct the line ?[3]

---

[1] *Or*, shewed. [2] Lord Bute.

[3] *Or*,

What generous passion can refine my breast ?
What besides interest has my mind possessed ?

And should a galling truth, like this, be told
By me, instructed here to slave for gold,
My prudent neighbours (who can read) would see
Another Savage[1] to be starved in me.
Faith is a powerful virtue everywhere;
By this once Bristol dressed, for Cato, Clare;
But now the blockheads grumble, Nugent's made
Lord of this idol, being lord of trade.[2]
They bawled for Clare, when little in their eyes,
But cannot to the titled villain rise.
This state-credulity, a bait for fools,
Employs his lordship's literary tools;
Murphy, a bishop of the chosen sect,
A ruling pastor of the Lord's elect,
Keeps journals, posts, and magazines in awe,
And parcels out his daily statute-law.
Would you the bard's veracity dispute?
He borrows persecution's scourge of Bute,
An excommunication-satire writes,
And the slow mischief trifles till it bites.
This faith, the subject of a late divine,
Is not as unsubstantial as his line;[3]
Though, blind and dubious to behold the right,
Its optics mourn a fixed Egyptian night,
Yet things unseen are seen so very clear,
She knew[4] fresh muster would begin the year;

---

[1] The celebrated Richard Savage, son to the Earl of Rivers, who died in jail at Bristol.—MS. note.

[2] *Or,* Lord of their choice, he being lord of trade.

[3] *Or,* This faith, a subject for a longer theme,
Is not the substance of a waking dream.

[4] So in the other copy; MS. "The new." It alludes to the change of ministry, Jan. 1770.

She knows that North, by Bute and conscience led,
Will hold his honours till his favour's dead,
She knows that Martin, ere he can be great,
Must practise at the target of the state:
If then his erring pistol should not kill,
Why Martin must remain a traitor still.
His gracious mistress, generous to the brave,
Will not neglect the necessary knave;
Since pious Chudleigh is become her[1] Grace,
Martin turns pimp, to occupy her place.
Say, Rigby, in the honours of the door,
How properly a rogue succeeds a whore!
She knows (the subject almost slipt my quill
Lost in that pistol of a woman's will)—
She knows that Bute will exercise his rod,
The worthiest of the worthy sons of God.

Ah! (exclaims Catcott)[2] this is saying much;
The Scripture tells us peace-makers are such.
Who can dispute his title? Who deny
What taxes and oppressions testify?[3]
Who of the Thane's beatitude can doubt?
Oh! was but North as sure of being out!
And (as I end whatever I begin)
Was Chatham but as sure of being in!
Bute, foster-child of fate, dear to a dame
Whom satire freely would, but dare not, name—
(Ye plodding barristers, who hunt a flaw,
What treason[4] would you from the sentence draw?
Tremble, and stand attentive as a dean,
Know, Royal Favour is the dame[5] I mean.
To sport with royalty my Muse forbears,

[1] So in other copy; MS. "his."
[2] *Or*, But (say the critics).
[3] *Or*, justify.
[4] *Or*, mischief.
[5] *Or*, thing.

And kindly takes compassion on my ears.
When once Shibbeare in glorious triumph stood
Upon a rostrum of distinguished wood,
Who then withheld his guinea or his praise,
Or envied him his crown of English bays?
But now Modestus,[1] truant to the cause,
Assists the pioneers who sap the laws,
Wreaths infamy around a sinking pen,
Who could withhold the pillory again?)—
Bute, lifted into notice by the eyes
Of one whose optics always set to rise[2]—
Forgive a pun, ye rationals, forgive
A flighty youth, as yet unlearnt to live;
When I have conned each sage's musty rule,
I may with greater reason play the fool;
Burgum and I, in ancient lore untaught,
Are always with our natures in a fault;
Though Camplin would instruct us in the part,
Our stubborn morals will not err by art.
Having in various starts from order strayed,
We'll call imagination to our aid—
See Bute astride upon a wrinkled hag,
His hand replenished with an opened bag,
Whence fly the ghosts of taxes and supplies,
The sales of places, and the last excise!
Upon the ground, in seemly order laid,
The Stuarts stretched[3] the majesty of plaid;
Rich with the peer, dependants bowed[4] the head,

---

[1] The signature of a writer in the newspapers of the time.—MS. note.

[2] So in other copy; MS. "setting rise."

[3] So in the other copy; MS. "stretch."

[4] MS. "poor dependance bow;" other copy, "peer, dependance bow'd."

And saw their hopes arising from the dead.
His countrymen were mustered into place,
And a Scotch piper rose above his Grace.
But say, astrologers, could this be strange?
The lord of the ascendant ruled the change;
And music, whether bagpipes, fiddles, drums,
All that has sense or meaning overcomes.
See now this universal favourite Scot,
His former native poverty forgot,
The highest member of the car[1] of state,
Where well he plays at blindman's buff with fate;
If fortune condescends to bless his play,
And drop a rich Havannah in his way,
He keeps it, with intention to release
All conquests at the general day of peace:
When first and foremost to divide the spoil,
Some millions down might satisfy his toil;
To guide the car of war he fancied not,
Where honour and no money could be got.
The Scots have tender honours to a man:
Honour's the tie that bundles up the clan:
They want one requisite to be divine,
One requisite in which all others shine;
They're very poor; then who can blame the hand
Which polishes by wealth its native land?
And to complete the worth possessed before,
Gives every Scotchman one perfection more;
Nobly bestows the infamy of place,
And Campbell struts about in doubled lace?
Who says Bute bartered peace, and wisely sold
His king, his unioned countrymen, for gold?

---

[1] So in other copy; MS. "corse." Look eight lines lower.

When ministerial hirelings proofs deny,
If Musgrave[1] could not prove it, how can I?
No facts unwarranted shall soil my quill,
Suffice it there's a strong suspicion still.
When Bute his iron rod of favour shook,
And bore his haughty temper in his look;
Not yet contented with his boundless sway,
Which all perforce must outwardly obey,
He thought to throw his chain upon the mind;
Nor would he leave conjecture unconfined.
We saw his measures wrong, and yet, in spite
Of reason, we must think those measures right;
Whilst curbed and checked by his imperious reign,
We must be satisfied, and not complain.
Complaints are libels, as the present age
Are all instructed by a law-wise sage,
Who, happy in his eloquence and fees,
Advances to preferment by degrees:
Trembles to think of such a daring step
As from a tool to Chancellor to leap;
But, lest his prudence should the law disgrace,
He keeps a longing eye upon the mace.
Whilst Bute was suffered to pursue his plan,
And ruin freedom as he raised the clan;
Could not his pride, his universal pride,
With working undisturbed be satisfied?
But when we saw the villany and fraud,
What conscience but a Scotchman's could applaud?

---

[1] Dr. Samuel Musgrave, who, in 1769, exhibited a charge against some great persons, of having sold the peace concluded in 1762. He was examined before the House of Commons, 29th January, 1770, when his information was voted frivolous.—MS. note.

But yet 'twas nothing—cheating in our sight,
We should have hummed ourselves, and thought
him right!
This faith, established by the mighty Thane,
Will long outlive the system of the Dane;
This faith—but now the number must be brief,
All human things are centred in belief;
And (or the philosophic sages dream)
All our most true ideas only seem:[1]
Faith is a glass to rectify our sight,
And teach us to distinguish wrong from right.
By this corrected, Bute appears a Pitt,
And candour marks the lines which Murphy writ;
Then let this faith support our ruined cause,
And give us back our liberties and laws:
No more complain of favourites made by lust,
No more think Chatham's patriot reasons just,
But let the Babylonish harlot see
We to her Baal bow the humble knee.
Lost in the praises of that favourite Scot,
My better theme, my Newton, was forgot:
Blessed with a pregnant wit, and never known
To boast of one impertinence his own,
He warped his vanity to serve his God,
And in the paths of pious Fathers trod.
Though genius might have started something new,
He honoured lawn, and proved his scripture true;
No literary worth presumed upon,
He wrote, the understrapper of St. John;
Unravelled every mystic simile,
Rich in the faith, and fanciful as me;

[1] *Or,* Nothing is really so as it may seem.

Pulled Revelation's sacred[1] robes aside,
And saw what priestly[2] modesty would hide;
Then seized the pen, and with a good intent
Discovered hidden meanings never meant.
The reader who, in carnal notions bred,
Has Athanasius without reverence read,
Will make a scurvy kind of Lenten feast
Upon the tortured offals of The Beast:
But if, in happy superstition taught,
He never once presumed to doubt in thought;
Like Catcott, lost in prejudice and pride,
He takes the literal meaning for his guide;
Let him read Newton, and his bill of fare:—
What prophecies unprophesied are there!
In explanations he's so justly skilled,
The pseudo-prophet's mysteries are fulfilled;
No superficial reasons have disgraced
The worthy prelate's sacerdotal taste;
No flimsy arguments he holds to view,
Like Camplin, he affirms it, and 'tis true.
Faith, Newton, is the tottering churchman's crutch,
On which our blest religion builds so much;
Thy fame would feel the loss of this support,
As much as Sawney's instruments at court;
For secret services without a name,
And mysteries in religion, are the same.
But to return to state, from whence the Muse
In wild digression smaller themes pursues;
And rambling from his Grace's magic rod,
Descends to lash the ministers of God.

---

[1] So in other copy; MS. "secret."
[2] So in other copy; MS. "priestish."

Both are adventures perilous and hard,
And often bring destruction on the bard;
For priests, and hireling ministers of state,
Are priests in love, infernals in their hate:
The church, no theme for satire, scorns the lash,
And will not suffer scandal in a dash:
Not Bute so tender in his spotless fame,[1]
Not Bute so careful of his lady's name.

Has sable lost its virtue? Will the bell
No longer scare[2] a straying sprite to hell?
Since souls, when animating flesh,[3] are sold
For benefices, bishoprics, and gold;
Since mitres, nightly laid upon the breast,
Can charm the night-mare conscience into rest;
And learn'd exorcists very lately made
Greater improvements in the living trade;
Since Warburton (of whom in future rhymes)
Has settled reformation on the times;
Whilst from the teeming press his numbers fly,
And, like his reasons, just exist and die;
Since, in the steps of clerical degree,
All through the telescope of fancy see;
(Though Fancy under Reason's lash may fall,
Yet Fancy in Religion's all in all):
Amongst these cassocked worthies, is there one
Who has the conscience to be Freedom's son?
Horne, patriotic Horne, will join the cause,
And tread on mitres to procure applause.
Prepare thy book and sacerdotal dress
To lay a walking spirit of the press,

---

[1] *Or,* juggling game. [2] *Or,* send.
[3] *Or,* animate with life.

Who knocks at midnight at his lordship's door,
And roars in hollow voice—"a hundred more!"
"A hundred more!" his rising greatness[1] cries,
Astonishment and terror in his eyes;
"A hundred more! by G—d, I won't comply!"
"Give," quoth the voice, "I'll raise a hue and cry;
On a wrong scent the leading beagle's gone,
Your interrupted measures may go on;
Grant what I ask, I'll witness to the Thane,
I'm not another Fanny of Cock Lane."
"Enough," says Mungo, "re-assume the quill;
And what we can afford to give, we will."

When Bute, the ministry and people's head,
With royal favour pensioned Johnson dead;
His works, in undeserved oblivion sunk,
Were read no longer, and the man was drunk.
Some blockhead, ever envious of his fame,
Massacred Shakespeare in the doctor's name:
The public saw the cheat, and wondered not—
Death is of all mortality the lot.
Kenrick has wrote his elegy, and penned
A piece of decent praise for such a friend;
And universal cat-calls testified
How mourned the critics when the genius died.
But now, though strange the fact to deists seem,
His ghost is risen in a venal theme,
And emulation maddened all the Row
To catch the strains which from a spectre flow,
And print the reasons of a bard deceased,
Who once gave all the town a weekly feast.
As beer, to every drinking purpose dead,

---

[1] *Or*, lordship.

Is to a wondrous metamorphose led,
And opened to the actions of the winds,
In vinegar a resurrection finds;
His genius dead, and decently interred,
The clamorous noise of duns sonorous heard,
Soured into life, assumed the heavy pen,
And saw existence for an hour again;
Scattered his thoughts spontaneous from his brain,
And proved we had no reason to complain;
Whilst from his fancy figures budded out,
As hair on humid carcases will sprout.
Horne! set this restless, shallow spirit still,
And from his venal fingers snatch the quill.
If, in defiance of the priestly word,
He still will scribble floridly absurd,
North is superior in a potent charm
To lay the terrors of a "False Alarm:"
Another hundred added to his five,
No longer is the stumbling-block alive;
Fixed in his chair, contented and at home,
The busy "Rambler" will no longer roam.
Released from servitude (such 'tis to think)
He'll prove it perfect happiness to drink:
Once (let the lovers of Irene[1] weep)
He thought it perfect happiness to sleep.
Irene, wondrous[2] composition, came,
To give the audience rest,[3] the author fame;
A snore was much more grateful than a clap,
And pit, box, gallery, proved[4] it in a nap.
Hail Johnson! chief of bards, thy rigid laws
Bestowed due praise, and critics snored applause.

---

[1] A tragedy, by Dr. Johnson; cf. p. 146. [2] *Or*, perfect.
[3] *Or*, To give us happiness. [4] *Or*, owned.

If from the humblest station, in a place
By writers fixed eternal in disgrace,
Long in the literary world unknown
To all but scribbling blockheads of its own;
Then only introduced, unhappy fate!
The subject of a satire's little[1] hate;
Whilst equally the butt of ridicule,
The town was dirty, and the bard a fool:—
If from this place, where catamites are found
To swarm like Scots on honorary ground,[2]
I may presume to exercise the pen,
And write a greeting to the best of men:
Health to the ruling minister I send,
Nor has that minister a better friend.
Greater, perhaps, in titles, pensions, place,
He inconsiderately prefers his Grace.
Ah, North! a humble bard is better far,
Friendship was never found near Grafton's star;
Bishops are not by office orthodox:
Who'd wear a title, when they've titled Fox?
Nor does the honorary shame stop here,
Have we not Weymouth, Barrington, and Clare?
If noble murders, as in tale we're told,
Made heroes of the ministers of old,
In noble murders Barrington's divine,
His merit claims the laureated line.
Let officers of train-bands wisely try
To save the blood of citizens, and fly
When some bold urchin beats his drum in sport,
Or tragic trumpets entertain the court;

---

[1] *Or*, deadly.
[2] *Or*, like Scotchmen Sawney's shade around.

The captain flies through every lane in town,
And safe from danger wears his civic crown:
Our noble Secretary scorned to run,
But with his magic wand[1] discharged the gun.
I leave him to the comforts of his breast,
And midnight ghosts, to howl him into rest.
Health to the minister, of [Bute] the tool,
Who with the little vulgar seems to rule.
But since the wiser maxims of the age
Mark for a noddy Ptolemy the sage;
Since Newton and Copernicus have taught
Our blundering senses ever are in fault;
The wise look further, and the wise can see
The hands of Sawney actuating thee;
The clock-work of thy conscience turns about,
Just as his mandates wind thee in and out.
By this political machine, my rhymes
Conceive an estimation of the times;
And, as the wheels of state in measures move,
See how time passes in the world above:
Whilst tottering on the slippery edge of doubt,
Sir Fletcher sees his train-bands flying out:
Thinks the minority, acquiring state,
Will undergo a change, and soon be great.
North issues out his hundreds to the crew,
Who catch the atoms of the golden dew;
The etiquette of wise Sir Robert takes,
The doubtful stand resolved, and one forsakes;
He shackles every vote in golden chains,
And Johnson in his list of slaves maintains.
Rest, Johnson, hapless spirit, rest and drink,

---

[1] So in other copy; MS. "word."

No more defile thy claret-glass with ink:
In quiet sleep repose thy heavy head,
* * * * disdains to —— upon the dead:
Administration will defend thy fame,
And pensions add importance to thy name.
When sovereign judgment owns thy works divine,
And every writer of reviews is thine,
Let busy Kenrick vent his little spleen,
And spit his venom in a magazine.
Health to the minister! nor will I dare
To pour out flattery in his noble ear;
His virtue, stoically great, disdains
Smooth adulation's entertaining strains,
And, red with virgin modesty, withdraws
From wondering crowds and murmurs of applause.
Here let no disappointed rhymer say,
Because his virtue shuns the glare of day,
And, like the conscience of a Bristol dean,
Is never by the subtlest optic seen,
That virtue is with North a priestish jest,
By which a mere nonentity's expressed.
No, North is strictly virtuous, pious, wise,
As every pensioned Johnson testifies.
But, reader, I had rather you should see
His virtues from another than from me:
Bear witness, Bristol, nobly prove that I
By thee or North was never paid to lie.
Health to the minister! his vices known,
(As every lord has vices of his own,
And all who wear a title think to shine
In forming follies foreign to his line;)
His vices shall employ my ablest pen,
And mark him out a miracle of men.

Then let the Muse the healing[1] strain begin,
And stamp[2] repentance upon every sin.
Why this recoil?—And will the dauntless Muse
To lash a minister of state refuse?
What! is his soul so black, thou canst not find
Aught like a human virtue in his mind?
Then draw him so, and to the public tell
Who owns this representative of hell:
Administration lifts her iron chain,
And truth must abdicate her lawful reign.[3]

Oh, Prudence! if, by friends or counsel swayed,
I had thy saving institutes obeyed,
And, lost to every love but love of self,
A wretch like Harris, living but in pelf;
Then, happy in a coach or turtle-feast,
I might have been an alderman at least.
Sage are the arguments by which I'm taught
To curb the wild excursive flights of thought:
Let Harris wear his self-sufficient air,
Nor dare remark, for Harris is a mayor;
If Catcott's flimsy system[4] can't be proved,
Let it alone, for Catcott's much beloved;
If Burgum bought a Bacon for a Strange,
The man has credit, and is great on 'change;
If Camplin ungrammatically spoke,
'Tis dangerous on such men to break[5] a joke;
If you from satire could withhold the line,
At every public hall perhaps you'd dine.

---

[1] *Or,* lashing. [2] *Or,* mark. [3] *Or,* strain.
[4] Catcott on the Deluge.—MS. note. [5] *Or,* pass.

"I must confess," exclaims a[1] prudent sage,
"You're really something clever for your age:
Your lines have sentiment, and now and then
A dash of satire stumbles from your pen:
But ah! that satire is a dangerous thing,
And often wounds the writer with its sting;
Your infant Muse should sport with other toys,
Men will not bear the ridicule of boys.
Some of the aldermen, (for some, indeed,
For want of education cannot read;
And those who can, when they aloud rehearse
What Collins,[2] happy genius! 'titles verse,
So spin the strains sonorous through the nose,
The hearer cannot call it verse or prose,)
Some of the aldermen may take offence
At your maintaining them devoid of sense;
And if you touch their aldermanic pride,
Bid dark reflection tell how Savage died![3]
Go to * * * * and copy worthy * * * *
Ah! what a sharp experienced genius that:
Well he prepares his bottle and his jest,
An alderman is no unwelcome guest;
Adulterate talents and adulterate wine
May make another draw[l]ing rascal shine;
His known integrity outvies a court,
His the dull tale, original the port:
Whilst loud he entertains the sleepy cits,
And rates his wine according to his wits,
Should a trite pun by happy error please,

---

[1] *Or*, rejoins the. [2] *Or*, Fowler.

[3] The next thirty-six lines do not occur in the shorter version.

His worship thunders at the laughing Mease;[1]
And * * * inserts this item in his bill,
Five shillings for a jest with every gill.
How commendable this, to turn at once
To good account the vintner and the dunce,
And, by a very hocus-pocus hit,
Dispose of damaged claret and bad wit,
Search through the ragged tribe who drink small
beer,
And sweetly echo in his worship's ear,—
"What are the wages of the tuneful nine,
What are their pleasures when compared to mine?
Happy I eat, and tell my numerous pence,
Free from the servitude of rhyme or sense:
The sing-song Whitehead ushers in the year
With joy to Briton's king and sovereign dear,
And, in compliance to an ancient mode,
Measures his syllables into an ode;
Yet such the sorry merit of his Muse,
He bows to deans and licks his lordship's shoes.
Then leave the wicked, barren way of rhyme,
Fly far from poverty—be wise in time—
Regard the office more—Parnassus less—
Put your religion in a decent dress;
Then may your interest in the town advance,
Above the reach of muses or romance.
Besides, the town (a sober, honest town,
Which smiles on virtue, and gives vice a frown)[2]
Bids censure brand with infamy your name,

[1] Matthew Mease, vintner. He kept the Bush, and was succeeded by John Weeks, who married his sister. Mease's father kept the Nag's Head, in Wine Street.—Dix.

[2] *Or,* Gives virtue her desert, and vice her frown.

I, even I, must think you are to blame.
Is there a street within this spacious place
That boasts the happiness of one fair face,
Where conversation does not turn on you,
Blaming your wild amours, your morals too?
Oaths, sacred and tremendous oaths you swear,
Oaths that might shock a Luttrell's soul to hear;
These very oaths, as if a thing of joke,
Made to betray, intended to be broke;
Whilst the too tender and believing maid,
(Remember pretty Fanny) is betrayed;
Then your religion—ah, beware! beware!
Although a deist is no monster here,
Yet hide your tenets—priests are powerful foes,
And priesthood fetters justice by the nose:
Think not the merit of a jingling song
Can countenance the author's acting wrong;
Reform your manners, and with solemn air
Hear Catcott bray, and Robins squeak in prayer.[1]
Robins, a reverend, cully-mully puff,
Who thinks all sermons, but his own, are stuff;
When harping on the dull, unmeaning text,
By disquisitions he's so sore perplexed,
He stammers, instantaneously is drawn
A bordered piece of inspiration-lawn,
Which being thrice unto his nose applied,
Into his pineal gland the vapours glide;
And now we hear the jingling doctor roar
On subjects he dissected thrice before.

---

[1] The next ten lines do not appear in the other version; but eight of them are made to begin the fragment entitled "Sunday." See p. 134.

Honour the scarlet robe, and let the quill
Be silent when old Isaac[1] eats his fill.
Regard thy interest, ever love thyself,
Rise into notice as you rise in pelf;
The Muses have no credit here, and fame
Confines itself to the mercántile name.
Then clip Imagination's wing, be wise,
And great in wealth, to rëal greatness rise.
Or if you must persist to sing and dream,
Let only panegyric be your theme;[2]
With pulpit adulation tickle Cutts,[3]
And wreathe with ivy Garden's tavern-butts;
Find sentiment in Dampier's empty look,
Genius in Collins, harmony in Rooke;
Swear Broderip's horrid noise the tuneful spheres,
And rescue Pindar from the songs of Shears.
Would you still further raise the fairy ground,
Praise Broughton,—for his eloquence profound,
His generosity, his sentiment,
His active fancy, and his thoughts on Lent:
Make North a Chatham, canonize his Grace,
And beg a pension, or procure a place."

Damned narrow notions! notions which disgrace
The boasted reason of the human race:
Bristol may keep her prudent maxims still,
I scorn her prudence, and I ever will:
Since all my vices magnified are here,
She cannot paint me worse than I appear;

---

[1] *Or,* his worship.
[2] The next ten lines are not in the other version.
[3] Dr. Cutts Barton, Dean of Bristol.—Dix.

When raving in the lunacy of ink,
I catch my pen, and publish what I think.[1]

[The poem was afterwards made to end as follows. See note 2, p. 153.]

Damned narrow notions! tending to disgrace
The boasted reason of the human race.
Bristol may keep her prudent maxims still,
But know, my saving friends, I never will.
The composition of my soul is made
Too great for servile, avaricious trade;
When raving in the lunacy of ink,
I catch the pen, and publish what I think.

---

[1] "We have to thank Mr. Gutch and Mr. Dix conjointly for the poem called 'Kew Gardens;' it is printed from the MS. of Mr. Isaac Reed, being contained in the late Mr. Haslewood's collection, now in the possession of Mr. Gutch. With the exception of some fragments, it was supposed to have been entirely lost. It consists of about 1200 lines, and is a great curiosity. The poet rambles mercilessly from London to Bristol—from the Ministry to our Corporation—from national affairs to our domestic and civic tittle-tattle; one while abusing the bench of Bishops, and then condescending to throw his ink at the clergy of this diocese, abusing one after another, all without discrimination. The poem is altogether indeed a great acquisition, although he is dreadfully severe upon many who are known to have been of the highest respectability."—*Bristol Paper.* The MS. is now in the British Museum.

"Successful attempts at satire were among the earliest manifestations of Chatterton's temperament and prematurity. A production of a more advanced age, entitled 'Kew Gardens,' contains many pointed lines and couplets: but who were the culprits under infliction is so well concealed behind rows of asterisms, that they might afterwards make their appearance with all effrontery as honest men, and nobody the wiser."—*Eclectic Review.*

North is a creature, and the king's misled;
Mansfield and Norton came as justice fled;
Few of our ministers are over wise:—
Old Harpagon's a cheat, and Taylor lies.
When cooler judgment actuates my brain,
My cooler judgment still approves the strain;
And if a horrid picture greets your view,
Where it continues still, if copied true.
Though in the double infamy of lawn
The future bishopric of Barton's drawn,
Protect me, fair ones, if I durst engage
To serve ye in this catamitish age,
To exercise a passion banished hence,
And summon satire in to your defence.
Woman, of every happiness the best,
Is all my heaven,—religion is a jest.
Nor shall the Muse in any future book
With awe upon the chains of favour look:
North shall in all his vices be displayed,
And Warburton in lively pride arrayed;
Sandwich shall undergo the healing lash,
And read his character without a dash;
Mansfield, surrounded by his dogs of law,
Shall see his picture drawn in every flaw;
Luttrell (if satire can descend so low)
Shall all his native little vices show;
And Grafton, though prudentially resigned,
Shall view a striking copy of his mind;
Whilst iron Justice, lifting up her scales,
Shall weigh the Princess Dowager of Wales.

COLIN INSTRUCTED. (1770.)

[Printed in the Supplement to the Miscellanies, 1784.]

YOUNG Colin was as stout a boy
As ever gave a maiden joy;
But long in vain he told his tale
To black-eyed Biddy of the Dale.

"Ah why," the whining shepherd cried,
"Am I alone your smiles denied?
I only tell in vain my tale
To black-eyed Biddy of the Dale."

"True, Colin," said the laughing dame,
You only whimper out your flame;
Others do more than sigh their tale
To black-eyed Biddy of the Dale."

He took the hint, &c.

A BURLESQUE CANTATA. (1770.)

[Printed in the Supplement to the Miscellanies, 1784.]

RECITATIVE.

MOUNTED aloft in Bristol's narrow streets,
Where pride and luxury with meanness meets,
A sturdy collier pressed the empty sack,
A troop of thousands swarming on his back;

When sudden to his rapt ecstatic view
Rose the brown beauties of his red-haired Sue
Music spontaneous echoed from his tongue,
And thus the lover rather bawled than sung.

AIR.

Zaunds! Pri'thee, pretty Zue, is it thee!
  Odzookers, I mun have a kiss!
A sweetheart should always be free,
  I whope you wunt take it amiss.
Thy peepers are blacker than caul,
  Thy carcase is sound as a sack,
Thy visage is whiter than ball,
  Odzookers, I mun have a smack!

RECITATIVE.

The swain descending, in his raptured arms
Held fast the goddess, and despoiled her charms.
Whilst, locked in Cupid's amorous embrace,
His jetty *skinnis* met her red bronzed face,
It seemed the sun when labouring in eclipse;
And on her nose he stamped his sable lips,
Pleased * * * * *

SONG.

FANNY OF THE HILL.[1] 1770.

[Printed in 1784.]

IF gentle Love's immortal fire
Could animate the quill,
Soon should the rapture-speaking lyre
Sing Fanny of the Hill.

My panting heart incessant moves,
No interval 'tis still;
And all my ravished nature loves
Sweet Fanny of the Hill.

Her dying soft expressive eye,
Her elegance must kill;
Ye Gods! how many thousands die
For Fanny of the Hill.

A love-taught tongue, angelic air,
A sentiment, a skill
In all the graces of the fair,
Mark Fanny of the Hill.

Thou mighty Power, eternal Fate,
My happiness to fill,
O! bless a wretched lover's state
With Fanny of the Hill.

---

[1] Miss F. B * * *, on Redcliff Hill, Bristol.

The name of *Fanny*, which was first written, was afterwards cancelled, and that of *Betsy* substituted in its stead; but for what reason was best known to the author.—Southey's *Edition*.

B * * * may very well mean *Bush*; he addresses a poem to Miss Bush, of Bristol.

NARVA AND MORED,

AN AFRICAN ECLOGUE.[1]

[First printed in the London Magazine for May, 1770.]

RECITE the loves of Narva and Mored,
The priest of Chalma's triple idol said.
High from the ground the youthful warriors sprung,
Loud on the concave shell the lances rung:
In all the mystic mazes of the dance,
The youths of Bonny's burning sands advance,
Whilst the soft virgin panting looks behind,
And rides upon the pinions of the wind;
Ascends the mountain's brow, and measures round
The steepy cliffs of Chalma's sacred ground:
Chalma, the god whose noisy thunders fly
Through the dark covering of the midnight sky,
Whose arm directs the close-embattled host,
And sinks the labouring vessels on the coast;
Chalma, whose excellence is known from far,
From Lupa's rocky hill to Calabar:
The guardian god of Afric and the isles,
Where nature in her strongest vigour smiles;
Where the blue blossom of the forky thorn
Bends with the nectar of the opening morn:
Where ginger's aromatic, matted root,
Creep through the mead, and up the mountains shoot.

---

[1] In a letter to his friend Cary, written on June 29 or July 1, 1770, Chatterton tells him, "In the last London magazine, and the magazine coming out to-morrow, are the only two pieces I have the vanity to call poetry." These were the two last African Eclogues, printed in the Miscellanies, 1778.

Three times the virgin, swimming on the breeze,
Danced in the shadow of the mystic trees:
When, like a dark cloud spreading to the view,
The first-born sons of war and blood pursue;
Swift as the elk they pour along the plain;
Swift as the flying clouds distilling rain.
Swift as the boundings of the youthful roe,
They course around, and lengthen as they go.
Like the long chain of rocks, whose summits rise
Far in the sacred regions of the skies,
Upon whose top the blackening tempest lours,
Whilst down its side the gushing torrent pours;
Like the long cliffy mountains which extend
From Lorbar's cave, to where the nations end,
Which sink in darkness, thickening and obscure,
Impenetrable, mystic, and impure;
The flying terrors of the war advance,
And round the sacred oak repeat the dance.
Furious they twist around the gloomy trees,
Like leaves in autumn twirling with the breeze.
So, when the splendour of the dying day
Darts the red lustre of the watery way,
Sudden beneath Toddida's whistling brink
The circling billows in wild eddies sink,
Whirl furious round, and the loud bursting wave
Sinks down to Chalma's sacerdotal cave,
Explores the palaces on Zira's coast,
Where howls the war-song of the chieftain's ghost;
Where the artificer, in realms below,
Gilds the rich lance or beautifies the bow,
From the young palm-tree spins the useful twine,
Or makes the teeth of elephants divine;
Where the pale children of the feeble sun,

In search of gold, through every climate run:
From burning heat to freezing torments go,
And live in all vicissitudes of woe.
Like the loud eddies of Toddida's sea,
The warriors circle the mysterious tree:
Till, spent with exercise, they spread around
Upon the opening blossoms of the ground.
The priestess, rising, sings the sacred tale,
And the loud chorus echoes through the dale.

PRIESTESS.

Far from the burning sands of Calabar;
Far from the lustre of the morning-star;
Far from the pleasure of the holy morn;
Far from the blessedness of Chalma's horn:
Now rest the souls of Narva and Mored,
Laid in the dust, and numbered with the dead.
Dear are their memories to us, and long,
Long shall their attributes be known in song.
Their lives were transient as the meadow-flower,
Ripened in ages, withered in an hour.
Chalma reward them in his gloomy cave,
And open all the prisons of the grave!
Bred to the service of the godhead's throne,
And living but to serve his god alone,
Narva was beauteous as the opening day
When on the spangling waves the sunbeams play,
When the mackaw, ascending to the sky,
Views the bright splendour with a steady eye.
Tall, as the house of Chalma's dark retreat,
Compact and firm, as Rhadal Ynca's fleet,
Completely beauteous as a summer's sun,
Was Narva, by his excellence undone.

Where the soft Togla creeps along the meads,
Through scented calamus and fragrant reeds;
Where the sweet Zinsa spreads its matted bed,
Lived the still sweeter flower, the young Mored;
Black was her face, as Togla's hidden cell;
Soft, as the moss where hissing adders dwell.
As to the sacred court she brought a fawn,
The sportive tenant of the spicy lawn,
She saw and loved! and Narva too forgot
His sacred vestment and his mystic lot.
Long had the mutual sigh, the mutual tear,
Burst from the breast and scorned confinement there;
Existence was a torment! O my breast!
Can I find accents to unfold the rest?
Locked in each other's arms, from Hyga's cave
They plunged relentless to a watery grave;
And, falling, murmured to the powers above,
"Gods! take our lives, unless we live to love."

C.

Shoreditch, May 2, 1770.

A SONG,

ADDRESSED TO MISS C—AM, OF BRISTOL.

[Printed in the "Miscellanies," 1778.]

AS Spring now approaches with all his gay train,
And scatters his beauties around the green plain,
Come then, my dear charmer, all scruples remove,
Accept of my passion, allow me to love.

Without the soft transports which love must inspire,
Without the sweet torment of fear and desire,
Our thoughts and ideas are never refined,
And nothing but winter can reign in the mind.

But love is the blossom, the spring of the soul,
The frosts of our judgments may check, not control;
In spite of each hindrance, the spring will return,
And nature with transports refining will burn.

This passion celestial by heav'n was designed
The only fixed means of improving the mind;
When it beams on the senses, they quickly display
How great and prolific, how pleasing the ray.

Then come, my dear charmer, since love is a flame
Which polishes nature, and angels your frame,
Permit the soft passion to rise in your breast,—
I leave your good nature to grant me the rest.

Shall the beautiful flow'rets all blossom around,
Shall Flora's gay mantle enamel the ground,
Shall the red-blushing blossom be seen on the tree,
Without the least pleasure or rapture for me?

And yet, if my charmer should frown when I sing,
Ah! what are the beauties, the glories of spring?
The flow'rs will be faded, all happiness fly,
And clouds veil the azure of every bright sky.

C.

London, May 4, 1770.

ENQUIRY AFTER HAPPINESS.[1]

[Written on a blank leaf in a copy of Lucas's "Enquiry after Happiness."]

THOUGH happiness be each man's darling aim,
Yet folly too, too often plays the game;
To that one centre all our wishes tend,
We fly the means but still pursue the end.
No wonder then we find our hopes were vain;
The wretch who shuns his cure must still complain.
In labyrinths of crooked error lost,
Or on life's sea with raging tempest tossed,
We by no compass steer, but blindly stray,
And, knowing we are wrong, ne'er ask the way.
"How hard, how very hard to walk," they cry,
"In thorny roads while flowery meads are nigh!"
But know, deluded mortals, virtue's race
Is run in paths of pleasantness and peace;
Though narrow, yet sufficient for the few
Who have this pearl of price alone in view.
"But how," they ask, "can we this gem obtain?"
Be that thy task, O Lucas, to explain.
As Milton, eyeless bard, has sweetly sung
The fatal course[2] whence all our woes first sprung,
So he has taught, though not in measured phrase,
A lesson which deserves full greater praise;
How man (as once in Eden) may be blest,

---

[1] Printed in the Gospel Magazine, Nov. 1770, p. 600. Probably written in the preceding May. See Wilson's Life of Chatterton, p. 271.

[2] Probably for *cause*.

And paradise be found in every breast.
O! may you find it there, may you obtain
The bliss which too much knowledge rendered vain,
By tasting boldly the fair fruit again.

Lucas like Milton, wondrous bard, was blind,
Like Milton too, illumined was his mind:
Then ask thy Guide, for he who seeks shall find.

D. B.

HAPPINESS. 1770.

[From "Love and Madness;" corrected (in 1803) from Mr. Catcott's copy.]

SINCE happiness was not ordained for man,
Let's make ourselves as easy as we can;
Possessed with fame or fortune, friend or w——e,
But think it happiness—we want no more.

Hail, Revelation! sphere-enveloped dame,
To some divinity, to most a name,
Reason's dark-lantern, superstition's sun,
Whose cause mysterious and effect are one—
From thee, ideal bliss we only trace,
Fair as Ambition's dream, or Beauty's face,
But, in reality, as shadowy found
As seeming truth in twisted mysteries bound.
What little rest from over-anxious care
The lords of Nature are designed to share,

To wanton whim and prejudice we owe.
Opinion is the only God we know.
Our furthest wish, the Deity we fear,
In different subjects, differently appear.
Where's the foundation of religion placed?
On every individual's fickle taste.

The narrow way the priest-rid mortals tread,
By superstitious prejudice misled.—
This passage leads to heaven—yet, strange to tell!
Another's conscience finds it lead to hell.
Conscience, the soul-chameleon's varying hue,
Reflects all notions, to no notion true.—
The bloody son of Jesse, when he saw
The mystic priesthood kept the Jews in awe,
He made himself an ephod to his mind,
And sought the Lord, and always found him kind:
In murder, horrid cruelty, and lust,
The Lord was with him, and his actions just.

Priestcraft! thou universal blind of all,
Thou idol, at whose feet all nations fall;
Father of misery, origin of sin,
Whose first existence did with fear begin;
Still sparing deal thy seeming blessings out,
Veil thy Elysium with a cloud of doubt.
Since present blessings in possession cloy,
Bid hope in future worlds expect the joy:
Or, if thy sons the airy phantoms slight,
And dawning Reason would direct them right,
Some glittering trifle to their optics hold;
Perhaps they'll think the glaring spangle gold,
And, madded in the search of coins and toys,
Eager pursue the momentary joys.

Mercator worships Mammon, and adores
No other deity but gold and w——es.
Catcott is very fond of talk and fame—
His wish, a perpetuity of name;
Which to procure, a pewter altar's made,
To bear his name and signify his trade;
In pomp burlesqued the rising spire to head,
To tell futurity a pewterer's dead.
Incomparable Catcott, still pursue
The seeming happiness thou hast in view:
Unfinished chimneys, gaping spires complete,
Eternal fame on oval dishes beat;
Ride four-inch bridges, clouded turrets climb,
And bravely die—to live in after-time.
Horrid idea! if on rolls of fame
The twentieth century only find thy name,
Unnoticed this, in prose or tagging flower,
He left his dinner to ascend the tower!
Then, what avails thy anxious spitting pain?
Thy laugh-provoking labours are in vain.
On matrimonial pewter set thy hand;
Hammer with every power thou canst command;
Stamp thy whole self, original as 'tis,
To propagate thy whimsies, name, and phiz—
Then, when the tottering spires or chimneys fall,
A Catcott shall remain admired by all.

Eudo, who has some trifling couplets writ,
Is only happy when he's thought a wit—
Thinks I've more judgment than the whole Reviews,
Because I always compliment his Muse.
If any mildly would reprove his faults,
They're critics envy-sickened at his thoughts.

To me he flies, his best-belovèd friend,
Reads me asleep, then wakes me to commend.

Say, sages—if not sleep-charmed by the rhyme—
Is flattery, much-loved flattery, any crime?
Shall dragon Satire exercise his sting,
And not insinuating Flattery sing?
Is it more noble to torment than please?
How ill that thought with rectitude agrees!

Come to my pen, companion of the lay,
And speak of worth where merit cannot say;
Let lazy Barton undistinguished snore,
Nor lash his generosity to Hoare;
Praise him for sermons of his curate bought,
His easy flow of words, his depth of thought;
His active spirit, ever in display,
His great devotion when he drawls to pray;
His sainted soul distinguishably seen,
With all the virtues of a modern dean.

Varo, a genius of peculiar taste,
His misery in his happiness is placed;
When in soft calm the waves of Fortune roll,
A tempest of reflection storms the soul;
But what would make another man distressed
Gives him tranquillity and thoughtless rest:
No disappointment can his peace invade,
Superior to all troubles not self-made.
This character let gray Oxonians scan,
And tell me of what species he's a man;
Or be it by young Yeatman criticised,
Who damns good English if not latinized.

In Aristotle's scale the Muse he weighs,
And damps her little fire with copied lays!
Versed in the mystic learning of the schools,
He rings bob-majors by Leibnitzian rules.

Pulvis, whose knowledge centres in degrees,
Is never happy but when taking fees.
Blessed with a bushy wig and solemn grace,
Catcott admires him for a fossil face.

When first his farce of countenance began,
Ere the soft down had marked him almost man,
A solemn dulness occupied his eyes,
And the fond mother thought him wondrous wise;—
But little had she read in Nature's book,
That fools assume a philosophic look.

O Education, ever in the wrong,
To thee the curses of mankind belong;
Thou first great author of our future state,
Chief source of our religion, passions, fate:
On every atom of the Doctor's frame
Nature has stamped the pedant with his name;
But thou hast made him (ever wast thou blind)
A licensed butcher of the human kind.

Mouldering in dust the fair Lavinia lies;
Death and our Doctor closed her sparkling eyes.
O all ye Powers, the guardians of the world!
Where is the useless bolt of vengeance hurled?
Say, shall this leaden sword of plague prevail,
And kill the mighty where the mighty fail?
Let the red bolus tremble o'er his head,
And with his cordial julep strike him dead!

But to return—in this wide sea of thought,
How shall we steer our notions as we ought?
Content is happiness, as sages say—
But what's content? The trifle of a day.
Then, friend, let inclination be thy guide,
Nor be by superstition led aside.
The saint and sinner, fool and wise attain
An equal share of easiness and pain.[1]

ELEGY.[2]

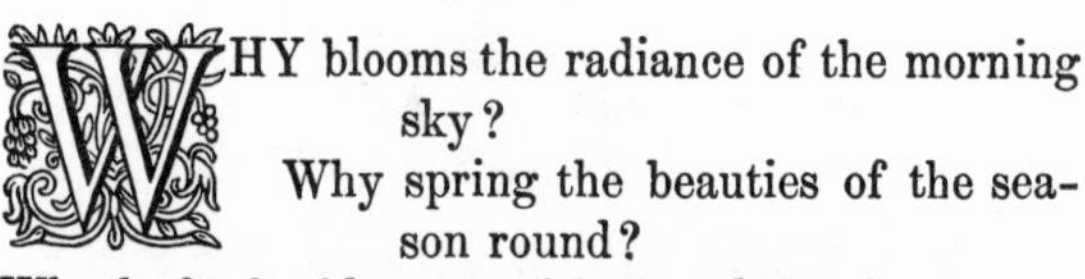

WHY blooms the radiance of the morning sky?
Why spring the beauties of the season round?
Why buds the blossom with the glossy dye?
Ah! why does nature beautify the ground?

Whilst, softly floating on the zephyr's wing,
The melting accents of the thrushes rise,
And all the heavenly music of the spring,
Steal on the sense, and harmonize the skies;

---

[1] When or how Chatterton was unfortunate enough to receive a tincture of infidelity we are not informed. Early in the year 1769 [rather 1770] it appears from a poem on "Happiness," addressed to Mr. Catcott, that he had drunk deeply of the poisoned spring. And in the conclusion of a letter to the same gentleman, after he left Bristol, he expresses himself, "Heaven send you the comforts of Christianity; I request them not, for I am no Christian."
—Dr. Gregory.

[2] This poem was printed in the Town and Country Magazine for May, 1770.

When the racked soul is not attuned to joy,
  When sorrow an internal monarch reigns:
In vain the choristers their powers employ,
  'Tis hateful music, and discordant strains.

The velvet mantle of the skirted mead,
  The rich varieties of Flora's pride,
Till the full bosom is from trouble freed,
  Disgusts the eye, and bids the big tear glide.

Once, ere the gold-haired sun shot the new ray
  Through the grey twilight of the dubious morn,
To woodlands, lawns, and hills, I took my way,
  And listened to the echoes of the horn;

Dwelt on the prospect, sought the varied view,
  Traced the meanders of the bubbling stream:
From joy to joy uninterrupted flew,
  And thought existence but a fairy dream.

Now through the gloomy cloister's lengthening way,
  Through all the terror superstition frames,
I lose the minutes of the lingering day,
  And view the night light up her pointed flames.

I dare the danger of the mouldering wall,
  Nor heed the arch that totters o'er my head;
O! quickly may the friendly ruin fall,
  Release me of my love, and strike me dead.

M———! cruel, sweet, inexorable fair,
  O! must I unregarded seek the grave?
Must I from all my bosom holds repair,
  When one indulgent smile from thee would save?

Let mercy plead my cause; and think, oh! think!
A love like mine but ill deserves thy hate:
Remember, I am tottering on the brink,
Thy smile or censure seals my final fate.

C.

Shoreditch, May 20, [1770].

THE METHODIST.

[Printed in the Supplement to the Miscellanies, 1784.]

SAYS Tom to Jack, "'tis very odd,
These representatives of God,
In colour, way of life, and evil,
Should be so very like the devil."
Jack, understand, was one of those,
Who mould religion in the nose,
A red-hot methodist; his face
Was full of puritanic grace,
His loose lank hair, his slow gradation,
Declared a late regeneration;
Among the daughters long renowned,
For standing upon holy ground;
Never in carnal battle beat,
Though sometimes forced to a retreat.
But Catcott,[1] hero as he is,
Knight of incomparable phiz,
When pliant doxy seems to yield,
Courageously forsakes the field.

---

[1] See Notes and Queries, 2nd S. vi. 182.

Jack, or to write more gravely, John,
Through hills of Wesley's works had gone;
Could sing one hundred hymns by rote,
Hymns which will sanctify the throat:
But some indeed composed so oddly,
You'd swear 'twas bawdy songs made godly.

May, 1770.

THE PROPHECY.

" *When times are at the worst they will certainly mend.*"

[First printed in the Political Register for June, 1770; and reprinted in the Miscellanies, 1778.]

I.

THIS truth of old was Sorrow's friend,
" Times at the worst will surely mend,"
The difficulty's then, to know
How long Oppression's clock can go;
When Britain's sons may cease to sigh,
And hope that their redemption's nigh.

II.

When Vice exalted takes the lead,
And Vengeance hangs but by a thread;
Gay peeresses turned out o' doors;
Whoremasters peers, and sons of whores;
Look up, ye Britons! cease to sigh,
For your redemption draweth nigh.

III.

When vile Corruption's brazen face
At council-board shall take her place,
And lords and commoners resort
To welcome her at Britain's court;
Look up, ye Britons! cease to sigh,
For your redemption draweth nigh.

IV.

See Pension's harbour, large and clear,
Defended by St. Stephen's pier!
The entrance safe, by current led,
Tiding round G[rafton]'s jetty-head;
Look up, ye Britons! cease to sigh,
For your redemption draweth nigh.

V.

When civil-power shall snore at ease,
While soldiers fire—to keep the peace;
When murders sanctuary find,
And petticoats can Justice blind;
Look up, ye Britons! cease to sigh,
For your redemption draweth nigh.

VI.

Commerce o'er bondage will prevail,
Free as the wind that fills her sail;
When she complains of vile restraint,
And power is deaf to her complaint;
Look up, ye Britons! cease to sigh,
For your redemption draweth nigh.

VII.

When raw projectors shall begin
Oppression's hedge, to keep her in;

She in disdain will take her flight,
And bid the Gotham fools good-night.
Look up, ye Britons! cease to sigh,
For your redemption draweth nigh.

VIII.

When tax is laid, to save debate,
By prudent ministers of state;
And what the people did not give
Is levied by prerogative;
Look up, ye Britons! cease to sigh,
For your redemption draweth nigh.

IX.

When popish bishops dare to claim
Authority, in George's name;
By treason's hand set up, in spite
Of George's title, William's right;
Look up, ye Britons! cease to sigh,
For your redemption draweth nigh.

X.

When popish priest a pension draws
From starved exchequer, for the cause;
Commissioned proselytes to make
In British realms, for Britain's sake;
Look up, ye Britons! cease to sigh,
For your redemption draweth nigh.

XI.

When snug in power, sly recusants
Make laws for British protestants;
And d—g William's revolution,
As justices, claim execution;

Look up, ye Britons! cease to sigh,
For your redemption draweth nigh.

XII.

When soldiers, paid for our defence,
In wanton pride slay innocence;
Blood from the ground for vengeance reeks,
Till Heaven the inquisition makes;
Look up, ye Britons! cease to sigh,
For your redemption draweth nigh.

XIII.

When at Bute's feet poor Freedom lies,
Marked by the priest for sacrifice,
And doomed a victim for the sins
Of half the *outs*, and all the *ins*;
Look up, ye Britons! cease to sigh,
For your redemption draweth nigh.

XIV.

When stewards pass a *boot* account,
And credit for the gross amount;
Then, to replace exhausted store,
Mortgage the land to borrow more;
Look up, ye Britons! cease to sigh,
For your redemption draweth nigh.

XV.

When scrutineers, for private ends,
Against the vote declare their friends;
Or judge, as you stand there alive,
That five is more than forty-five;[1]

---

[1] This probably alludes to the famous No. 45 of Wilkes's "North Briton," which was suppressed by the government.

Look up, ye Britons! cease to sigh,
For your redemption draweth nigh.

XVI.

When George shall condescend to hear
The modest suit, the humble prayer;
A Prince, to purpled pride unknown!
No favourites disgrace the throne!
Look up, ye Britons! sigh no more,
For your redemption's at the door.

XVII.

When time shall bring your wish about,
Or seven-years lease, *you sold,* is out,
No future contract to fulfil;
Your tenants holding at your will;
Raise up your heads! your right demand!
For your redemption's in your hand.

XVIII.

Then is your time to strike the blow,
And let the *slaves* of Mammon know
Briton's true sons A BRIBE can scorn,
And die as *free* as they were born.
VIRTUE again shall take her seat,
And your redemption stand complete.

FABLES FOR THE COURT.

Addressed to Mr. Michael Clayfield, of Bristol.

[Transcribed by Mr. Catcott, Oct. 19, 1796, from Chatterton's MS. Printed in 1803.]

THE SHEPHERDS.

MORALS, as critics must allow,
Are almost out of fashion now;
And, if we credit Dodsley's word,
All applications are absurd.
What has the author to be vain in
Who knows his fable wants explaining,
And substitutes a second scene
To publish what the first should mean?
Besides, it saucily reflects
Upon the reader's intellects.
When, armed in metaphors and dashes,
The bard some noble villain lashes,
'Tis a direct affront, no doubt,
To think he cannot find it out.
The sing-song trifles of the stage,
The happy favourites of the age,
Without a meaning crawl along,
And, for a moral, give a song.
The tragic Muse, once pure and chaste,
Is turned a whore, debauched by taste:
Poor Juliet never claims the tear
Till borne triumphant on the bier;

And Ammon's son is never great
Till seated in his chair of state.
And yet the harlot scarce goes down,
She's been so long upon the town,
Her morals never can be seen.
Not rigid Johnson seems to mean,
A tittering epilogue contains
The cobweb of a poet's brains.
If what the Muse prepares to write
To entertain the public sight
Should in its characters be known,
The knowledge is the reader's own.
When villany and vices shine,
You won't find Sandwich in the line;
When little rascals rise to fame,
Sir Fletcher cannot read his name;
Nor will the Muse digressive run
To call the king his mother's son,
But, plodding on the beaten way,
With honest North prepares the lay:
And should the meaning figures please
The dull reviews of laughing ease,
No politician can dispute
My knowledge of the Earl of Bute.

A flock of sheep, no matter where,
Was all an aged shepherd's care;
His dogs were watchful, and he took
Upon himself the ruling crook:
His boys who wattled in the fold
Were never bought and never sold.
'Tis true, by strange affection led,
He visited a turnip-bed;

And, fearful of a winter storm,
Employed his wool to keep it warm;
But that, comparatively set
Against the present heavy debt,
Was but a trifling piece of state,
And hardly make a villain great.
The shepherd died—the dreadful toll
Entreated masses for his soul.
The pious bosom and the back
Shone in the farce of courtly black.
The weeping Laureate's ready pen
Lamented o'er the best of men;
And Oxford sent her load of rhyme
In all varieties of chime,
Administering due consolation,
Well seasoned with congratulation.
Cambridge her ancient lumber wrote,
And what could Cambridge do but quote?
All sung, though very few could read,
And none but mercers mourned indeed.
The younger shepherd caught the crook,
And was a monarch in his look.
The flock rejoiced, and could no less
Than pay their duty and address;
And Edinburgh was heard to sing,
"Now heaven be praised for such a king!"
All joined in joy and expectation,
And "Union!" echoed through the nation.
A council called——— * * *

THE DEATH OF NICOU.

AN AFRICAN ECLOGUE.

[First printed in the London Magazine, June, 1770; and reprinted in the "Miscellanies," 1778.]

N Tiber's banks, Tiber, whose waters glide
In slow meanders down to Gaigra's side;
And circling all the horrid mountain round,
Rushes impetuous to the deep profound;
Rolls o'er the ragged rocks with hideous yell;
Collects its waves beneath the earth's vast shell:
There for a while in loud confusion hurled,
It crumbles mountains down, and shakes the world,
Till borne upon the pinions of the air,
Through the rent earth the bursting waves appear;
Fiercely propelled the whitened billows rise,
Break from the cavern and ascend the skies:
Then lost and conquered by superior force,
Through hot Arabia holds its rapid course:
On Tiber's banks, where scarlet jasmines bloom,
And purple aloes shed a rich perfume;
Where, when the sun is melting in his heat,
The reeking tigers find a cool retreat,
Bask in the sedges, lose the sultry beam,
And wanton with their shadows in the stream;
On Tiber's banks, by sacred priests revered,
Where in the days of old a god appeared;
'Twas in the dead of night, at Chalma's feast,
The tribe of Alra slept around the priest.
He spoke; as evening-thunders, bursting near,

His horrid accents broke upon the ear;
Attend, Alraddas, with your sacred priest!
"This day the sun is rising in the east;
The sun which shall illumine all the earth
Now, now is rising, in a mortal birth."
He vanished like a vapour of the night,
And sunk away in a faint blaze of light;
Swift from the branches of the holy oak,
Horror, confusion, fear, and torment broke:
And still, when midnight trims her mazy lamp,
They take their way through Tiber's watery swamp.
On Tiber's banks, close ranked, a warring train,
Stretched to the distant edge of Galca's plain:
So, when arrived at Gaigra's highest steep,
We view the wide expansion of the deep,
See, in the gilding of her watery robe,
The quick declension of the circling globe,
From the blue sea a chain of mountains rise,
Blended at once with water and with skies,
Beyond our sight in vast extension curled,
The check of waves, the guardians of the world.
Strong were the warriors as the ghost of Cawn,
Who threw the Hill-of-archers to the lawn,
When the soft earth at his appearance fled,
And rising billows played around his head:
When a strong tempest, rising from the main,
Dashed the full clouds unbroken on the plain.
Nicou, immortal in the sacred song,
Held the red sword of war, and led the strong;
From his own tribe the sable warriors came,
Well tried in battle, and well known in fame.
Nicou, descended from the god of war
Who lived coeval with the morning star:
Narada was his name; who cannot tell

How all the world through great Narada fell!
Vichon, the god who ruled above the skies,
Looked on Narada, but with envious eyes:
The warrior dared him, ridiculed his might,
Bent his white bow, and summoned him to fight.
Vichon, disdainful, bade his lightnings fly,
And scattered burning arrows in the sky;
Threw down a star, the armour of his feet,
To burn the air with supernatural heat;
Bid a loud tempest roar beneath the ground;
Lifted the sea, and all the earth was drowned.
Narada still escaped; a sacred tree
Lifted him up, and bore him through the sea.
The waters still ascending fierce and high,
He towered into the chambers of the sky:
There Vichon sat, his armour on his bed,
He thought Narada with the mighty dead.
Before his seat the heavenly warrior stands,
The lightning quivering in his yellow hands.
The god astonished dropped; hurled from the shore,
He dropped to torments, and to rise no more.
Headlong he falls; 'tis his own arms compel,
Condemned in ever-burning fires to dwell.
From this Narada, mighty Nicou sprung;
The mighty Nicou, furious, wild, and young,
Who led th' embattled archers to the field,
And bore a thunderbolt upon his shield:
That shield his glorious father died to gain,
When the white warriors fled along the plain,
When the full sails could not provoke the flood,
Till Nicou came and swelled the seas with blood.
Slow, at the end of his robust array,
The mighty warrior pensive took his way,
Against the son of Nair, the young Rorest,

Once the companion of his youthful breast.
Strong were the passions of the son of Nair,
Strong, as the tempest of the evening air;
Insatiate in desire; fierce as the boar;
Firm in resolve as Cannie's rocky shore.
Long had the gods endeavoured to destroy
All Nicou's friendship, happiness, and joy:
They sought in vain, till Vicat, Vichon's son,
Never in feats of wickedness outdone,
Saw Nica, sister to the Mountain-king,
Dressed beautiful, with all the flowers of spring:
He saw, and scattered poison in her eyes;
From limb to limb in varied forms he flies;
Dwelt on her crimson lip, and added grace
To every glossy feature of her face.
Rorest was fired with passion at the sight,
Friendship and honour sunk to Vicat's right;
He saw, he loved, and burning with desire,
Bore the soft maid from brother, sister, sire.
Pining with sorrow, Nica faded, died,
Like a fair aloe in its morning pride.
This brought the warrior to the bloody mead,
And sent to young Rorest the threatening reed.
He drew his army forth: oh! need I tell
That Nicou conquered, and the lover fell:
His breathless army mantled all the plain,
And Death sat smiling on the heaps of slain.
The battle ended, with his reeking dart
The pensive Nicou pierced his beating heart:
And to his mourning valiant warriors cried,
"I, and my sister's ghost are satisfied."

C.

Brooke Street, Holborn, June 12, 1770.

TO MISS BUSH, OF BRISTOL.[1]

BEFORE I seek the dreary shore
Where Gambia's rapid billows roar,
And foaming pour along,
To you I urge the plaintive strain,
And though a lover sings in vain,
Yet you shall hear the song.

Ungrateful, cruel, lovely maid,
Since all my torments were repaid
With frowns or languid sneers;
With assiduities no more
Your captive will your health implore,
Or tease you with his tears.

Now to the regions where the sun
Does his hot course of glory run,
And parches up the ground;
Where o'er the burning cleaving plains,
A long eternal dog-star reigns,
And splendour flames around:

---

[1] "Written," says Dr. Gregory, "in the style of Cowley—that is, with too much affectation of wit for real feeling." He had now in contemplation "the miserable hope of securing the very ineligible appointment of a surgeon's mate to Africa." In a letter to his sister, dated July 11, 1770, he alludes to his piece "To Miss Bush," as having been printed in June. See the Town and Country Magazine for June, 1770.

There will I go, yet not to find
A fire intenser than my mind,
Which burns a constant flame:
There will I lose thy heavenly form,
Nor shall remembrance, raptured, warm,
Draw shadows of thy frame.

In the rough element, the sea,
I'll drown the softer subject, thee,
And sink each lovely charm:
No more my bosom shall be torn,
No more, by wild ideas borne,
I'll cherish the alarm.

Yet, Polly, could thy heart be kind,
Soon would my feeble purpose find
Thy sway within my breast:
But hence, soft scenes of painted woe!
Spite of the dear delight I'll go,
Forget her, and be blest.

CELORIMON.

THE REVENGE.[1]

A BURLETTA;

Acted at Marylebone Gardens, 1770; *with additional Songs.*

[First printed, with the five songs following, in 1795, from a MS. in the possession of Mr. Atterbury.]

DRAMATIS PERSONÆ.

JUPITER	MR. REINHOLD.
BACCHUS	MR. BANNISTER.
CUPID	MASTER CHENEY.
JUNO	MRS. THOMPSON.

ACT I. SCENE I.

JUPITER.

Recitative.

I SWEAR by Styx, this usage is past bearing;
My lady Juno ranting, tearing, swearing!
Why, what the devil will my godship do,
If blows and thunder cannot tame a shrew?

---

[1] Among the MSS. of Chatterton in the British Museum [MS. Addit. 5766. B. 68] there is the first outline of this Burletta under the title of "Amphitryon," the *dramatis personæ* of which are as follows:—*Celestials,* Jupiter, Mercury, Juno, Nox.—*Mortals,* Amphitryon, Sosia, Phocyon, Dorus, Alcmena, Phrygia. It differs very widely from the printer's text. Chatterton received five guineas for "The Revenge" from Mr. Atterbury, of the Marylebone Gardens, where it was performed shortly after his death.—Chatterton's re-

Air.

Though the loud thunder rumbles,
Though storms rend the sky;
Yet louder she grumbles,
And swells the sharp cry.

Her jealousy teasing,
Disgusting her form:
Her music as pleasing
As pigs in a storm.

I fly her embraces,
To wenches more fair;
And leave her wry faces,
Cold sighs, and despair.

Recitative.

And oh! ye tedious minutes, steal away;
Come evening, close the folding doors of day;
Night, spread thy sable petticoat around,
And sow thy poppies on the slumbering ground;
Then raving into love, and drunk with charms,
I'll lose my Juno's tongue in Maia's arms.

Air.

Sighing,
Dying,

---

ceipt for the amount is dated July 6, 1770. In Southey's Edition of his poems, the MS. is said to have been lost at the printing-office, but the Editor of the Cambridge edition, 1842, says that he had a distinct recollection of having observed a notice of its sale some six or seven years previously (to 1842), for the sum of ONE HUNDRED AND FIFTY POUNDS. In fact, the MS. was recovered by Mr. Upcott from a cheesemonger's. See Wilson's Life, p. 277.

Lying,
Frying,
In the furnace of desire;
Creeping,
Sleeping,
Oh! how slow the hours retire!

When the busy heart is beating,
When the bosom's all on fire,
Oh! how welcome is the meeting!
Oh! how slow the hours retire!

Recitative.

But see—my Fury comes; by Styx, I tremble:
I'll creep aside—'tis folly to dissemble.

Scene II.

Juno, Jupiter.

JUNO.

Recitative.

See, see, my good man steals aside!
In spite of his thunder,
I make him knock under,
And own the superior right of a bride.

Air.

How happy the life
Of a governing wife,
How charming, how easy, the swift minutes pass;
Let her do what she will,
The husband is still,
And but for his horns you would think him an ass.

How happy the spouse
In his dignified brows;
How worthy with heroes and monarchs to class:
Both above and below,
Experience will shew,
But take off the horns, and each husband's an ass.

JUPITER.

Recitative. [*Aside.*

Zounds, I'll take heart of grace, and brave her clapper;
And, if my courage holds, egad, I'll strap her:
Through all Olympus shall the thunders roll,
And earth shall echo to the mustard-bowl;
Should she prove sturdy, by the Lord, I'll heave hence,
Down to some brandy shop, this noisy grievance.

Air.

What means this horrid rattle?
And must that tongue of riot
Wage one eternal battle
With happiness and quiet?

JUNO.

Air continued.

What means your saucy question?
D'ye think I mind your bluster?
Your godship's always best in
Words, thunder, noise, and fluster.

JUPITER.

Recitative.

Hence, thou eternal tempest, from our regions,
And yell in concert with infernal legions:
Hence, or be calm—our will is fate—away hence,
Or on the lightning's wings you'll find conveyance.

JUNO.

Recitative.

I brave your vengeance—

JUPITER.

Oh! 'tis most provoking!

JUNO.

Should not my spirit better my condition,
I've one way left—remonstrance and petition
To all the gods in senate: 'tis no joking—

Air.

I will never tamely bear
All my wrongs and slights, sir;
Heaven and all the gods shall hear
How you spend your nights, sir:
Drinking, swearing,
Roaring, tearing,
Wenching, roving everywhere;
Whilst poor I
At home must lie,
Wishing, scheming,
Sighing, dreaming,
Grasping nothing but the air.

JUPITER.

Recitative.

O how shall I escape the swelling clatter—
I'll slit her tongue, and make short work o' th' matter.

Air.

Fury, cease,
Give me peace,

Still your racket,
Or your jacket
I'll be drubbing,
For your snubbing;
By the gods, you shall knock under.
Must you ever
Thus endeavour,
Rumbling,
Grumbling,
Rowling,
Growling,
To outsound the noisy thunder?

JUNO.

Recitative. [*Aside.*

Ah! I'm quite out here—plaguily mistaken—
The man's in earnest—I must save my bacon;
Since scolding but provokes him,
A method I'll pursue..
I'll soothe him, tickle, coax him,
Then I shall have my due.

Air.

Ah, cruel, cruel Jove,
And is it thus a love,
So pure, so chaste, so strong as mine,
Is slighted, disrespected,
Unnoticed and neglected,
Returned with such a love as thine?

JUPITER.

Air.

Did the foolish passion tease ye,
Would you have a husband please ye,

Suppliant, pliant, amorous, easy?
Never rate him like a fury:
By experience I'll assure ye,
Kindness, and not rage, must cure ye.

JUNO.

Recitative. [*Aside.*

He's in the right on't—hits it to a tittle—
But Juno must display her tongue a little.

Air.

I own my error, I repent;
Let thy sparkling eyes behold me,
Let thy lovely arms infold me;
Let thy stubborn heart relent.

JUPITER.

Recitative.

Egad, why this is more than I desire,
'Tis from the frying-pan to meet the fire;
Zounds, I've no stomach to the marriage-bed;
But something must be either sung or said.

Air.

What is love? the wise despise it;
'Tis a bubble blown for boys:
Gods and heroes should not prize it,
Jove aspires to greater joys.

JUNO.

Air continued.

What is love? 'tis nature's treasure,
'Tis the storehouse of her joys;
'Tis the highest heaven of pleasure,
'Tis a bliss which never cloys.

JUPITER.

Air continued.

What is love? an air-blown bubble,
Only silly fools receive it:
'Tis a magazine of trouble;
'Tis but folly—thus I leave it.

[*Jupiter runs off.*

Scene III.

JUNO.

Recitative.

Well, he is gone, and I may curse my fate,
That linked my gentle love to such a mate;
He neither fills my freezing bed, my heart, nor
My vainly-folding arms: oh! such a partner!

Air.

When a woman's tied down
To a spiritless log,
Let her fondle or frown,
Yet still he's a clog.
Let her please her own mind,
Abroad let her roam;
Abroad she may find
What she can't find at home.

Scene IV.

Juno *and* Cupid.

CUPID.

Recitative.

Ho! mistress Juno—here's a storm a-brewing—
Your devil of a spouse is always doing—

Pray step aside—this evening, I protest,
Jove and Miss Maia—you may guess the rest—

JUNO.

How! what? when? where?—nay, pri'thee now, unfold it.

CUPID.

'Gad—so I will; for, faith, I cannot hold it.
His mighty godship in a fiery flurry
Met me just now—confusion to his hurry!
I stopt his way, forsooth, and, with a thwack,
He laid a thunderbolt across my back:
Bless me! I feel it now—my short ribs ache yet—
I vowed revenge, and now, by Styx, I'll take it.
Miss Maia, in her chamber, after nine,
Receives the thunderer, in his robes divine.
I undermined it all; see, here's the letter—
Could dukes spell worse, whose tutors spelt no better?
You know false spelling now is much the fashion—

JUNO.

Lend me your drops—oh! I shall swoon with passion!
I'll tear her eyes out! oh! I'll stab—I'll strangle!
And worse than lover's English, her I'll mangle!

CUPID.

Nay, pray be calm; I've hit off an expedient
To do you right—

JUNO.

Sweet Cupid, your obedient—

CUPID.

Tie Maia by the leg; steal in her stead
Into the smuggled raptures of her bed;
When the god enters, let him take possession.

JUNO.

An excellent scheme! My joy's beyond expression!

CUPID.

Nay, never stay; delaying may confute it.

JUNO.

O happy thought! I fly to execute it.

[*Exit Juno.*

SCENE V.

CUPID.

Recitative.

See how she flies, whilst warring passions shake her,
Nor thought nor lightning now can overtake her.

Air.

How often in the marriage state
The wise, the sensible, the great,
  Find misery and woe;
Though, should we dive in nature's laws
To trace the first primæval cause,
  The wretch is self-made so.

Air changes.

Love's a pleasure, solid, rëal,
Nothing fanciful, ideal,
  'Tis the bliss of human kind;
All the other passions move
In subjection under Love,
  'Tis the tyrant of the mind.

Scene VI.

Cupid, Bacchus *with a bowl.*

BACCHUS.

Recitative.

'Odsniggers, t'other draught, 'tis devilish heady,
Olympus turns about; (*staggers*) steady, boys, steady!

Air.

If Jove should pretend that he governs the skies,
I swear by this liquor his thundership lies;
A slave to his bottle, he governs by wine,
And all must confess he's a servant of mine.

Air changes.

Rosy, sparkling, powerful wine,
All the joys of life are thine!
Search the drinking world around,
Bacchus everywhere sits crowned:
Whilst we lift the flowing bowl,
Unregarded thunders roll.

Air changes.

Since man, as says each bearded sage,
Is but a piece of clay,
Whose mystic moisture lost by age,
To dust it falls away;
'Tis orthodox beyond a doubt,
That drought will only fret it;
To make the brittle stuff hold out,
Is thus to drink and wet it.

Recitative.

Ah! Master Cupid, 'slife, I did not s'ye,
'Tis excellent champagne, and so here's t'ye:

I brought it to these gardens as imported,
'Tis monstrous strong—you need not twice be courted.
Come drink, my boy—

CUPID.

Hence, monster, hence! I scorn thy flowing bowl,
It prostitutes the sense, degenerates the soul.

BACCHUS.

Gadso, methinks the youngster's woundy moral!
He plays with ethics like a bell and coral.

Air.

'Tis madness to think
To judge ere you drink,—
The bottom all wisdom contains:
Then let you and I
Now drink the bowl dry,
We both shall grow wise for our pains.

CUPID.

Pray keep your distance, beast, and cease your bawling,
Or with this dart I'll send you catterwauling.

Air.

The charms of wine cannot compare
With the soft raptures of the fair:
Can drunken pleasures ever find
A place with love and womankind?

Can the full bowl pretend to vie
With the soft languish of the eye?
Can the mad roar our passions move,
Like gentle breathing sighs of love?

BACCHUS.

Go whine and complain
To the girls of the plain,
And sigh out your soul ere she come to the mind ;
My mistress is here,
And, faith, I don't fear—
I always am happy, she always is kind.

Air changes.

A pox o' your lasses !
A shot of my glasses
Your arrow surpasses ;
For nothing but asses
Will draw in your team ;
Whilst thus I am drinking,
My misery sinking,
The cannikin clinking,
I'm lost to all thinking,
And care is a dream.

CUPID.

Provoking insolence !

BACCHUS.

What words it utters !
Alas ! poor little creature, how it sputters !

CUPID.

Away, you drunkard wild—

BACCHUS.

Away, you silly child—

CUPID.

Fly, or else I'll wound thy soul.

BACCHUS.

Zounds, I'll drown thee in the bowl !

CUPID.

You rascally broacher,
You hogshead of liquor—

BACCHUS.

You shadow, you poacher!
Aha!—bring me a stick here—.
I'll give you a trimmer,
You bladder of air—

CUPID.

You soul of a brimmer—

BACCHUS.

You tool of the fair—

CUPID.

You moveable tun,
You tippler, you sot—

BACCHUS.

Nay, then the work's done,
My arrow is shot.

[*Bacchus throws the contents of the bowl in Cupid's face, and runs off.*

SCENE VII.

CUPID.

Recitative.

Kind usage this—it sorely shall befall him—
Here's my best arrow, and, by heaven, I'll maul him.
Revenge! revenge! Oh, how I long to wound him;
Now all the pangs of slighted love confound him!

Air.

No more in the bowl
His brutalized soul
Shall find a retreat from the lass:
I'll pay him,
And slay him,
His love shall be dry as his glass. [*Exit.*

END OF THE FIRST ACT.

ACT II. SCENE I.

BACCHUS, *with his bowl on his head.*

Air.

ALAS, alas! how fast
I feel my spirits sinking;
The joys of life are past,
I've lost the power of drinking.
'Egad, I find at last
The heavenly charms of tinking,
And in the sound I cast
The miseries of thinking.

Recitative.

I'm plaguy ill—in devilish bad condition—
What shall I do?—I'll send for a physician:
But then the horrid fees—aye, there's the question—
'Tis losing all a man's estate in jesting,
Whilst nurses and apothecaries pártake—
Zounds, this will never do, 'twill make my heart ache.
Come then, ye fiddlers, play up t'other bout,
I've a new nostrum, and I'll sing it out.

Air.

Scrape, ye fiddlers, tinkle, tinkle.
Music makes my twinklers twinkle;
Humming,
Thrumming,
Groaning,
Toning,
Squeaking,
Shrieking,
Bawling,
Squalling,
O the sweet charms of tinkle, tinkle!

Recitative.

But this is trifling with the hot disease,
Nor wine nor brandy now can give me ease.

Air.

When a jolly toper ails,
And his nectar-bottle fails,
He's in a most heavenly condition:
Unless he can drink,
To the grave he must sink,
And Death be his only physician.

Recitative.

Zounds, can't I guess the cause—hum—could I say a
Short prayer or two, with pretty Mistress Maia?
Ah! there it is! why, I was woundy stupid—
Faith, this is all the handy-work of Cupid.

Since I'm in love then, over ears and head in,
'Tis time to look about for bed and bedding;
But first uncovering, in this magic helmet
I'll shew the God that love and wine are well met.

Air.

Fill the bowl, and fill it high,
Vast as the extended sky!
Since the dire disease is found,
Wine's a balm to cure the wound.
O the rapturous delights,
When with women wine unites!

Recitative.

O here, my satyrs, fill the mighty cup,
Haste, fly, begone! I'm dying for a sup.

Air.

I'll fly to her arms,
And rifle her charms,
In kisses and compliments lavish:
When heated by wine,
If she should not incline,
I'll try all my courage, and ravish.

SCENE II. *A dark Room.*

JUNO.

Recitative.

Now, Master Jupiter, I'll catch you napping—
'Gad, you'll be finely hamper'd your own trap in.
Would every husband follow your example,
And take upon himself his own adorning,
No more would wives upon their trammels trample,
No more would stand the ancient trade of horning.

Air.

What wife but, like me,
Her husband would see
A rakehelly fellow, a ranter, a rover,

If, mistaking her charms,
He should die in her arms,
And lose the cold spouse in the warmth of the lover?

Recitative.

Impatiently I wait—

Air.

Hark, hark! the God approaches,
He longs to ease his pain;
Oh, how this love encroaches
Through every trembling vein.
Oh, how my passion's rising,
And thumping in my breast!
'Tis something most surprising,
I shall be doubly blest.

Recitative.

He's here—Now prosper, Love, my undertaking.
I'll steal aside—I'm in a piteous quaking.

SCENE III.

JUNO *and* BACCHUS.

BACCHUS.

Recitative.

Now, pretty Mistress Maiá, I'm your humble—
But faith, I'd better look before I tumble:
For should the little gipsy make resistance,
And call in witnesses to her assistance,
Then, Bacchus, should your friends or sister fail ye,
You'll look confounded queer at the Old Bailey.

Air.

The man that has no friend at court,
Must make the laws confine his sport;
But he that has, by dint of flaws,
May make his sport confine the laws.

Recitative.

Zounds! I've a project, and a fine one too—
What will not passion and invention do?
I'll imitate the voice and sound of Jove,
The girl's ambition won't withstand his love.
But should she squawl, and cry a rape, and scream on't,
Presto, I'm gone, and Jove will bear the blame on't.
The farce begins, the prologue's wonderous teasing,
Pray Cupid, the catastrophe be pleasing!

Air.

Oh! where is my Maia? O say
What shadow conceals the fair maid?
Bring hither the lantern of day,
And shew me where Maia is laid.
Envious vapours, fly away;
Come, ye streaming lights, discover,
To an ardent, dying lover,
Maia and the charms of day.

JUNO.

Recitative. [*Aside.*

I have you fast—by all my wrongs, I'll fit ye—
Wise as you are, perhaps I may outwit ye.

Air.

Here thy longing Maia lies,
Passion flaming in her eyes;

Whilst her heart
Is thumping, beating,
All in a heat, in
Every part:
Like the ocean,
All commotion,
Through her veins the billows roll,
And the soft tempest ruffles all her soul.

BACCHUS.

Recitative. [*Aside.*

Gods! I have struck upon the very minute;
I shall be happy, or the devil's in it:
It seems some assignation was intended,
I'd pump it—but least said is soonest mended.

Air.

Happy, happy, happy hour!
Cupid now exalts his power;
In my breast the passion raging,
All my trembling frame engaging,
Sets my every sense on fire;
Let us, Maia, now retire.

JUNO.

Recitative.

But say, should I resign my virgin charms,
Would you be ever constant to my arms?
Would not your Juno rob me of your kindness?
Must you not truckle to her royal highness?

BACCHUS.

No! by the dirty waves of Styx I swear it,
My love is yours—my wife shall never share it.

JUNO, *aside.*

'Tis a sad compliment, but I must bear it.

BACCHUS.

Air.

Then let's away,
And never delay,
'Tis folly to stay
From rapture and love:
I sicken, I die;
O come, let us fly,
From the blue vaulted sky
To the Paphian Grove.

JUNO.

Then away!
I obey
Love and nature.

BACCHUS.

Since 'tis so,
Let us go,
Dearest creature!

SCENE IV.

JUNO, BACCHUS, JUPITER.

JUPITER.

Recitative.

I heard a voice within, or else I'm tipsy—
Maia, where are you? Come, you little gipsy.

BACCHUS.

Maia's with me, sir; who the devil are ye?
Sirrah, be gone; I'll trim you if you tarry.

JUPITER.

Fine lingo this to Jupiter!—why truly
I'm Jove the thunderer—

JUNO.

Out, you rascal, you lie—

BACCHUS.

'Tis I am Jupiter, I wield the thunder!
Zounds, I'll sneak off before they find the blunder.
[*Aside.*

JUPITER.

Breaking from above, below,
Flow, ye gleams of morning, flow;
Rise, ye glories of the day,
Rise at once with strengthened ray!
[*Sudden light; all astonished.*

BACCHUS.

Zounds! what can this mean?

JUNO.

I am all confusion!

JUPITER.

Your pardon, Juno, for this rude intrusion.
Insatiate monster! I may now be jealous;
If I've my mistresses, you have your fellows:
I'm now a very husband without doubt,
I feel the honours of my forehead sprout.

Air.

Was it for this, from morning to night,
Tempests and hurricanes dwelt on your tongue;
Ever complaining of coldness and slight,
And the same peal was eternally rung?
Was it for this I was stinted of joy,
Pleasure and happiness banished my breast,
Poisoned with fondness which ever must cloy,
Pinned to your sleeve, and denied to be blest?

Recitative.

I swear by Styx, and that's a horrid oath,
I'll have revenge, and that upon you both.

JUNO.

Nay, hear me, Jove, by all that's serious, too,
I swear I took the drunken dog for you.

BACCHUS.

And with as safe a conscience, I can say, as
I now stand here, I thought the chamber Maia's.

JUPITER.

It cannot be—

Air.

I'll not be cheated,
Nor be treated
Like the plaything of your will.

JUNO.

I'll not be slighted,
I'll be righted,
And I'll keep my spirits still.

JUPITER. [*To Bacchus.*

You pitiful cully—

JUNO AND BACCHUS. [*To Jupiter.*

You rakehelly bully,
Your blustering,
Clattering,
Flustering,
Spattering,
Thundering,
Blundering,
I defy.

JUPITER.

Go mind your toping,
Never come groping
Into my quarters, I desire, sir:
Here you come horning,
And adorning—

JUNO.

You are a liar, sir.

BACCHUS.

You lie, sir, you lie.

SCENE V.

JUNO, BACCHUS, JUPITER, CUPID.

CUPID.

Recitative.

Here are the lovers all at clapper-clawing;
A very pretty scene for Collett's drawing.
Oh, oh, immortals, why this catterwauling?
Through all Olympus I have heard your bawling.

JUNO.

Ah! Cupid, your fine plotting, with a pox,
Has set [your victims] all in the wrong box.[1]
Unravel quickly, for the Thunderer swears
To pull creation down about our ears.

CUPID.

Air.

Attend! attend! attend!
God, demi-god, and fiend,
Mortals and immortals see,
Hither turn your wondering eyes,
See the rulers of the skies
Conquered all, and slaves to me!

JUPITER.

Recitative.

Pox o' your brawling! haste, unriddle quickly,
Or, by the thunder of my power, I'll tickle ye!

CUPID.

You, Jove, as punctual to your assignation,
Came here, with Maia to be very happy;
But Juno, out of a fond inclination,
Stepped in her room, of all your love to trap ye.
Struck by my power, which the slave dared despise,
Bacchus was wounded too by Maia's eyes,
And hither stealing to appease his love,
Thought Juno Maia; she thought Bacchus Jove.
Here rests the matter:—are you all contented?

JUNO.

No, no! not I—

BACCHUS. [*Aside.*

I'm glad I was prevented.

---

[1] An imperfect line.

JUPITER.

A lucky disappointment, on my life,
All love is thrown away upon a wife:
How sad! my interruption could not please her.
She moves my pity—

CUPID.

Soften, Jove, and ease her.

JUPITER.

Juno, thy hand, the girls no more I'll drive at,
I will be ever thine—or wench more private.
[*Aside.*

Air.

Smooth the furrows of thy brow,
Jove is all the lover now:
Others he'll no more pursue,
But be ever fixed to you.

JUNO.

Then contented I resign
My prerogative of scolding;
Quiet when thy love is mine,
When my arms with thine are folding.

CUPID.

Then, jolly Bacchus, why should we stand out?
If we have quarrelled, zounds! we'll drink about.

Air.

Love and wine uniting
Rule without control,
Are to the sense delighting,
And captivate the soul.

Love and wine uniting
Are everywhere adored;
Their pleasures are inviting,
All heaven they can afford.

BACCHUS.

Zounds, I agree, 'tis folly to oppose it:
Let's pay our duty here, and then we'll close it.

Air. [*To the audience.*

To you, ye brave, ye fair, ye gay,
Permit me from myself to say—
The juicy grape for you shall rise
In all the colours of the skies;
For you the vine's delicious fruit
Shall on the lofty mountains shoot;
And every wine to Bacchus dear
Shall sparkle in perfection here.

CUPID.

For you, ye fair, whose heavenly charms
Make all my arrows useless arms,
For you shall Handel's lofty flight
Clash on the listening ear of night,
And the soft, melting, sinking lay
In gentle accents die away:
And not a whisper shall appear
Which modesty would blush to hear.

JUNO.

Ye brave, the pillars of the state,
In valour and in conduct great,
For you the rushing clang of arms,
The yell of battle and alarms

Shall from the martial trumpets fly,
And echo through the mantling sky.

JUPITER.

From you, ye glories of mankind,
We hope a firm support to find;
All that our humble powers can do
Shall be displayed to pleasure you:
On you we build a wished success,
'Tis yours, like deities, to bless;
Your smiles will better every scene,
And clothe our barren waste in green.

CHORUS.

So, when along the eastern skies
The glories of the morning rise,
The humble flower which slept the night,
Expands its beauties to the light,
Glows in its glossy new array,
And shines amidst the shining day.

THE HAPPY PAIR.

[See note prefixed to "The Revenge."]

STREPHON.

LUCY, since the knot was tied,
Which confirmed thee Strephon's bride,
All is pleasure, all is joy,
Married love can never cloy;
Learn, ye rovers, learn from this,
Marriage is the road to bliss.

LUCY.

Whilst thy kindness every hour
Gathers pleasure with its power,
Love and tenderness in thee
Must be happiness to me.
Learn, ye rovers, learn from this,
Marriage is substantial bliss.

BOTH.

Godlike Hymen, ever reign,
Ruler of the happy train,
Lift thy flaming torch above
All the flights of wanton love;
Peaceful, solid, blest, serene,
Triumph in the married scene.

STREPHON.

Blest with thee, the sultry day
Flies on wings of down away.

Labouring o'er the yellow plain
Open to the sun and rain,
All my painful labours fly,
When I think my Lucy's nigh.

LUCY.

O my Strephon, could my heart
Happiness to thee impart,
Joy should sing away the hour,
Love should every pleasure shower:
Search my faithful breast, and see,
I am blest in loving thee.

BOTH.

Godlike Hymen, ever reign,
Ruler of the happy train,
Lift thy flaming torch above
All the flights of wanton love;
Peaceful, solid, blest, serene,
Triumph in the married scene.

SONGS.

A BACCHANALIAN.

SUNG BY MR. REINHOLD.

BACCHUS, ever smiling power,
Patron of the festive hour!
Here thy genuine nectar roll
To the wide capacious bowl,
While gentility and glee
Make these gardens worthy thee.

Bacchus, ever mirth and joy,
Laughing, wanton, happy boy!
Here advance thy clustered crown,
Send thy purple blessings down;
With the Nine to please conspire,
Wreathe the ivy round the lyre.

THE INVITATION.

TO BE SUNG BY MRS. BARTHELEMON AND MASTER CHENEY.

AWAY to the woodlands, away!
The shepherds are forming a ring
To dance to the honour of May,
And welcome the pleasures of Spring.
The shepherdess labours a grace,
And shines in her Sunday's array,
And bears in the bloom of her face
The charms and the beauties of May.
Away to the woodlands, away!
The shepherds are forming a ring, &c.

Away to the woodlands, away!
And join with the amorous train:
'Tis treason to labour to-day,
Now Bacchus and Cupid must reign.
With garlands of primroses made,
And crowned with the sweet blooming spray,
Through woodland, and meadow, and shade,
We'll dance to the honour of May.
Away, &c.

A BACCHANALIAN.

WHAT is war and all its joys?
Useless mischief, empty noise.
What are arms and trophies won?
Spangles glittering in the sun.
Rosy Bacchus, give me wine,
Happiness is only thine!

What is love without the bowl?
'Tis a languor of the soul:
Crowned with ivy, Venus charms;
Ivy courts me to her arms.
Bacchus, give me love and wine,
Happiness is only thine!

THE VIRGIN'S CHOICE.

YOUNG Strephon is as fair a swain
As e'er a shepherd of the plain
In all the hundred round;
But Ralph has tempting shoulders too,[1]
And will as quickly buckle to
As any to be found.

Young Colin has a comely face,
And cudgels with an active grace,
In everything complete;

[1] Southey's edition has "shoulders, true;" but "too" seems intended.

But Hobbinol can dance divine,
Gods! how his manly beauties shine,
When jigging with his feet!

Roger is very stout and strong,
And Thyrsis sings a heavenly song,
Soft Giles is brisk and small.
Who shall I choose? who shall I shun?
Why must I be confined to one?
Why can't I have them all?

THE WOMAN OF SPIRIT.

A BURLETTA. 1770.

DRAMATIS PERSONÆ.

DISTORT	MR. BANNISTER.
COUNSELLOR LATITAT . . .	MR. REINHOLD.
ENDORSE	MASTER CHENEY.
LADY TEMPEST	MRS. THOMPSON.

ACT I. SCENE I.

LADY TEMPEST AND LATITAT.

LATITAT.

I TELL you, Lady Tempest—

LADY TEMPEST.

And I tell you, Mr. Latitat, it shall not be.—I'll have no Society of Antiquaries meet here. None but the honourable Members of the Coterie shall assemble here, you shall know.

LATITAT.

Suspend your rage, Lady Tempest, and let me open my brief. Have you not this day, moved by the instigation of the devil, and not having the fear of God before your eyes, wilfully and wittingly and maliciously, driven all my friends out of my house? Was it done like a Woman of Quality?

LADY TEMPEST.

It was done like a Woman of Spirit: a character, it shall ever be my task to maintain.

Air.

Away with your maxims, and dull formal rules,
The shackles of pleasure, and trammels of fools;
For wisdom and prudence I care not a straw,
I'll act as I please, for my will is my law.

LATITAT.

But upon my soul, Madam, I have one more consideration which should especially move you to bridle your passion: for it spoils your face. When you knocked down Lord Rust with the bust of Marcus Aurelius, you looked the very picture of the Alecto last taken out of the Herculaneum.

Air.

Passion worse than age will plough
Furrows on the frowning brow;
Rage and passion will disgrace
Every beauty of the face;
Whilst good-nature will supply
Beauties, which can never die.

LADY TEMPEST.

Mr. Latitat, I won't be abused—Did I for this condescend to forget my quality and marry such a tautology of nothing?—I will not be abused.

Scene II.

Distort, Latitat, Lady Tempest.

DISTORT.

Pray, Madam, what has enraged you? May I have the honour of knowing?

LATITAT.

Mr. Distort shall be our referee.

LADY TEMPEST.

That is, if I please, sir.

LATITAT.

Pray, my Lady, let me state the case, and you may afterwards make a reply—you must know, sir—

LADY TEMPEST.

Yes, sir, you must know, this morning Mr. Latitat had invited all his antiquated friends, Lord Rust, Horatio Trefoil, Col. Tragedus, Professor Vase, and Counterfeit the Jew, to sit upon a brass half-penny, which being a little worn, they agreed, *nem. con.*, to be an Otho.

LATITAT.

And it is further necessary to be known, that, while we were all warm in debate upon the premises, my lady made a forcible entry into the parlour, and seizing an antique bust of Marcus Aurelius, of malice prepense and aforethought, did, with three blows of the said bust, knock down Anthony, Viscount Rust, and—

LADY TEMPEST.

And drove them all out of the house.

LATITAT.

And furthermore—

LADY TEMPEST.

Silence, Mr. Latitat,—I insist on the privilege of English wife.

LATITAT.

And moreover—

DISTORT.

Nay, Counsellor, as I am your referee, I command silence: pray what do you lay your damages at?

LATITAT.

My lady has in her cabinet a Jupiter Tonans, which, in spite of all my endeavours to open her eyes, she persists in calling an Indian Pagod, and upon condition of my receiving that, I drop the prosecution.

DISTORT. [*Aside to Lady.*

'Tis a trifle, Madam, let him have it, it may turn to account.

LADY TEMPEST.

A very toy: he shall have it instantly, on condition I have the use of my tongue.

Air.

What are all our[1] favourite joys?
What are [all] our pleasures?

[*The rest is wanting.*]

---

[1] Printed "your."

AN ELEGY,

On the Much Lamented DEATH of WILLIAM BECKFORD, Esq., Late LORD-MAYOR of, and REPRESENTATIVE in PARLIAMENT FOR, THE CITY OF LONDON.[1] [Died June 21, 1770.]

I.

WEEP on, ye Britons—give your gen'ral Tear;
But hence, ye Venal—Hence, each titled Slave;
An honest pang should wait on *Beckford*'s Bier,
And patriot Anguish mark the Patriot's Grave.

II.

When, like the Roman, to his Field retir'd,
'Twas you, (surrounded by unnumber'd Foes)
Who call'd him forth, his Services requir'd,
And took from Age the Blessing of Repose.

---

[1] "To the Editor of *Felix Farley's Journal.*

"SIR,—As the columns of your Paper gave the earliest effusions of the highly-gifted *Chatterton* to the public eye, it may form a ground for claiming a space for an entire copy of an Elegy by him, of which only the first twelve stanzas, gathered from a contemporary review, are to be found in any edition of his works. It was advertised in the *Middlesex Journal* (the patriotic paper of that period, to which Chatterton made many communications), on the 3rd July, 1770, and was published in quarto, by Mr. Kearsley, of Fleet-street, price one shilling. It is probable the author received

III.

With Soul impell'd by Virtue's sacred Flame,
To stem the Torrent of corruption's Tide,
He came, heav'n-fraught with LIBERTY! he came,
And nobly in his Country's Service died.

IV.

In the last awful, the departing Hour,
When Life's poor Lamp more faint, and fainter grew;
As Mem'ry feebly exercis'd her Pow'r,
He only felt for LIBERTY and you.

V.

He view'd Death's Arrow with a Christian Eye,
With Firmness only to a Christian known;
And nobly gave your Miseries that Sigh
With which he never gratified his own.

VI.

Thou breathing Sculpture, celebrate his Fame,
And give his Laurel everlasting Bloom;
Record his Worth while Gratitude has Name,
And teach succeeding Ages from his Tomb.

---

for this production two guineas, according to his current account, inserted in his life, of the balance in favour of the Lord Mayor's death. The obtainment of a copy of the original publication was an object of search for above ten years.

Yours, &c. EU. HOOD."

The punctuation, capital letters, numerals, &c. are here reproduced as they occur in Kearsley's edition above referred to, excepting that a few superfluous commas have been omitted.

VII.

The Sword of Justice cautiously he sway'd,
His Hand for ever held the Balance right;
Each venial Fault with Pity he survey'd,
But MURDER found NO MERCY in his Sight.

VIII.

He knew, when Flatterers besiege a Throne,
Truth seldom reaches to a Monarch's Ear;
Knew, IF OPPRESS'D a LOYAL PEOPLE GROAN,
'Tis not the COURTIER'S Int'rest HE SHOULD HEAR.

IX.

Hence, honest to his Prince, his manly Tongue
The PUBLIC WRONG and LOYALTY convey'd,
While TITLED TREMBLERS, ev'ry Nerve unstrung,
Look'd all around, confounded and dismay'd;

X.

Look'd all around, astonish'd to behold
(Train'd up to Flatt'ry from their early Youth)
An ARTLESS, FEARLESS Citizen unfold
To ROYAL Ears a MORTIFYING Truth.

XI.

Titles to him no Pleasure could impart,
No Bribes his rigid Virtue could controul;
The Star could never gain upon his Heart,
Nor turn the Tide of Honor in his Soul.

XII.

For this his Name our Hist'ry shall adorn,
Shall soar on Fame's wide Pinions, all sublime,
'Till Heaven's own bright and never-dying Morn
Absorbs our little Particle of Time.

XIII.

Far other Fate the venal Crew shall find,
  Who sigh for Pomp, or languish after Strings;
And sell their native Probity of Mind,
  For Bribes from Statesmen, or for Smiles from
    Kings.

XIV.

And here a long inglorious List of Names
  On my disturb'd Imagination croud;
"O! let them perish (loud the Muse exclaims)
  Consign'd for ever to Oblivion's Cloud.

XV.

"White be the Page that celebrates his Fame,
  "Nor let one Mark of Infamy appear;
"Let not the Villain's mingle with his Name,
  "Lest Indignation stop the swelling Tear.

XVI.

"The swelling Tear should plenteously descend,
  "The delug'd Eye should give the Heart Relief;
"Humanity should melt for Nature's Friend,
  "In all the richest Luxury of Grief."

XVII.

He, as a Planet with unceasing Ray,
  Is seen in one unvaried Course to move,
Through Life pursued but one illustrious Way,
  And all his Orbit was his Country's Love.

XVIII.

But he is gone!—And now, alas! no more
  His generous Hand neglected Worth redeems;
No more around his Mansion shall the Poor
  Bask in his warm, his charitable Beams.

XIX.

No more his grateful Countrymen shall hear
His manly Voice, in martyr'd Freedom's Cause;
No more the courtly Sycophant shall fear
His poignant Lash for violated Laws.

XX.

Yet say, Stern Virtue, who'd not wish to die,
Thus greatly struggling, a whole Land to save?
Who would not wish, with Ardor wish to lie,
With *Beckford*'s Honor, in a *Beckford*'s Grave?

XXI.

Not Honor, such as Princes can bestow,
Whose breath a Reptile to a Lord can raise;
But far the brightest Honor here below,
A grateful Nation's unabating Praise.

XXII.

But see! where Liberty, on yonder Strand,
Where the Cliff rises, and the Billows roar,
Already takes her melancholy Stand,
To wing her Passage to some happier Shore.

XXIII.

Stay, Goddess! stay, nor leave this once-bless'd Isle,
So many Ages thy peculiar Care,
O! stay, and cheer us ever with thy Smile,
Lest quick we sink in terrible Despair.

XXIV.

And lo! she listens to the Muse's Call;
She comes, once more, to cheer a wretched Land;
Thou, Tyranny, shall tremble to thy Fall!
To hear her high, her absolute Command:—

XXV.

"Let not, my Sons, the Laws your Fathers bought,
"With such rich Oceans of undaunted Blood,
"By TRAITORS, thus be basely set at Nought,
"While at your Hearts you feel the purple Flood.

XXVI.

"Unite in firm, in honorable Bands;
"Break ev'ry Link of Slav'ry's hateful Chain:
"Nor let your Children, at their Fathers' Hands,
"Demand their Birthright, and demand in vain.

XXVII.

"Where e'er the Murd'rers of their Country hide,
"Whatever Dignities their Names adorn;
"It is your Duty—let it be your Pride,
"To drag them forth to universal Scorn.

XXVIII.

"So shall your lov'd, your venerated Name,
"O'er Earth's vast Convex gloriously expand;
"So shall your still accumulating Fame
"In one bright Story with your *Beckford* stand."[1]

---

[1] In the Town and Country Magazine for November, 1769, there is a full-length portrait of Alderman Beckford in his magisterial robes; and a Sketch for his Statue in the number for August, 1770. The Alderman, as is well known, was father to Wm. Beckford, Esq., the talented author of "Vathek." "Chatterton," says Dr. Gregory, "had, it seems, addressed an essay to the patriotic Lord Mayor, W. Beckford, which was so well received that it encouraged him to wait upon his Lordship in order to obtain his approbation to address a second letter to him, on the subject of the city remonstrance, and its reception. 'His Lordship (adds he) received me as politely as a citizen could, and warmly invited me to call on him again. The rest is a secret.' His

THE ART OF PUFFING.

BY A BOOKSELLER'S JOURNEYMAN.

[Copied from a MS. of Chatterton. Printed in 1803.]

ERSED by experience in the subtle art,
The mysteries of a title I impart:
Teach the young author how to please the town,
And make the heavy drug of rhyme go down.
Since Curl, immortal never-dying name!
A double pica in the book of fame,
By various arts did various Dunces prop,
And tickled every fancy to his shop,
Who can, like Pottinger, ensure a book?
Who judges with the solid taste of Cooke?
Villains, exalted in the midway sky,
Shall live again to drain your purses dry:
Nor yet unrivalled they; see Baldwin comes,
Rich in inventions, patents, cuts, and hums:

---

inclination doubtless led him to espouse the party of opposition; but he complains that 'no money is to be got on that side the question; interest is on the other side. But he is a poor author that cannot write on both sides. I believe I may be introduced (and if I am not, I'll introduce myself) to a ruling power in the court party.' When Beckford died, he is said to have been almost frantic, and to have exclaimed that he was ruined. The elegy, however, in which he has celebrated him, contains more of frigid praise than of ardent feeling; nor is there a single line which appears to flow from the heart."—*Pref. to* SOUTHEY'S *Edition*; vol. i. p. lx.

The honourable Boswell writes, 'tis true,
What else can Paoli's supporter do?[1]
The trading wits endeavour to attain,
Like booksellers, the world's first idol—gain.
For this they puff the heavy Goldsmith's line,
And hail his sentiment, though trite, divine;
For this the patriotic bard complains,
And Bingley binds poor liberty in chains:
For this was every reader's faith deceived,
And Edmunds swore what nobody believed:
For this the wits in close disguises fight;
For this the varying politicians write;
For this each month new magazines are sold,
With dullness filled and transcripts of the old.
The "Town and Country" struck a lucky hit,
Was novel, sentimental, full of wit:
Aping her walk the same success to find,
The "Court and City" hobbles far behind.
Sons of Apollo, learn: merit's no more
Than a good frontispiece to grace the door:
The author who invents a title well
Will always find his covered dullness sell:
Flexney and every bookseller will buy—
Bound in neat calf, the work will never die.

VAMP.

July 22, 1770.

---

[1] General Paoli, a Corsican, was Boswell's great friend. Bingley was printer and proprietor of the Political Register. Edmunds was editor of the Middlesex Journal. Curl is immortalised in that "book of fame" named Pope's Dunciad.

TO A FRIEND,

ON HIS INTENDED MARRIAGE.

[Printed in 1803.]

I.

MARRIAGE, dear M—,[1] is a serious thing;
'Tis proper every man should think it so;
'Twill either every human blessing bring,
Or load thee with a settlement of woe.

II.

Sometimes indeed it is a middle state,
Neither supremely blest, nor deeply curst;
A stagnant pool of life, a dream of fate—
In my opinion, of all states the worst.

III.

Observe the partner of thy future state:
If no strong vice is stamped upon her mind,
Take her; and let her ease thy amorous pain:
A little error proves her human-kind.

IV.

What we call vices are not always such;
Some virtues scarce deserve the sacred name;
Thy wife may love, as well as pray too much,
And to another stretch her rising flame.

---

[1] Possibly *Mason*. Chatterton had a friend of that name; see Works, ed. 1803, iii. 494.

V.

Choose no religionist; whose every day
Is lost to thee and thine—to none a friend:
Know too, when pleasure calls the heart astray,
The warmest zealot is the blackest fiend.

VI.

Let not the fortune first engross thy care,
Let it a second estimation hold;
A Smithfield-marriage is of pleasures bare,
And love, without the purse, will soon grow cold.

VII.

Marry no lettered damsel, whose wise head
May prove it just to graft the horns on thine:
Marry no idiot, keep her from thy bed—
What the brains want will often elsewhere shine.

VIII.

A disposition good, a judgment sound,
Will bring substantial pleasures in a wife:
Whilst love and tenderness in thee are found,
Happy and calm will be the married life.

THOMAS CHATTERTON.

HORATIUS: Lib. I. Carm. V.[1]

WHAT gentle youth, my lovely fair one, say,
With sweets perfumed, now courts thee to the bower,
Where glows with lustre red the rose of May,
To form thy couch in love's enchanting hour?

---

[1] Ad Pyrrham.

Quis multâ gracilis te puer in rosâ
Perfusus liquidis urget odoribus
Grato, Pyrrha, sub antro?
Cui flavam religas comam,
Simplex munditiis? heu, quotiens fidem
Mutatosque Deos flebit, et aspera
Nigris æquora ventis
Emirabitur insolens,
Qui nunc te fruitur credulus aureâ:
Qui semper vacuam, semper amabilem
Sperat, nescius auræ
Fallacis! miseri, quibus
Intemptata nites! me tabulâ sacer
Votivâ paries indicat uvida
Suspendisse potenti
Vestimenta maris Deo.

Hor. Lib. i. Carm. 5.

"Who, Pyrrha, is this slender young gallant, perfumed with rich odours, that caresses you on a bed of roses in a pleasant grotto? For whom, pray, do you bind up your golden locks, genteelly dressed, though plain? Poor unexperienced youth! how oft will he have cause to complain of your treachery, and to lament his own hard fate! How will he stand amazed to see your smooth temper all on a sudden ruffled as the sea with stormy winds! he who now enjoys

By zephyrs waved, why does thy loose hair sweep
  In simple curls around thy polished brow?
The wretch that loves thee now too soon shall weep
  Thy faithless beauty and thy broken vow.

Though soft the beams of thy delusive eyes
  As the smooth surface of th' untroubled stream;
Yet, ah! too soon th' ecstatic vision flies—
  Flies like the fairy paintings of a dream.

---

your charms without fear, and who, unacquainted with your coquette airs, fondly thinks you are solely his, and that you will be always the same. Thrice wretched they, who, strangers to your arts, are allured with your beauty. But as trophies of my narrow escape, I have, as I vowed, hung up my tablet, and dripping wet clothes in the temple of Neptune, that great ruler of the sea."—WATSON'S *Translation*, published in 1741.

The reader may desire to compare with Chatterton's version of the above, the same Ode rendered by Milton "almost word for word, without rhyme, according to the Latin measure, as near as the language will permit."

What slender youth, bedew'd with liquid odours,
Courts thee on roses in some pleasant cave,
  Pyrrha? For whom bind'st thou
  In wreaths thy golden hair,
Plain in thy neatness? Oh, how oft shall he
On faith and changèd gods complain, and seas
  Rough with black winds and storms
  Unwonted shall admire!
Who now enjoys thee credulous, all gold,
Who always vacant, always amiable
  Hopes thee, of flattering gales
  Unmindful. Hapless they
To whom thou untried seem'st fair! Me in my vow'd
Picture, the sacred wall declares t' have hung
  My dank and dropping weeds
  To the stern god of sea.

Unhappy youth, oh, shun the warm embrace,
  Nor trust too much affection's flattering smile;
Dark poison lurks beneath that charming face,
  Those melting eyes but languish to beguile.

Thank heaven, I've broke the sweet but galling chain,
Worse than the horrors of the stormy main!

D. B.

HORATIUS: Lib. I. Carm. XIX.[1]

YES! I am caught, my melting soul
  To Venus bends without control,
    I pour the empassioned sigh.
  Ye Gods! what throbs my bosom move,
Responsive to the glance of love,
  That beams from Stella's eye.

---

[1] "These translations from Horace were made by Chatterton, from Watson's literal version; a book which his friend Mr. Edward Gardner lent him for the express purpose."—Southey's *Edition*. As Mr. E. Gardner only knew Chatterton during the latter's last three months at Bristol, the date of these translations cannot be far from Feb. 1770.

De Glycera.

Mater sæva Cupidinum,
  Thebanæque iubet me Semeles puer,
Et lasciva licentia,
  Finitis animum reddere amoribus.
Urit me Glyceræ nitor
  Splendentis Pario marmore puriùs;
Urit grata protervitas,

Oh, how divinely fair that face,
And what a sweet resistless grace
On every feature dwells!
And on those features all the while
The softness of each frequent smile
Her sweet good-nature tells.

O Love! I'm thine—no more I sing
Heroic deeds—the sounding string
Forgets its wonted strains;
For aught but love the lyre's unstrung,

Et vultus nimiùm lubricus aspici.
In me tota ruens Venus
Cyprum deseruit; nec patitur Scythas,
Et versis animosum equis
Parthum dicere, nec quæ nihil attinent.
Hic vivum mihi cespitem, hic
Verbenas, pueri, ponite, turaque,
Bimi cum paterâ meri:
Mactatâ veniet lenior hostiâ.

Watson's Translation of this ode is as follows:—

"Of Glycera.

"The cruel Queen of Love, and Bacchus, son of the Theban Semele, assisted by licentious desires, conspire to rekindle in me the passion of love, which I thought had been quite extinguished. I am ravished with the beauty of Glycera, which far excels the finest Parian marble. I am struck with her agreeable humour and fine complexion, which cannot be looked on without manifest danger. Venus hath left Cyprus to reign in my heart, and will not permit me to sing of either the warlike Scythians, or of the Parthians, who fight so boldly while they are flying; or of anything else, but what relates to her. Bring me then, boys, some green turf, vervain, incense, and a cup of two-year-old wine: when I have offered this goddess a sacrifice, she will be more mild and tractable."

Love melts and trembles on my tongue,
And thrills in every vein.

Invoking the propitious skies,
The green-sod altar let us rise,
Let holy incense smoke:
And if we pour the sparkling wine,
Sweet, gentle peace may still be mine,
This dreadful chain be broke!

D. B.

THE COMPLAINT.

ADDRESSED TO MISS P— L—, OF BRISTOL.[1]

[Reprinted, without alteration of spelling, from the Universal Magazine for Nov. 1769.]

OVE, lawless tyrant of my breast,
When will my passions be at rest,
And in soft murmurs roll—
When will the dove-ey'd goddess, Peace,
Bid black despair and torment cease,
And wake to joy my soul?

---

[1] In the *Universal Magazine* for November, 1769, I find a poem which has every claim to be by Chatterton, though not included in any edition of his works. The external and internal evidences all point that way. The external evidences are (1) the date of its appearance; (2) the mention of Bristol and the Severn; (3) the signature "C," which he adopted about this time, in preference to "T. C.," which were also the initials of Thomas Cary; and (4) the address to Miss L—, who may have been the same as the person of whom he afterwards wrote in one of his letters home, dated May 14, 1770—"If Miss Love has no

Adieu! ye flow'r-bespangled hills;
Adieu! ye softly-purling rills,
That through the meadows play;
Adieu! the cool refreshing shade,
By hoary oaks and woodbines made,
Where oft with joy I lay.

No more beneath your boughs I hear,
With pleasure unallayed by fear,
The distant Severne roar—
Adieu! the forest's mossy side
Deck'd out in Flora's richest pride:
Ye can delight no more.

---

objection to having a crambo song on her name published, it shall be done." It is even possible that the poem here printed, beginning, be it observed, with the word *Love*, is the very "crambo song" referred to; for it was a common practice with Chatterton to alter a poem very slightly, and to produce it a second time. The internal evidences are supplied by comparison with other poems. For example, he writes to Miss Hoyland, in the same metre, as follows:—

O! haste to give my passion ease
And bid the perturbation *cease*
That harrows up my *soul!*
The joy such happiness to find
Would make the functions of my mind
In peace and love to *roll*. (p. 15.)

Again, the "noxious vapours" and the snakes occur also in his "Burlesque Elegy on Lady Betty's Cat":—

Ye noxious vapours, fall upon my head,
Ye writhing adders, round my feet entwine;
Ye toads, your venom in my foot-path spread; (p. 130)

whilst the spellings of *Severne* and *eccho* occur in the Rowley Poems.

After writing this note, I found that Dr. Maitland has also recorded his belief that this poem is by Chatterton.

Oft at the solitary hour
When Melancholy's silent power
  Is gliding through the shade ;
With raging Madness by her side,
Whose hands, in blood and murder dy'd,
  Display the reeking blade,

I catch the eccho of their feet,
And follow to their drear retreat
  Of deadliest nightshade wove :
There, stretch'd upon the dewy ground,
Whilst noxious vapours rise around,
  I sigh my tale of love.

Oft has the solemn bird of night,
When rising to his gloomy flight,
  Unseen against me fled !
Whilst snakes in curling orbs uproll'd,
Bedrop'd with azure, flame, and gold,
  Hurl'd poison at my head.

O say ! thou best of womankind,
Thou miracle, in whom we find
  Wit, charms, and sense unite,
Can plagues like these be always borne ?
No ; if I still must meet your scorn,
  I'll seek the realms of night.

C.

AN EPITAPH ON AN OLD MAID.[1]

ERE lies, her debt of nature paid,
A[2] handsome, proud, and ancient maid,
Who used (you'll think it strangely odd)
This as a plea to cheat her God:
That few are blest who fondly wed,
So rare the joys of marriage-bed;
Thus broke the law that first was given
By the kind hand of parent heaven.
Be wise, ye fair, and this apply—
God orders you to multiply.

ELEGY

ON MR. WILLIAM SMITH.[3]

ASCEND, my Muse, on sorrow's sable plume,
Let the soft number meet the swelling sigh;
With laureated chaplets deck the tomb,
The blood-stained tomb where Smith and comfort lie.

---

[1] This epitaph, hitherto unprinted, is from a MS. scrap in the possession of Mr. Bell. It is certainly genuine, being in Chatterton's own handwriting.

[2] MS. "An;" the fourth word following is spelt "antient" in the MS.

[3] Happily mistaken, having since heard, from good authority, it is Peter [William's brother].—CHATTERTON.

I loved him with a brother's ardent love,
 Beyond the love which tenderest brothers bear;
Though savage kindred bosoms cannot move,
 Friendship shall deck his urn and pay the tear.

Despised, an alien to thy father's breast,
 Thy ready services repaid with hate;
By brother, father, sisters, all distressed,
 They pushed thee on to death, they urged thy fate.

Ye callous-breasted brutes in human form,
 Have you not often boldly wished him dead?
He's gone, ere yet his fire of man was warm,
 O may his crying blood be on your head!

ON THE IMMORTALITY OF THE SOUL.[1]

[From G. Pryce's "Memorials of the Canynges' Family," p. 303.]

SAY, O my soul, if not allowed to be
Immortal, whence the mystery we see
Day after day, and hour after hour,
But to proclaim its never-ceasing power?
If not immortal, then our thoughts of thee
Are visions but of non-futurity.
Why do we live to feel of pain on pain,
If, in the midst of hope, we hope in vain?

---

[1] These lines were written impromptu by Chatterton in the presence of his friend William Smith, at Bristol, probably in 1769. See Wilson's Life of Chatterton, p. 233.

Perish the thought in night's eternal shade:
To live, then die, man was not only made.
There's yet an awful something else remains
Either to lessen or increase our pains.
Whate'er it be, whate'er man's future fate,
Nature proclaims there is another state
Of woe, or bliss. But who is he can tell?
None but the good, and they that have done well.
Oh! may that happiness be ours, my friend,
The little we have now will shortly end;
When joy and bliss more lasting will appear,
Or all our hopes translated into fear.
Oh! may our portion in that world above,
Eternal Fountain of Eternal Love,
Be crowned with peace that bids the sinner live;
With praise to Him who only can forgive—
Blot out the stains and errors of our youth;
Whose smile is mercy, and whose word is truth.

THE RESIGNATION.[1]

[From Sir H. Croft's "Love and Madness."]

GOD, whose thunder shakes the sky,
Whose eye this atom globe surveys,
To thee, my only rock, I fly,
Thy mercy in thy justice praise.

---

[1] James Montgomery, the author of "The Wanderer of Switzerland," in a letter to Mr. Dix, alluded to by that gentleman in his Life of Chatterton, says with reference to these verses that they "show at least some 'light from

The mystic mazes of thy will,
The shadows of celestial light,
Are past the power of human skill,—
But what th' Eternal acts is right.

O teach me in the trying hour,
When anguish swells the dewy tear,
To still my sorrows, own thy power,
Thy goodness love, thy justice fear.

If in this bosom aught but Thee
Encroaching sought a boundless sway,
Omniscience could the danger see,
And Mercy look the cause away.

Then why, my soul, dost thou complain?
Why drooping seek the dark recess?
Shake off the melancholy chain,
For God created all to bless.

---

heaven' breathing through the darkness of his soul, which affected me so deeply, when, as a young man, I read them, that I responded to them from the depth of my heart, with a sympathy which I endeavoured to express in one of my earlier poems."

The following are Mr. Montgomery's verses:—

A dying swan of Pindus sings
In wildly-mournful strains;
As Death's cold fingers snap the strings,
His suffering lyre complains.

Soft as the mist of evening wends
Along the shadowy vale;
Sad as in storms the moon ascends,
And turns the darkness pale;

So soft the melting numbers flow
From his harmonious lips;
So sad his woe-wan features show,
Just fading in eclipse.

But ah! my breast is human still;
The rising sigh, the falling tear,
My languid vitals' feeble rill,
The sickness of my soul declare.

But yet, with fortitude resigned,
I'll thank th' inflicter of the blow;
Forbid the sigh, compose my mind,
Nor let the gush of misery flow.

The gloomy mantle of the night,
Which on my sinking spirit steals,
Will vanish at the morning light
Which God, my East, my Sun, reveals.[1]

The Bard to dark despair resign'd,
With his expiring art
Sings 'midst the tempest of his mind
The shipwreck of his heart.

If Hope still seem to linger nigh,
And hover o'er his head,
Her pinions are too weak to fly;
Or Hope ere now had fled.

Rash Minstrel! who can hear thy songs,
Nor long to share thy fire?
Who read thine errors and thy wrongs,
Nor execrate the lyre?

The lyre that sunk thee to the grave
When bursting into bloom,
That lyre the power to genius gave
To blossom in the tomb.

Yes; till his memory fail with years,
Shall Time thy strains recite;
And while thy story swells his tears,
Thy song shall charm his flight.

[1] "Within four months Chatterton's London career began and closed, yet it witnessed all the most fitful extremes of

LAST VERSES.[1]

FAREWELL, Bristolia's dingy piles of brick,
Lovers of Mammon, worshippers of Trick!
Ye spurned the boy who gave you antique lays,
And paid for learning with your empty praise.

---

hope and despair. In the hectic gaiety with which he struggles to conceal the latter feeling from his poor friends, and in the buoyant certainty of greatness to which he shows himself lifted by the most trifling success, his letters are models of the profoundest pathos. The "seething brains and shaping fantasies, which apprehend more than cooler reason can," were indeed Chatterton's; but these, we cannot help thinking, included also in his case qualities which redeem his short and unhappy life from the more ordinary class of literary miseries. His pride and his honour never deserted him. He did not die after descending to make his talents instruments of evil to others, or of disgrace to himself. Panting and jaded as he was, and pursued to the extremest verge of despair by the dogs of hunger and necessity, literature still remained a refreshment and a hope to him, when madness suddenly terminated all. His poison draught is not to be compared to Boyse's blanket, or to the prison of Savage, or even to the loaf of the starving Otway."

MRS. S. C. HALL.

[1] These "Last Verses," bearing date on the day of the poet's death, first appeared in an edition of his works published in Boston, U.S., in 1857. A note, signed "C." (presumably the initial of the editor) gives us the following account of them. "J. R. Dix, Esq., has politely communicated to us the following lines (never before published),

Farewell, ye guzzling aldermanic fools,
By nature fitted for Corruption's tools!
I go to where celestial anthems swell;
But you, when you depart, will sink to hell.
Farewell, my mother!—cease, my anguished soul,
Nor let Distraction's billows o'er me roll!
Have mercy, Heaven! when here I cease to live,
And this last act of wretchedness forgive.

T. C.

August 24, 1770.

CHATTERTON'S WILL.[1]

[Hitherto the parts of this piece have been misarranged. They here appear in their right order.]

LL this wrote between 11 and 2 o'clock Saturday, in the utmost distress of mind. April 14, 1770.

Burgum, I thank thee, thou hast let me see
That Bristol has impressed her stamp on thee,
Thy generous spirit emulates the Mayor's,
Thy generous spirit with thy Bristol's pairs.

---

which he states to have been found in Chatterton's pocket-book after his death. They were given to Mr. Dix by Joseph Cottle, who received them from Mrs. Newton [Chatterton's sister], but too late for insertion in his edition of Chatterton's works."

[1] "It was the accidental sight of this Will which occasioned Mr. Lambert to part with Chatterton; when the latter, a few days after, set off for London.—Without this

Gods! what would Burgum give to get a name,
And snatch his blundering dialect from shame!
What would he give, to hand his memory down
To time's remotest boundary?—A Crown.[1]
Would you ask more, his swelling face looks blue;
Futurity he rates at two pound two.
Well, Burgum, take thy laurel to thy brow;
With a rich saddle decorate a sow,
Strut in Iambics, totter in an Ode,
Promise, and never pay, and be the mode.

Catcott, for thee, I know thy heart is good,
But ah! thy merit's seldom understood;
Too bigoted to whimsies, which thy youth
Received to venerate as Gospel truth,
Thy friendship never could be dear to me,
Since all I am is opposite to thee.
If ever obligated to thy purse,
Rowley discharges all—my first, chief curse!
For had I never known the antique lore,
I ne'er had ventured from my peaceful shore
To be the wreck of promises and hopes,
A Boy of Learning, and a Bard of Tropes;

---

intimation, and attending to the *date*, the reader might suppose that the above was the will which Chatterton wrote immediately preceding his death."—Cottle (1803). Dr. Gregory states, that he was informed on good authority, that this will "was occasioned by the refusal of a gentleman [viz. Mr. Burgum], whom he had occasionally complimented in his poems, to accommodate him with a supply of money." The MS. in Chatterton's handwriting is preserved in the Library of the Bristol Institution.

[1] The sum given to Chatterton by Mr. Burgum for his pedigree; see vol. ii. p. 308.

But happy in my humble sphere had moved,
Untroubled, unrespected, unbeloved.[1]

To Barrett next, he has my thanks sincere
For all the little knowledge I had here.
But what was knowledge? Could it here succeed
When scarcely twenty in the town can read?
Could knowledge bring in interest to maintain
The wild expenses of a poet's brain?
Disinterested Burgum never meant
To take my knowledge for his gain per cent.
When wildly squandering every thing I got
On books and learning, and the Lord knows what,
Could Burgum then, my critic, patron, friend,

---

[1] "Such was Chatterton's firmness of perseverance, that he seems to attest the originality of Rowley, even in the *Will* which he wrote before his projected suicide. This circumstance is much founded on by the believers. To me it only affords an additional proof of the unconquerable and haughty perseverance of his character. I attach no implicit faith to dying declarations; for upon points in which fame is implicated, the voice of the passions is heard even in the hour of death. I disclaim every application of the illustration which can be disrespectful to the memory of Chatterton; but it is well known, that criminals, whose crimes are not of a nature to meet public sympathy, often at their death endeavour, by a denial of guilt most satisfactorily proved, to avert the odium attached to their persons and memory. It may be thought that Chatterton would have better consulted his own fame by avowing these beautiful poems; but the pride of every one is not sustained by the same nutriment. He probably deprecated the doubtful fame of an ingenious but detected impostor, and preferred the internal consciousness, that, by persisting in the deception he had commenced, future ages might venerate the poems of Chatterton, under patronage of the fictitious Rowley."—SIR WALTER SCOTT; in Edinb. Review, vol. iv. April, 1804.

Without security attempt to lend?
No, that would be imprudent in the man;
Accuse him of imprudence if you can.
He promised, I confess, and seemed sincere;
Few keep an honorary promise here.
I thank thee, Barrett—thy advice was right,
But 'twas ordain'd by fate that I should write.
Spite of the prudence of this prudent place,
I wrote my mind, nor hid the author's face.
Harris ere long, when, reeking from the press,
My numbers make his self-importance less,
Will wrinkle up his face, and damn the day,
And drag my body to the triple way.
Poor superstitious mortals! wreak your hate
Upon my cold remains——

This is the last Will and Testament of me, Thomas Chatterton, of the city of Bristol; being sound in body, or it is the fault of my last surgeon: the soundness of my mind, the coroner and jury are to be judges of, desiring them to take notice, that the most perfect masters of human nature in Bristol distinguish me by the title of the Mad Genius; therefore, if I do a mad action, it is conformable to every action of my life, which all savoured of insanity.[1]

---

[1] "Chatterton *was* insane,—better proof of this than the coroner's inquest is, that there was insanity in his family. (His sister, Mrs. Newton, was for some period confined in a mad-house.) His biographers were not informed of this important fact; and the editors of his collected works forbore to state it, because the collection was made for the benefit of his surviving relations, a sister and niece, in both of whom the disease had manifested itself."—SOUTHEY.

Item. If after my death, which will happen to-morrow night before eight o'clock, being the Feast of the Resurrection,[1] the coroner and jury bring it in lunacy, I will and direct, that Paul Farr, Esq. and Mr. John Flower, at their joint expense, cause my body to be interred in the tomb of my fathers, and raise the monument over my body to the height of four feet five inches, placing the present flat stone on the top, and adding six tablets.

On the *first*, to be engraved in Old English characters:—

Vous qui par ici pasez
Pur l'ame Guateroine Chatterton priez
Le Cors di oi ici gist
L'ame receyve Jhu Crist. MCCX.[2]

On the *second* tablet, in Old English characters:—

Orate pro animabus Alanus Chatterton, et Alicia Uxoris ejus, qui quidem Alanus obiit x die mensis Novemb. MCCCCXV, quorum animabus propitietur Deus Amen.

---

[1] Easter-day fell upon April 15 in 1770.

[2] "Whatever obsolete spelling or mistakes may be observed here, either in the French or the Latin, the reader is desired to consider as the author's, not the editor's." —*Note by* Cottle. Yet I have ventured to put *Ihu, Uxoris, obiit, propitietur* in place of *Thu, Uxeris, obict,* and *propinetur*.

On the *third* tablet, in Roman characters:—

SACRED TO THE MEMORY OF

THOMAS CHATTERTON,[1]

Subchaunter of the Cathedral of this city, whose ancestors were residents of St. Mary Redcliffe since the year 1140. He died the 7th of August, 1752.

On the *fourth* tablet, in Roman characters:—

TO THE MEMORY OF

THOMAS CHATTERTON.

Reader, judge not; if thou art a Christian, believe that he shall be judged by a superior Power. To that Power alone is he now answerable.

On the *fifth* and *sixth* tablets, which shall front each other:—

Atchievements: viz. on the one, vert, a fess, or; crest, a mantle of estate, gules, supported by a spear, sable, headed, or. On the other, or, a fess vert, crest, a cross of Knights Templars.—And I will and direct that if the coroner's inquest bring it in *felo-de-se*, the said monument shall be notwithstanding erected. And if the said Paul Farr and John Flower have souls so Bristolish as to refuse this my request, they will transmit a copy of my Will to the Society for supporting the Bill of Rights, whom I hereby empower to build the said

[1] The poet's father.

monument according to the aforesaid directions. And if they the said Paul Farr and John Flower should build the said monument, I will and direct that the second edition of my Kew Gardens shall be dedicated to them in the following dedication:— To Paul Farr and John Flower, Esqrs. this book is most humbly dedicated by the Author's Ghost.

Item. I give all my vigour and fire of youth to Mr. George Catcott, being sensible he is most in want of it.

Item. From the same charitable motive, I give and bequeath unto the Reverend Mr. Camplin senior, all my humility. To Mr. Burgum all my prosody and grammar,—likewise one moiety of my modesty; the other moiety to any young lady who can prove without blushing that she wants that valuable commodity. To Bristol, all my spirit and disinterestedness; parcels of goods unknown on her quay since the days of Canning and Rowley! 'Tis true, a charitable gentleman, one Mr. Colston, smuggled a considerable quantity of it, but it being proved that he was a papist, the Worshipful Society of Aldermen endeavoured to throttle him with the Oath of Allegiance. I leave also my religion to Dr. Cutts Barton, Dean of Bristol, hereby empowering the sub-sacrist to strike him on the head when he goes to sleep in church. My powers of utterance I give to the Reverend Mr. Broughton, hoping he will employ them to a better purpose than reading lectures on the immortality of the soul. I leave the Reverend Mr. Catcott some little of my free-thinking, that he may put on [the] spectacles of Reason, and see how vilely he is duped in believing the Scriptures literally. I wish he and his brother George would know how far I am their real enemy; but I have an unlucky way of raillery, and when the strong fit of satire is upon me, I spare neither friend nor foe. This is my excuse for what I have said of them elsewhere. I leave Mr. Clayfield the sincerest thanks my gratitude can give; and I will and direct that, whatever any person may think the pleasure of reading my works worth, they immediately pay their own valuation to him, since it is then become a lawful debt to me, and to him as my executor in this case.

I leave my moderation to the politicians on both sides of the question. I leave my generosity to our present Right Worshipful Mayor, Thomas Harris, Esq. I give my abstinence to the company at the Sheriffs' annual feast in general, more particularly the Aldermen.

Item. I give and bequeath to Mr. Matthew Mease a mourning ring with this motto, "Alas, poor Chatterton!" provided he pays for it himself. Item. I leave the young ladies all the letters they have had from me, assuring them that they need be under no apprehensions from the appearance of my ghost, for I die for none of them.—Item. I leave all my debts, the whole not five pounds, to the payment of the charitable and generous Chamber of Bristol, on penalty, if refused, to hinder every member from a good dinner by appearing in the form of a bailiff. If in defiance of this terrible spectre, they obstinately persist in refusing to discharge my debts, let my two creditors apply to the supporters of the Bill of Rights.—Item. I leave my mother and sister to the protection of my friends, if I have any.

Executed in the presence of Omniscience this 14th of April, 1770.

THOS. CHATTERTON.

CODICIL.

It is my pleasure that Mr. Cocking and Miss Farley print this my Will the first Saturday after my death.—T. C.

N. B.—In a dispute concerning the character of David, Mr. ——— argued that he must be a holy man, from the strains of piety that breathed through his whole works. I being of a contrary opinion, and knowing that a great genius can affect everything;[1] endeavouring in the foregoing Poems[2] to represent an enthusiastic Methodist, intended to send it to Romaine, and impose it upon the infatuated world as a reality; but thanks to Burgum's generosity, I am now employed in matters of more importance.

Saturday, April 20[3], 1770.

---

[1] Cottle prints "effect anything;" which can hardly have been intended here.

[2] What poems are here meant is uncertain. Yet see pp. 42, 192.

[3] Read 21. This last paragraph, obviously added a week later, (during which period Mr. Burgum had become *generous*), is wrongly placed at the *beginning* of the Will in the editions.

THE ARTICLES OF THE BELIEF OF ME, THOMAS CHATTERTON.

THAT God being incomprehensible, it is not required of us to know the mysteries of the Trinity, &c., &c., &c., &c.

That it matters not whether a man is a Pagan, Turk, Jew, or Christian, if he acts according to the Religion he professes.

That if a man leads a good moral life, he is a Christian.

That the Stage is the best School of Morality.
and

That The Church of Rome (some Tricks of Priestcraft excepted) is certainly the true Church.

T. CHATTERTON.

ANTIQUITY OF CHRISTMAS GAMES.[1]

IN the days of our ancestors, Christmas was a period sacred to mirth and hospitality. Though not wholly neglected now, it cannot boast of the honours it once had; the veneration for religious seasons fled with popery, and old English hospitality is long since deceased. Our modern playthings of fortune, who make the whole year a revolution of dissipation and joyless festivity, cannot distinguish this season; unless by resting from their laborious pleasures, and (if they can think) find a happy serenity in solitude and reflection, unknown in the tumult of hurricanes.—The ancient Christmas gambols were, in my opinion, superior to our modern spectacles and amusements; wrestling, hurling the ball, and dancing in the woodlands, were pleasures for men; it is true, the conversation of the hearthside was the tales of superstition;

---

[1] The MS. of the Christmas Games is preserved in the British Museum; but on comparing it with the "Antiquity of Christmas Games," printed by Southey in his Edition of 1803, I discovered such a striking difference in the construction of the sentences, so much omitted in the MS. that is to be found in the printed copy, that it seems probable that there were two MSS. in Chatterton's handwriting in existence, and that Southey's text was printed from the missing document. I have retained the article as it has hitherto appeared in previous editions.—EDITOR (1842).

the fairies, Robin Goodfellow, and hobgoblins, never failed to make the trembling audience mutter an Ave Maria, and cross their chins; but the laughable exercises of blindman's-buff, riddling, and question and command, sufficiently compensated for the few sudden starts of terror. Add to these amusements, the wretched voices of the chanters and sub-chanters; howling carols in Latin; the chiming of consecrated bells; the burning consecrated wax-candles; curiously representing the Virgin Mary; praying the saint whose monastery stood nearest; the munching consecrated cross-loaves, sold by the monks; all which effectually eradicated the spectres of their terrific stories. Nor were these the only charms against the foul fiends and night-mare; sleeping cross-legged, like the effigies of Knights Templars and warriors, and the holy bush and church-yard yew, were certain antidotes against those invisible beings. After this representation, I may be thought partial to my own hobby-horse, as an antiquary, in giving the preference to the amusements of the days of old; but let the sentimental reader consider that the tales of superstition, when believed, affect the soul with a sensation pleasurably horrid; we may paint in more lively colours to the eye, they spoke to the heart.

The great barons and knights usually kept open house during this season, when their villains, or vassals, were entertained with bread, beef, and beer, and a pudding, wastel cake, or Christmas kitchel, and a groat in silver at parting; being obliged, in return, to wave the full flaggon round their heads, in honour of the master of the house. Sometimes the festival continued till Twelfth-day, when the baron, or his steward, took the deis or upper seat of the table, and after dinner gave every man a new gown of his livery, and two Christmas kitchels.—This kind of liberality endeared the barons to the common people, and made them ever ready to take up arms under their banners.

A register of the nunnery of Keynsham relates, that William, Earl of Gloucester, entertained two hundred knights with tilts and fortunys, at his great manor of Keynsham, provided thirty pies of the eels of Avon, as a curious dainty; and on the Twelfth-day began the plays for the knights by the monks; with miracles and maumeries for the henchmen and servants, by minstrels.

Here is plainly a distinction made between maumeries and miracles, and the more noble representations comprehended under the name plays. The first were the holiday entertainments of the vulgar; the other of the barons and nobility. The private exhibitions at the manors of the barons were usually family histories; the monk, who represented the master of the family, being arrayed in a tabard (or herald's coat without sleeves) painted with all the hatchments of the names. In these domestic performances, absurdities were unavoidable; and in a play wrote by Sir Tibbet Gorges,[1]

---

[1] Who was Sir Thybbot Gorges? He was one of that bright galaxy of bards who flourished in the fourteenth and fifteenth centuries, and who were unknown to the world till Chatterton generously introduced them to posterity and fame.—Editor (1842). See vol. ii. p. 275.

Constance, countess of Bretagne and Richmond, marries and buries her three husbands in the compass of an hour. Sometimes these pieces were merely relations, and had only two characters of this kind, as that in Weever's 'Funeral Monuments.' None but the patrons of monasteries had the service of monks in performing plays on holidays; provided the same contained nothing against God or the church. The public exhibitions were superior to the private; the plot, generally, the life of some pope, or the founder of the abbey the monks belonged to. I have seen several of these pieces, mostly Latin, and cannot think our ancestors so ignorant of dramatic excellence as the generality of modern writers would represent: they had a good moral in view, and some of the maumeries abound with it, which though low now, was not so then. Minstrels, jesters, and mummers, was the next class of performers: every knight had two or three minstrels and jesters, who were maintained in his house, to entertain his family in their hours of dissipation; these Chaucer mentions in the following passages:

Doe comme, he saied, mye mynstrales,
And jestours for to tellen us tales,
Anon in myne armynge.
Of Romaunces yatte been royals,
Of popes and of cardinals,
And eke of love-longynge.
Rime of Sir Thopas.

Of all manere of mynstrales,
And jestours thatte tellen tales,
Both of weepynge and of yame,
And of all thatte longeth unto fame.
Third Book of Fame.

ON THE ORIGIN, NATURE, AND DESIGN OF SCULPTURE.

[From the Town and Country Magazine, August, 1770.
Accompanied with a design for a statue
of Wm. Beckford.]

SCULPTURE is an art which, by design and solid matter, imitates the palpable objects of nature. It is difficult to ascertain the epocha of its origin; it is lost in the most remote antiquity. The arts of imitation in general, as painting, architecture, sculpture, &c. were the first invented. Sculptors began to work upon clay and wax, which are more flexible, and more pliable than wood and stone. They soon made statues of trees which were neither subject to corruption nor worms, as the lemon-tree, the cypress, the palm, the olive, the ebony, and the vine: at last they made use of metals, ivory, and the hardest stones; marble especially became the most precious matter, and the most esteemed for works of sculpture.

The nations amongst which this fine art was in the greatest honour were the Ægyptians; those people, so celebrated by the monuments of their gratitude towards the memory of the kings their benefactors. It was to perpetuate their names that they erected, in the earliest ages, the two Colossean statues of Moeris,[1] and the Queen his spouse.

---

[1] Printed "Mocrus."

The Ægyptian sculptors excelled all others in exactness of proportion; the different parts of a statue were often formed by divers artists; and these parts united made the whole perfect.

The Greek historians boast of the invention of that art in their country, which they attribute to love: however, it is certain that the first essays of sculpture in Greece were very unpolished; but Dedalus, having travelled in Ægypt, improved himself in this art, and formed afterwards pupils who became the admiration of a people whose taste was not yet refined by the elegant statues of Phydias, Myron, Lysippus, &c.

The Greeks, subdued by the Romans, degenerated insensibly; and the arts vanished with their freedom.

Sculpture was an exotic which never could thrive in victorious Rome; its transient glory was eclipsed by the other arts in the reign of Augustus; it declined under Tiberius, Caius, and Claudius; and re-appeared with an enormous magnitude under Nero.

The Gothic sculpture sprung afterwards from a wild imagination, unassisted by nature.

The epocha of sculpture is the same in France and Italy. The celebrated Michael Angelo worked in Rome under the pontificate of Leo X., whilst John Goujon was admired at Paris, under the patronage of Francis I.

The English advanced by slow degrees to the perfection of that art, in which they now rival their ancient masters.

The sculptors gave the name of statue to a figure

in embossed work, that stands by itself in wood, stone, marble, or metal, of persons conspicuous by their birth, their rank, or their merit.

The ancients often represented figures of men, kings, and even Gods, under a species of statues smaller than the natural size.

Those of persons who had distinguished themselves by their superior knowledge, their virtues, or some important services to the commonwealth, were erected at the public expence in statues of human size.

The third species of statues was designed for kings and emperors: they were taller than men commonly are; and those which personated heroes were larger in proportion.

As for the Colossean statues, they represented Gods; and often kings and emperors, desirous to magnify themselves by these stupendous works, reared at their own expense monuments of their vanity and folly.

An equestrian statue exhibits a man on horseback, as the statue of Charles I. at Charing-cross; the statue of Henry IV. at Paris; and that of Cosmo de Medicis, at Leghorn.

A Greek statue is naked and antique; thus called, because the Greeks displayed in that manner the Gods, the heroes, and the athlet[e]s of the Olympic games.

The Roman statues are all represented with a drapery.

A mausoleum is a pompous funeral monument, decorated with sculpture and architecture, with an epitaph sacred to the memory of some considerable personage. It derives its etymology from the magnificent tomb, which Queen Artemis[i]a caused to be erected for Mausolus, king of Caria, her husband.

Heroes, patriots, and statesmen, are not only entitled to the love and veneration of their co-temporaries during their lives, but their virtues and services ought to be transmitted to the latest posterity. This vanity of surviving our dust by lasting monuments of national gratitude, has prompted men to the most noble actions, and inspired them with the emulation of being enrolled, in the records of time, with those great heroes whose statues and inscriptions they contemplate with a sort of extacy. The tombs in Westminster-Abbey fill the mind with that awful reverence, which a magnificent and grateful nation testifies for its benefactors. The portraits of the illustrious warriors who have subdued our inveterate enemies in both hemispheres, exposed to public view in Vauxhall-gardens, create even in a dissipated multitude a kind of admiration greatly superior to that inspired by the enchantment of the place. The spirit and magnanimity of the incorruptible Beckford, so becoming the first magistrate of the metropolis of a powerful empire; his noble and animated speech to the throne, which was the last public testimony of his unwearied zeal for his country's cause, will be echoed with applause at the sight of his statue by the succeeding generation, to whom he tried to transmit our constitution restored to its pristine purity.

POLITICAL LETTERS.

LETTER I.

[From the Middlesex Journal, Feb. 24, 1770.]

To the Duke of G[rafto]n.[1]

SIR,

YOUR resignation is a step which will cause as much speculation in the political world, as any harlequinade you have already acted. Those who imagine you are at last convinced of your insufficiency to support the measures you have hitherto endeavoured to establish, forget that the most striking part of your character is an obstinate perseverance in the wrong. Others, who are so little acquainted with you as not to doubt your veracity, may be satisfied with your own reasons, and see the affair in whatever light you would choose to set it. But those who would know the

[1] The letters under the signature of "Decimus" were published in the Middlesex Journal for 1770, and were reprinted for the first time in 1837, in Mr. Dix's Life of Chatterton.

The Duke of Grafton resigned the premiership, Jan. 28, 1770.

real cause of your retreat, must trace it to the root of all authority and power—the Earl of Bute. It was the influence of this sun of state, that ripened your latent genius into life. He drew your talents out of obscurity; he raised you to the pinnacle of place, and you have (as in duty bound) been his pack-ass till your late retreat. 'Tis true, the measures which have set the nation in a flame, were executed by you: but they were planned by him, and his more inventive projectors. I would not seem to lessen your character as a minister; but it is well known your talent does not lie in scheming; and you are very incapable of guiding, but upon the lifeless, insipid plan you first set out on. These were qualifications in the eye of the Thane: a jesuitical minister, who has parts to intrigue for himself, will pay little regard to the instructions of another. Your happy vacuity of invention, raised you to that dignity you so nobly maintained. As an instrument, you acquitted yourself to general satisfaction. You bore the infamy of every unconstitutional measure with a temerity truly stoical; you have heard unmoved the cries of the wretched; and was pleased to countenance murder, by calling a just and commendable desire of liberty, riot and licentiousness. It was certainly a little galling to find, that, notwithstanding all your labour and public infamy, you could not be permitted to nominate a friend or dependant to a lucrative post, without the consent of the Thane first meanly obtained. Your little sense of honour might have been touched; but you submitted. After such a slavish submission to the evil genius of England, it was impossible to expect any other effects from your administration than what have happened. We saw every measure pursued with that erring obstinacy which characterizes the Earl of Bute: the ministry were ever in the wrong, and still insisting on the rectitude of their actions: but had their actions been right, we had been obliged to chance; for they cannot, dare not, assert the rectitude of their intentions.

But this may be wandering from the point, in regard to your late resignation. I will proceed to it immediately. The Thane grew weary of being obliged to dictate on every trifling occasion; if he was not continually advising, the helm was all confusion and mistake. He imagined, if he ordered the principal matters, your genius for jockeyship might manage the frivolous. But, though you could not proceed without a director, you had the ministerial vanity to seem to despise the assistance you depended on. The Thane nominated some of his trusty friends to assist you in such cases. Nothing is more natural, than for a beggarly Scot to forget himself in prosperity. Your worthy colleagues, conscious of their superior talents for guiding, were ever assuming an equality, which must disgust a person of less rank and haughtiness than the Duke of G[rafto]n.

This you took occasion to resent. The all-powerful Thane, enraged at such behaviour from a creature his hands had formed, began to exert his authority; and had you not timely resigned, we should have seen you kicked out, with as little ceremony as you were taken in. Thus have I endeavoured to set the matter in a true light, and beg pardon if I have offended in speaking truth.

It is something surprising to hear you complain of being linked in administration with wretches justly the detestation of the public: but was your Grace ever regarded in any other light? Did you give, or receive dishonour from your worthy assistants? That you have not been suffered to pursue your own lenient plans is no matter of wonder, when you were admitted as minister on condition that you proposed no plans of your own.

The people are indeed to be pitied. They have a king, (the best of kings, in the language of flattery,) who never hears the truth. They petition, and are not regarded; and if they assume a becoming spirit of freedom, it is licentiousness.

I shall conclude with observing, that your whole administration has been derogatory to the honour and dignity of the crown; for the honour of the crown is the liberty of the subject.

DECIMUS.

Bristol, Feb. 16, 1770.

LETTER II.

[From the Middlesex Journal, 17th April, 1770.]

To the Princess of Gotham.[1]

IT were an affront to your understanding, to suppose that you are unacquainted with the murmurs of the people concerning you. I hope that many of the aspersions thrown out against you, are as ill-founded as infamous. You cannot forget your dignity so far as to be the tool of power, by which a tyrannous favourite protects his wretches of administration. Your ridiculous vanity in assuming the statesman, and conveying orders dictated by that minion, may make you more contemptible than the meritorious peace-maker you copy from; but till you have his genius for vice, you never will be honoured as the inventor of these master-strokes of tyranny, which we have severely felt. You are reported to be the fountain which feeds the different streams of oppression through the kingdom.

By you, the right of election was, before its perpetration, contrived to be destroyed, the constitu-

[1] *i.e.* the Princess Dowager of Wales, mother of George III. See Letter IV.

tion perverted, and a venal parliament impowered to establish an infamous precedent for future ministers to act upon. By you, men of no principle were thrust into offices they did not know how to discharge, and honoured with trusts they only accepted to violate; being made more conspicuously mean, by communicating error, and often vice, to the character of the person who promoted them. None but a sovereign power can make little villains dangerous; the nobly vicious, the daringly ambitious, only rise from themselves. Without the influence of ministerial authority, Mansfield had been a pettifogging attorney, and Warburton a bustling country curate. The first had not lived to bury the substance of our laws in the shadow of his explanations; nor would the latter have confounded religion with deism, and proved of no use to either. By you, every measure of oppression is ushered into the world; and Sir Gilbert, happy in your private conversation, presumes to direct his lordship in the affairs of the nation: but all the above charges are trifling, when compared to that atrocious one of fomenting discords between the chief magistrate of the people and his subjects. That you possess the royal ear, and employ your influence there in the most dangerous manner, representing the complaints of an injured nation as the voice of faction, and advising a misled ruler to pursue measures which will end in the destruction of his fame: that you have carried ministerial tyranny farther than the most oppressive of the Stuarts dared to do. This is the voice of rumour; with what justice it accuseth you, I dare not singly avouch; but the thoughts of the multitude I have written: their suggestions, their murmurs, increase with their grievances. If a Remonstrance is a libel, the spirit of an Englishman will no more petition for redress, but redress himself. The state of affairs very much resembles the eve of the troubles of Charles the First. Unhappy monarch! thou hast a claim, a dear-bought claim, to our pity; nothing but thy death could purchase it. Hadst thou died quietly, and in peace, thou hadst died infamous: thy misfortunes were the only happy means of saving thee from the book of shame. What a parallel could the freedom of an English pen strike out! Both are misled, and both by women; but may the fate of the former never attend the present; may the future regulation of his conduct compensate for the injured credulity of his youth; may he see for himself, and remember he is a king. Though it may be doubtful, whether the favoured Earl of Bute hangs self-balanced on his own influence, or is greatly little through your partial indulgence; yet all agree that your authority in office supersedes that of the prime minister, who should be the head of the trusts, the three estates jointly repose in him. It would be an usurpation, even in a king, to nominate officers merely from motives of favour. As a magistrate, he should discharge his duty, by honouring with his confidence men of abilities and integrity. But what shall we say, if a woman presumes to intrude such tools as North and Sandwich into offices of the highest trust; and to prefer men to places which require abilities, who neither write nor speak English? What shall we say, but that we are slaves, and ever shall be so, till we know how to free ourselves?

DECIMUS.

Bristol, April 10, 1770.

LETTER III.

[From the Middlesex Journal, 10th May, 1770.]

To the Earl of H[illsboroug]h.[1]

MY LORD,

IF a constant exercise of tyranny and cruelty has not steeled your breast against all sensations of compunction and remorse, permit me to remind you of the recent massacre at Boston.[2] It is an infamous attribute of the ministry of the Thane, that what his tools begin in secret fraud and oppression, ends in murder and avowed assassination. Not contented to deprive us of our liberty, they rob us of our lives; knowing, from a sad experience, that the one without the other is an insupportable burden. Your lordship has bravely distinguished yourself among the ministers of the present reign. Whilst North, and the instruments of his r[oya]l mistress, settled the plan of operations, it was your part to execute; you was the assassin, whose knife was ever ready to finish the

---

[1] Lord Hillsborough, appointed as a third secretary of state, for the conduct of American affairs.

[2] On the 5th of March, 1770.

cause. If every feeling of humanity is not extinct in you, reflect, for a moment reflect, on the horrid task you undertook and perpetrated. Think of the injury you have done to your country, which nothing but the dissolution of a parliament, not representing the people, can ever erase. Think of the odium you and your coherents have thrown on the character of a [king], unhappy in the choice of his ministers, and blind obedience to maternal authority: that [king], whose innocent credulity is the ruin of our constitution; whose undesigning simplicity will injure us more than the most tyrannous incroachments of the Stuarts; who deserves to be beloved when by himself, but should not be permitted to run blindly into destruction, by adopting the violent proceedings of his unworthy ministers.

Think of the recent murders at Boston. O my lord! however you may force a smile into your countenance, however you may trifle in the train of dissipation, your conscience must raise a hell within. I cannot think you so hardened a ruffian as to view without concern the miseries you have occasioned. If greatly villainous, you could rejoice in the ruin of a nation—the distresses of a private family, the cries of the widow, must awaken the torture of your soul. Since your lordship first sold yourself to the infamy of a minister, to draw in the Team of the Witch of the Isle, what has been your reward? The Duke of Grafton had very little to give of anything, but disgrace and infamy: of that you greatly partook. But pecuniary recompenses were seldom to be met with: his Grace had a strong passion for gaming; the immense sums which his r[oya]l mistress issued out to pay the troop of titled vassals, and keep them from mutiny, were lavished by his Grace on the dice, Arabella, and Newmarket. You, and instruments of more consequence, have more than once been baulked of your pay. Mungo protests, no city porter could be more laborious or worse paid.—Titles were sufficiently prostituted in the dignified persons of Barrington, Grafton, and Clare; your lordship could incur no additional contempt by a ducal crown:—indeed, you sought it not; warned by the disappointment of Rigby, not to sollicit what you could never obtain. Poor Rigby! whose labour in carrying so long the burthen of state, could not entitle him to a barony, to stamp his infamy with his coat of arms on his posterity.

How then could your lordship receive reward, adequate to the merit of your services, but by place? There was no other method to recompense your former servitudes, than by engaging you in a new one which would be its own reward. In your department you have behaved consistently; tyranny made you a secretary, and you governed tyrannically: the last bloody transaction is written in characters indelible, and will make you detested to the latest posterity.

DECIMUS.

Bristol, April 27, [1770].

LETTER IV.

[From the Middlesex Journal, 15th May, 1770.]

To the P[rincess] D[owager] of W[ales].

YOU are called upon by the united voices of all the friends of liberty and their country, to vindicate your conduct. When the fate of the nation trembles upon a minute, it is no time to trifle: ceremony and an appearance of respect must give way to plain truth and sincerity. The constitution has already suffered too much by an ill-timed veneration for the [king]. 'Tis now the duty of an Englishman who is a loyal subject, to throw off the unnecessary covering, and attempt to open the eyes of his misled s[overeign]. To tell him boldly who are his enemies, and to assist him in removing those enemies from his confidence. I am willing to believe that you are not the principal agent in the misfortunes of the present reign: you may be duped by the artifices of a villain, who has found the way to impose on your good nature, and make himself of consequence in your eyes. You may be imposed upon as well as his [majesty]; but that you have been instrumental in those transactions is undoubted: your influence in the ministerial junto cannot be denied. I would wish your

R[oyal] H[ighness] would know how to act worthy your situation in life; and not debase yourself by mingling with a group of ministers, the most detestable that ever embroiled a kingdom in discord and commotion. Your consequence in the council can arise only from your power over his [majesty]; and that power you possess but by the courtesy of an unaccountable infatuation. Filial duty has nothing to do with the question; a king has no mother, no wife, no friend, considered as a king; his country, his subjects, are the only objects of his public concern. It is amazing to me that his [majesty] cannot, or at least does not, distinguish between private obligations and public: whatever respect you claim from the former, you have no title to any on the latter account: though as a mother you might be commendable, yet, as a subject you are highly blameable: you have associated with his enemies; avowedly and openly assisted those enemies in their most criminal designs; and did all you could do to bury the fortunes of the [king] in the constitution of the country: you have estranged from him the hearts of his subjects, and left him only the infamous approbation of a v—— c—— P———. One of the three kingdoms expressed themselves highly satisfied with your conduct: they might have said highly obliged to it, if conferring infamy with places or pensions is conferring an obligation. But the friendship of Scotland is not to be depended upon; it is ominous. His [majesty] has made but an ill exchange in bartering the hearts and approbations of two kingdoms; he might have trusted with safety for the pretended friendship of one, which never was trusted but to betray.

To your kind management of his infant years may, with justice, be attributed all the past, present, and future troubles and misfortunes of his reign. Bred to notions of despotism, and instructed to govern by a warm stickler for monarchy and tyranny, could we look for any milder measures than his [majesty] has taken? Our [sovereign] has been more unfortunate than he could possibly deserve, since his misfortunes began almost with his birth. Instead of being put under the care of an able tutor, who could teach him how to rule the hearts of his people, he was left to the tuition of one who, had he wished to do otherwise, could instruct him only how to make himself feared and hated. His [majesty]'s education may be considered as the foundation on which all his misfortunes are or will be raised. It was the interest of the Earl of Bute, as a firm friend to the house of Stuart, to instil into him principles which should not fail to ruin him in the love of the people, and make the throne totter under the house of Hanover. This was his plan. Let us now consider how he has succeeded. His [majesty] imbibed every pernicious tenet he was taught to support his regal dignity with: he looked upon his future crown as something which should exalt him above the state of mortal men, and was filled with every poison of absolute monarchy. Bute saw with rapture the improvement of the predestinated t[yrant]: he had studied the tempers of the English, and hoped to give them a [sovereign] who should disgust; such a [sovereign] whose behaviour should make his subjects wish for another. How unhappy must a m[onarch] be, thus destined to abuse his dignity! whose repeated lesson was, to maintain the authority of the crown at the expense of the rights of the subject: who was taught that kings are the representatives of God, and answerable to none for their conduct. But, thank heaven! though this pernicious doctrine is so deeply inculcated on the mind of our S[overeign], it has not had the desired effect; spite of the united efforts of you, the Earl of Bute, and the Cocoa-tree, an opposition too powerful for you to quash, will frustrate every design you can inflame. Mr. Wilkes stands now at the head of this opposition: in him you find an enemy, as long as you are an enemy to the constitution of this country; his enmity extends no further; it has nothing meanly personal. As he fights in a glorious cause, he scorns to debase that cause, by copying the littleness which characterised your resentment against him. Whilst the Duke of Cumberland lived, he checked the progress of your diabolical junto. Conscious of his integrity, you desponded of soothing him; and fearing his rigorous justice, you kept out of sight as much as the posture of affairs would permit you. Notwithstanding the many obligations this country was under to him, by his delivering us from the tyranny of a Stuart; and then preserving us from falling into the ministerial slavery of a friend to the Stuarts: you and the junto had the daring insolence to asperse his sacred character, and endeavoured to rob him of the love of the people;

but that love was founded on a basis your strongest endeavours could not shake—his virtue. The Earl of Bute gloried in the infamy of having manufactured the peace; he did not so avowedly confess that by your help he had established it. The Stuarts were ever fond of peace, and loved to bask in the sunshine of public tranquillity: intestine broils only dignify their annals. The granting this dishonourable peace, was the first means of beginning a domestic war: the nation was in general displeased at it; a revenge for the many undeserved injuries we had received from our continual enemies, was just, was laudable; and granting them a cessation of arms, was only giving them time to prepare themselves for future hostilities. The French, at the close of the war, were in the utmost distress; the navy but small, and out of repair; the army imbecilitated, and on the point of mutiny; and the whole nation trembling under the English flag, and dissatisfied with the conduct of their ministers. The best attribute of the king is mercy; but it was certainly here ill-timed. How can we sufficiently admire the clemency, which so royally condescended to stop the torrent of blood, and sheathe the ravaging sword of war, by ceding all our valuable conquests, which had cost us so much blood; (but, in the system of the present ministry, English blood is of no estimation:) whilst, in the humility of our desires, we retained whatever could be of no use to us, and was but an incumbrance to the enemy? This concession shall bear the name of Bute to posterity, and grace his monument with the infamy he so richly deserves. The French are again in high spirits; they see the prospect brighten on every side, and are vigorously preparing every necessary material for the carrying on a future war, with better accommodations, and, in all probability, better success. No sooner had our glorious monarch given peace to Europe, but he began to turn his thoughts on the ease which peace allowed him; but you, stung with resentment at the writings of a man obnoxious to your favoured minister, the Earl of Bute, disturbed his serenity. Unaccountable are the prejudices of age: what could so bias you to that enemy of this country, is to me a mystery I cannot dive into. The 'North Briton' contained facts, which could not be evaded by a plain denial. An affirmation that it was a seditious libel, was not sufficient to invalidate its arguments. However, Mr. Wilkes having gloriously headed the opposition, and given great disgust by divulging important truths which should not be told; you began a persecution which does honour to his fortitude, and displays how little it is in your power to injure his noble spirit. You have continued this persecution with all the littleness which distinguishes the creatures of the Ministry; you have humbled yourself to the meanest offices in the state, and acted only as a mere machine of convenience, by which the Thane received the approbation of — — May you be taught what your birth and royal alliances require; and make a better use of the gifts which fortune has so blindly lavished upon you.

DECIMUS.

May 10, 1770.

LETTER V.

[From the Middlesex Journal, 22nd May, 1770.]

To the Prime Minister.[1]

MY LORD,

AS a lover of justice, I cannot see you blamed for measures in which you act only in obedience to a higher power, without endeavouring to vindicate you. It is an unfortunate circumstance that you are saddled with the title of premier: people who know nothing of the matter think you act as such. —It shall be my task to inform them better, and rescue the reputation of an innocent servant from ruin. As character is all menial slaves have to depend upon, 'tis a cruelty beneath humanity to deprive you of your only support, by indulging the caprice of patriotism, and mistaking the servant for the master.

That we have suffered in regard to our liberties is undoubted; that the constitution is now falling to decay, nothing but the fee'd conscience of Sir Fletcher Norton can deny. But they are infants in politics who charge you, or even his Grace, with the whole infamy of these glorious transactions.— No—there are still higher powers, from whose hands we are to expect good or evil; and yet this is not the k[ing]. I am charitable enough to be-

[1] Lord North. See Letter IX.

lieve his majesty is no more a principal than your lordship: the only difference between you I take to be this, the one is paid and the other pays, and dearly too, for his labour. Who these higher powers are is no secret; their influence has been felt since the last memorable peace, and their influence is now laying in additional causes to increase the distractions of this unhappy kingdom.

As a servant to these powers I have nothing to accuse YOU with: you have implicitly obeyed every command which Jeremiah Dyson has honoured you with. I feel some little hurt to my pride, as an Englishman, in seeing a thing which represents a minister, the director of the affairs of the nation, degraded so low as to be the servant of titled valets and petty clerks.

Sir Gilbert mouths his orders like an oracle; he speaks by inspiration from above, and his word is fate. The merit of this favoured counsellor is a little uncommon; his talents are too contemptible for examination: in the mid-way state, between a city alderman and idiotcy, he has all that little cunning which distinguishes fools; his talkative qualifications are not worth notice; and yet he is a chief director in the first junto of the state. His only merit lies in what he has seen—what he has heard—and what he has read concerning certain matters of which we speak darkly. But how, in the name of wonder, can those accomplishments qualify him for the council-board? It might be the means of richly shutting his mouth, and none but a German genius would make it instrumental in learning him to speak. The insolence of this confidant is great: the Duke of Grafton thought it insupportable; but your lordship has less pride than his Grace, perhaps less commendable pride.

From him and his colleagues flow, through the channel of your office, every measure which meets with deserved opposition.

You are only the porter in these matters: it is not for your humble hopes to aspire to the assertion of your right.

Conscious of the influence of the personage, who took you from a dependent, menial service of the Duke of Bedford, and raised you to the empty dignity of state, you let that personage preside, and, conscious of what you was, learn to obey. Humility is a capital Christian virtue, but not a political one; a little constitutional pride would do your country more service than all the virtues your irreverend hireling can daub you with.

You may be a good husband—a good father—I cannot deny it, I know nothing of your concerns; but private virtues, or private vices, in a minister, are of no public account: I look not to the man, but to the tool of state, the slave of an infamous association, composed of creatures exalted out of obscurity only by their villainy; and headed by a person an Englishman must blush to name. But, my lord, as you are the instrument of conveyance, through you I lay before the junto the following queries, written by an Englishman, who dares to assert in person whatever he has advanced here.

Is there among the infamous association at Carlton-house, one member, daring enough to acknowledge himself a limb of that infernal body?

Has any one measure of consequence been taken since the accession of his present majesty, but what was planned, or approved of, by the Earl of Bute and the Princess Dowager of Wales?

Was Mr. Wilkes's offence the 'North Briton,' the 'Essay on Woman,' or only a private quarrel with the Princess Dowager—he, as an Englishman, having dared to assert what he knew?

Has the Carlton-house gang one man of repute among them? Or can the talents of any individual, or the whole string of rogues, be thought capable of directing the state?

Is there one honest man now in the administration of public affairs? If there is one, let him be pointed out, for the author cannot find him!

These queries are submitted to the consciences of the ministerial troop, though the writer fears that conscience has lost her force in the breast of that statesman, who could plunge his country into such a ruin as now seems to hang over it. You, my lord, how mean and servile soever your department is, may be of some use in averting the impending storm. Fly to the council, with your face whitened with fear: tell them, that justice is at the door, and the axe will do its office: tell them, whilst the spirit of English freedom exists, vengeance has also an existence; and when Britons are denied justice from the powers who have the trust of their rights, the constitution hath given them a power to do themselves justice.

DECIMUS.

May 15, 1770.

LETTER VI.

[From the Middlesex Journal, 26th May, 1770.]

AS we live to see the polite arts possess the place which liberty and the good of the constitution should be honoured with in his majesty's favour and protection, I flatter myself that the following criticisms on an exhibition of sign-paintings, may not be beneath the notice of the virtû.

DECIMUS.

May 17, 1770.

FIRST DAY'S EXHIBITION.

"1. *The Whore of Babylon, by the Whisperer.* This is an old piece new touched, and, by several masterly features, appears to have been once the P[rincess] D[owager] of W[ales].

"2. *A North Prospect of Carlton-House, by the same.* With what propriety can this be called a prospect? It represents three rogues in a gin-shop, sharing their last acquired booty; one, in the dress of an Highlander, is taking some innocent familiarities with the bawd, who sits above on an empty hogshead.

"3. *The Union, by the North Briton.* An Englishman sleeping, and a Scotchman picking his pocket.

"4. *The K[ing]*; a sign for a button maker. The painter, who has not fixed his name to this performance, is certainly a very loyal subject. His m[ajesty] has that innocent vacancy of countenance which distinguishes the representation of angels and cherubims; without guilt, without meaning; without every thing but an undesigning simplicity.

"5. *A Conversation-piece, by the Whisperer.* This is a daring performance: it represents the member of a certain council-board. The principal figures are, the president receiving instructions from an old woman; and the k[ing] chewing thistles.

"6. ———. A great personage, and a greater personage, receiving orders from the Earl of Bute.

"7. *The Marquis of Granby;* a sign for a turner. This is an old Janus, modernized by the addition of a regimental coat.

"8. *The modern Demosthenes.* An alderman reading a speech from the crown of his hat: the gravity of this orator's countenance is finely touched; and none but those who have seen Sir Richard Glynn, can form an idea of it.

"9. *We three Loggerheads, by Germanicus.* Represents the Czarina and the Grand Signor boxing. The former appears to have the advantage, and has a label coming out of her mouth, with these words, *I have learnt to drub.* The latter is frighted at the appearance of a candle in the tail of a kite, which he mistakes for a comet. The third figure is the King of Prussia, who is stripping for the combat, and seems eager to engage. There is great humour preserved throughout the whole piece.

"10. *Sir Robert Ladbroke;* a sign for a gin-shop. The revolutions of fortune are worthy the meditations of a Hervey. The father of the city, after having directed the affairs of the metropolis, can now only direct an old woman where to get drunk.

"11. *The genius of Bristol, by Bonner.* Represents a fish-woman sleeping on a cask; her shield a cheese, with her arms blazoned; three hogs couchant in the mire; her lance a spit, with a goose on it. There are several smaller figures in the groupe; a turn-spit dog, a sleeping alderman, and a Welch rabbit.

SECOND DAY'S EXHIBITION.

"12. *A Piece of Modern Antiquity, by Horace Walpole.* This is no other than a striking portrait of the facetious Mrs. Clive. Horace, finding it too large to be introduced in his next edition of Virtû, has returned it on the town.

"13. *The Dragoon dragooned, by Marplot.* This is an excellent piece, and has but one deficiency—it wants meaning. It represents Lord Barrington firing a musket with his eyes shut; and a great personage shooting at him with a bow and arrow; under the latter are these words, 'A fool's bolt is soon shot.'

"14. *Taste, by Phillipina Burton.* A complication of elegant figures: the design seems a little perplexed; colouring, very masterly and strong.

"15. *The Masquerade, by Truth.* Represents the court on a levee day: the company are masked in their own faces only.

"16. *The Jubilee, by Garrick.* The painter in the character of the bottle-conjurer. In his hand is a book, inscribed, 'The way to grow rich, a ballad farce.'

" 17. *Fortitude, by Hugh Kelly.* This has no relation to the fortitude of this unfortunate author, in bidding defiance to the censure of the town: the piece will turn to more account; it represents the ministry.

" 18. *A Word to the Wise, by the same.* The painter *in propriâ personâ*, holdin[illegible] purse in one hand, and a catcall in the othe[illegible]

" 19. *All in the Wrong,* [illegible] *Director.* The court of directors, fighting on t[illegible]ount of a certain general, who in the mea[illegible] is making off with the bullion.

STATUES, &c.

" 20. *The Earl of Bute.* The English and Scotch disagree concerning th[illegible] figure. The connoisseurs of the latter assert that it is not perfect, because it wants a head; whilst the opposite party as strenuously maintain that it could not be perfect unless it wanted a head.

" 21. *His M[ajesty].* Some sacrilegious villains having stolen the former head, which was lacquered with gold, the exhibitor hath supplied the deficiency with a wooden one.

" 22. *Mr. Wilkes in a Roman habit.* A bold majestic figure; in his right hand the Bill of Rights, and in the other the sword of justice.

" 23. *The Harlot's Progress, by the Duchess of K——, in Silk.* It were to be wished that ladies of quality would employ their time as well as her Grace has done. It is really surprising to see how well she has played her own cards, and kept one of the higher powers from losing the game.

"24. *The Keeper, by Miss R———.* Represents the notorious Jemmy Twitcher, licking the dust from the feet of his Dulcinea; whilst her fille-de-chambre conveys away her gallant. Jemmy, for the greater propriety, is black and all black.

"25. *The last Peace.* Modelled in gingerbread, and ready to fall in pieces with the slightest touch."

LETTER VII.

[From the Middlesex Journal, May 31, 1770.]

To the Freeholders of the City of Bristol.

Gentlemen,

As a fellow-citizen, I presume to address you on a subject, which I hoped would have animated an abler pen. At this critical situation, when the fate of the constitution depends upon the exertion of an English spirit, I confess my astonishment at finding you silent. The second city in England should not be ashamed to copy the first, in any laudable measure. Let not a false pride mislead you to neglect the care of your liberties. Tho' you were not the first in the spirited application to the throne, you will lose no glory in the imitation. Your silence cannot be attributed to your disapprobation of the proceedings of the Livery of London.

When an infamous set of wretches take shelter under the dignity of the crown, and from that sacred covert, wound the dearest rights of the subject; it is pusillanimity, it is a treason to our country, to view it with indifference.

The reception your petition met with, should animate you to demand a satisfactory answer to the grievances you complained of: and if you cannot have redress, know on what pretence you are denied that justice. The apostacy of one of your former leaders can be no detriment to your measures; he is too inconsiderable to disconcert an affair of so much importance as your liberty and the constitution of your country. Reflect on the importance of the measure you are under an obligation to take. It is not a transient emolument you seek: it is the inheritance of your posterity; an inheritance, without which all other possessions will be unserviceable.

Whilst thus you sit idly looking on, you do society the greatest injury it is in your power to do it. As subjects, Englishmen, and members of society, you are under a necessity to endeavour to preserve inviolate the freedom of an Englishman.

If, after every glorious attempt to rescue our invaluable rights from the wretches of power, the pernicious counsels of persons, who are a disgrace to their dignities, should still mislead an unhappy k[ing], and effectually prevent the purpose of your remonstrance; you have done your duty, and discharged your conscience.—But till you have done your duty by remonstrating, you are accessory to every future proceeding of the tools of administration; and equally concerned in every scene of murder and oppression, which the ruffians of state have chalked out in their plan of operations.

I do not address myself to the corporation: I know too well their selfish regard to interest. In the cause of liberty, they will gain nothing but the consciousness of having done a good action; a pleasure so long a stranger to the breast of any one of them, that none can know how to deserve it. They are too contemptible to injure the cause of liberty by their authority; and too mercenary to seduce any of its leaders by their generosity. How meanly infamous have they made themselves, in selling their consciences to the man, whose conscience they once bought. Lord C[lare], however titled and outwardly advanced in the world, is still internally the little wretch he ever was. It must be confessed he has cunning; but that is the common qualification of a pick-pocket: had he been born in a lower station in life, he must have been one. He is a slave to slaves; and has even his vices, though in large quantities, from second hand. Nothing can reflect with greater acrimony on the intellects of the corporation, than the whole tenor of their behaviour to Lord C[lare]: as it is generally known, so it is too ridiculous for recapitulation. No person could with greater propriety than Lord C[lare] represent the corporation of Bristol; he is their very counterpart, little, mean, and contemptible.—But I lose time upon them.

To you, then, ye citizens of Bristol, who look

above such mercenary examples—to you, who have honour and disinterestedness, I address myself. Be it your task to take off the load of shame, which your superiors in command throw upon the city. Look not to their superiority in office, but to their inferiority in principle, spirit, and real worth. Now is the moment to prove yourselves Englishmen, and disappoint the evil designs of the enemies of this country.

Remember the speech of the glorious CANYNGE,[1] in whose repeated mayoralties honour and virtue were not unknown in the corporation. When the unhappy dissensions first broke out between the houses of Lancaster and York, he immediately declared himself for the latter. His lady, fearful of the consequences, begged him to desist, and not ruin himself and family. "My family," replied the brave citizen, "is dear to me—Heaven can witness how dear! But when discord and oppressions begin to distract the realm, my country is my family; and THAT it is my duty to protect."

DECIMUS.

London, May 21, [1770.]

---

[1] Misprinted COMYNGE. See vol. ii. p. 211.

LETTER VIII.

[From the Political Register, June, 1770.]

To the Lord Mayor.[1]

My Lord,

THE steps you have hitherto taken in the service of your country, demand the warmest thanks the gratitude of an Englishman can give. That you will persevere in the glorious task, is the wish of every one who is a friend to the constitution of this country. Your integrity insures you from falling into the infamy of apostacy; and your understanding is a sufficient guard against the secret measures of the ministry, who are vile enough to stick at no villainy to complete their detestable purposes: nor can your British heart stoop to fear the contemptible threatenings of a set of hireling wretches, who have no power but what they derive from a person who engrosses every power and every vice. The spirit of the city has been displayed in that of its chief magistrate, in a general, as well as orderly endeavour to recover our liberties from the hands of a tyrannous junto of slaves, who would mutilate every shadow of right, law and justice. The military has been creeping upon us expedi-

[1] This letter is undoubtedly by Chatterton. It was addressed to Wm. Beckford, Esq., who died June 21, 1770, almost at the time of its publication. See Wilson's Life of Chatterton, p. 266.

tiously; it now begins to take large strides, in upholding the infamy of government, and inforcing that article of state faith, *passive obedience.* The massacres at St. George's-fields and Boston, still reek in our memories: the latter could not be glossed over with the least colour of excuse. They had been threatened with a military plague; they endeavoured to avert the curse, but in vain. Obstinacy is one of the first attributes of the administration of the creatures of the Earl of Bute; and this diabolical firmness, in every wrong step he has taken, has not a little sullied the character of his present M[ajest]y. Sent to protect their lives, and rob them of their liberty, every soldier had his commission. Insolence was to be observed to the inhabitants of the town, and implicit obedience to the commands of their villainous officers. What will not the resolution of a ruffian ministry effect! —We exist to see our countrymen wantonly murdered for the heinous offence of a pretended riot; and murderers, avowed murderers, pardoned, from doubts which arise from within or without the royal breast. If the massacre of the Bostonians was not concerted by the ministry, they were to be enslaved in consequence of a settled plan; and as the one was the result of the other, our worthy ministers were the assassins. Alas! the unhappy town had not a Beckford! He would have checked the audacious insolence of the army; and dared, as an Englishman, to make use of his freedom. Here, though under the eye of the secretary, no officer has had the fortitude to engage in the bloody cause, conscious that detestation and public hatred will attend the unsatisfactory promotion which the ministry could bestow. The city of London is too considerable to be treated with the forced contempt the hirelings of the crown attempt to look upon it with. Its petition may be considered as the voice of the nation; and none but a king, either lost to all feelings of humanity, or lost to himself in pride, would slight the petition of his subjects. His majesty's behaviour, when he received the complaints of his people, (not to redress them, indeed, but to get rid of them an easier way) was something particular: it was set, formal, and studied.—Should you address again, my lord, it would not be amiss to tell his Majesty, that you expect *his* answer, and not the answer of his mother or ministers.—You complain not to them, but of them; and, would they redress our grievances, they can only do it by doing justice on themselves, and being their own executioners. Your perseverance in the glorious cause will check the rapid progress of oppression, and extort a conclusive answer from the ministry, through the mouth of his Majesty, whether they are resolved to continue the system of tyranny, and brave the vengeance of an oppressed, but injured people; or, conscious of the danger of their situation, let the reins of arbitrary power relax, and endeavour to appease the fury of the public, by dissolving a parliament the most venal and contemptible that ever disgraced the nation? A parliament which, not representing the people, are continually heaping additional oppressions and impositions to the insupportable burthen laid on us before; who have given sanction to an act which deprives themselves of their liberties and privileges, in the most corrupt administration of former times, held sacred and inviolate. An Englishman, who petitions for a dissolution of this tainted body—and what Englishman, who has any regard for his own liberties, or the interest of his country, that does not?—The man who approves of the British spirit, which your lordship and your worthy assistants display, cannot be bound by laws made by a parliament, whose authority he does not allow, and to submit to laws issued from such a house, is acknowledging their legality; an acknowledgment, I hope, you will never make. Their mischiefs are now near being suspended for a time. Would his M[ajesty] take reason, and not prejudice, for his guide, that time might be prolonged, and a dissolution pave the way to a reformation in the state: a blessing which, I fear, whilst his M[ajesty]'s present infatuation continues, we shall never possess. The chief violation of the rights of the nation is in that of election. It is with propriety that this complaint is continually brought upon the carpet; since, in this one oppression is involved every other oppression tyranny could invent. The constitution could not be stabbed deeper, than by the proceedings of the ministry in the Middlesex election; the wound is mortal: palliatives are of no service: nothing but an amputation of the member which struck the blow can be beneficial: even that will fail, unless the k[ing] pursues a conduct quite opposite to that he is now erring in, and makes choice of ministers the reverse of the present creatures of administration.—The whole fabric of British Liberty is built on the Right of Election: how daring then must that minister be, who can, in defiance of conscience, law, and justice, violate this right, and support that despicable creature Col. Luttrell, in his pretensions to a seat in the House of Commons! What a gross affront to the freeholders of Middlesex, to suppose him their representative! I am sorry to say, there are many such representatives in the house; and, when we complain that Mr. Wilkes is not admitted, we have also sufficient reason to make an article of complaint, that many who were admitted are not expelled. It is not so much a matter of wonder, that we find many whose birth and fortune enable them to live independent, and in absolute freedom, selling those invaluable blessings for an empty title, or the greater meanness of mercenary views, as to find a man, whose elevated rank is temptation, preserve himself untainted with the too-general disease. Your lordship has proved the goodness of your heart, the soundness of your principles, and the merit of the cause in which you are engaged, by the rectitude of your conduct. Scandal maddens at your name, because she finds nothing to reproach you with; and the venal hirelings of the ministry despair of meriting their pay by blackening your character. Illiberal[1] abuse, and gross inconsistencies and absurdities, recoil upon the author; and only bear testimony of the weakness of his head, or the badness of his heart.

[1] Printed "Illiberate."

That man, whose enemies can find nothing to lay to his charge, may well dispense with the incoherent Billingsgate of a ministerial writer.

A man in a public character is in a very tender situation; his virtues are magnified, and his vices exaggerated. Your Lordship has maintained your reputation gloriously, though we are never at a loss to give your merit a proper share of applause: the opposite party must have recourse to fals[e]-hood, when they accuse you of vices. The city of London has, in an extraordinary manner, testified the opinion of your abilities; and at a time when Liberty, and all an Englishman holds sacred, was at stake, reposed a trust in you which, were you to betray, would inevitably ruin the constitution of this country.—I would ask a troop of gartered vassals, could the most misguided favour of a King, the greatest reward of a minister, bestow such an honour as has been bestowed upon you? Birth and fortune were not the bribes which purchased it: an unshaken fidelity, a tried integrity, and the spirit of a Briton, actuating a man whose private life is irreproachable; that and that only, deserved and received it. The important trusts thus reposed in you, could be nowhere in greater safety. Those accomplishments which made you worthy to receive it, continue to make you worthy of keeping it. Every step you have taken speaks the patriot; and your undaunted perseverance in insisting on redress, does honour to the choice of the city. Without such a check on their actions, whither might not the villainy of our ministers have carried them? Is there any privilege, ever so sacred, which they hesitate to violate? Your conduct, and the steady opposition of your friends, restrain the torrent of their arbitrary proceedings. Though they have too much power to be quelled in an instant, you have confined their illegal ravages within bounds; and may it be in your power to open the eyes of an unfortunate monarch, and restore liberty and tranquillity to an unfortunate people. As you only were thought capable of preserving the rights of the subject from the imminent danger which threatened us, exert your active spirit, and tell the tools of oppression, that the power of the chief magistrate of the city is capable of counteracting that of the servants of the Earl of Bute: and, with the same spirited resolution which has dignified your conduct hitherto, support the glorious cause in which you preside. If we must lose the birthright of Englishmen, let us not tamely lose it. However the misrepresentations of the enemies of this country may mislead his Majesty's judgment, he may be yet open to conviction; he may redeem the errors of his past conduct, by discarding his pernicious counsellors, dissolving an infamous parliament, and reposing confidence in his people: but it behoves us not to live idly in hope of this reformation: let us, as much as possible, put it forward ourselves. Let us with one united voice demand redress, if again refused: let us take the sword of justice in our hands and punish the wretches whose evil councils have estranged his Majesty from the good of the subject, and robbed him of his surest safeguard, the love of his people.

PROBUS.

LETTER IX.[1]

To the Right Hon. the Earl of Dartmouth.

My Lord,

AN honest, independent Englishman, who detests flattery and adulation, in sincerity of heart congratulates your lordship on your appointment to the important charge of conducting the affairs of the British colonies. The whole nation applauds the happy choice his majesty has made of so able, so conscientious, so temperate a minister. It is considered as a favourable presage of a change of sentiments at court. The public in general form the highest expectations, from your unspotted character, from your known attachment to the principles of religious and civil liberty, and from your generous concern for the welfare of your country, that you will exert the influence you cannot fail to acquire in the closet, to protect, to countenance, and support, the just pretensions of all his majesty's subjects to partake alike of his paternal care and affection.

In a future address I may have the honour to propose some conciliating measures, to be taken at home, to render every branch of administration

[1] From Dix's Life of Chatterton. Dix says it appeared in the Political Register, but I cannot find it there; and, notwithstanding the signature "Probus," I doubt if it is Chatterton's.

equally popular, and to make the people almost adore their sovereign: but for the present I shall confine myself to those objects which fall within your particular department.

There have been times, my lord, when an arbitrary minister would not have been permitted to steal out of office with impunity, after having shamefully oppressed one part of the British empire, still groaning beneath the tyranny of his dictatorial power. But we have now been long used to see the worst services the best rewarded; and the last instance is that of your predecessor, the scourge of America, who, if he had continued his notorious mal-administration of the colonies only a few months longer, would have found the weight of the just indignation of his American brethren too heavy for him to have borne. Apprehensive of this, he dexterously avoided the impending blow by stepping aside. In his native obscurity let us leave him, while I lay before your lordship the actual state of one of the British settlements, which, instead of being made a most valuable acquisition to the mother country, by the commercial benefits to be derived from it, has been rendered the seat of internal discord and commotion, through the violent measures of the abandoned tools of his power.

Your lordship cannot be a stranger to the disputes which have subsisted in the ceded island of GRANADA,[1] from the time that the form of government, established and amicably settled by the first governor, on the basis of the treaty of peace, and

[1] See the Political Register, Jan. 1770; p. 52.

in conformity to the king's proclamation, was altered, or rather subverted, by the mandates, private instructions, and other prerogative acts of the crown, impoliticly obtained, and illegally issued from your predecessor's office. The repeated petitions and memorials of the king's natural born subjects on this head ought to be found in your office: for persuaded as the injured parties are, that Lord Hillsborough never let them have access to the throne, they doubt not the preservation of them by the vigilance of the official secretary. These papers will save me the trouble of recapitulating the progress of despotism in Granada, till it arrived at its full height by the last acts of your predecessor's administration. The manœuvres of the lieutenant-governor Fitzmaurice (the prototype of Sir Francis Bernard), of his jesuitical secretary Staunton, and of all the abettors of the French party, Mr. Pownall has long since got by heart; and if your lordship wants further information relative to the same subject, I can refer you to abler and better authorities. It shall therefore be my business to take up the matter (in this matter) where my brother-writers seem to have left it; and to convince your lordship that it is highly expedient, from the present posture of affairs in Granada, to reverse all the measures of your predecessor respecting its government, without loss of time.

On the strength of a promise made by the Duke of Grafton, to seat as many as he possibly could of his jockey and gaming companions in ministerial saddles, Gordon was sent to Brussels, and Leybourne to Granada. The latter, a young man, who had never had the least experience of public affairs, was appointed to a government of the most delicate nature, rendered still more so by the odious measures that had been taken to enforce obedience to unconstitutional mandates. Without countenance, without any persuasive influence, without any fixed principle within himself, but that of making his fortune by an implicit submission to his singular instructions, he has dared to accomplish, to complete, as far as in him lies, Lord Hillsborough's illegal, oppressive plan.

The house of representatives of the British subjects of Granada, is at present composed of members chosen by the united interest of the French and Irish Roman Catholic subjects; persons of low and mean situations in life, needy dependants on the French adopted subjects, with but one Englishman amongst them, and he a man of no consequence, are the respectable legislative body of this unfortunate island. These men, under the direction of a raw governor, and an overbearing attorney-general, (who supplanted a modest, humane, equitable man) have no objection to act in conjunction with the French Roman Catholic members, who, contrary to the first constitution of the island, have been admitted to sit in the assembly, and have been sworn into the king's council by prerogative mandates.

But all the British subjects of property in the island, who are animated by a sense of their duty to their native country, are determined not to acknowledge the legality of any acts passed by such an assembly. They positively refuse, and will persist, to the last extremity, in refusing to pay any taxes imposed upon them by disqualified members of the council and house of representatives; and the universal disgust taken to the governor increases the confusion: in short it has overpowered him and his master. Mr. Leybourne is in a languid state of health, and Lord Hillsborough has wisely retired to Ireland.

In this state of affairs no public business can proceed, for no act of the government will be deemed valid so long as Mr. Leybourne enforces his instructions, and commands British subjects to admit French Roman Catholic subjects to privileges appertaining solely to Protestant natives. The necessity, therefore, of recalling the present governor, of dissolving the present assembly, and of restoring the first, the only legal form of government established in this island, shall be made apparent, and some other obnoxious steps of which I have just received advice, shall be laid before your lordship in my next; the friends of the natural-born subjects in London being well assured that they shall find in you, my lord, an impartial judge, who will not add to their sufferings by misrepresenting their conduct to his majesty.

PROBUS.

LETTER X.

[From the Freeholder's Magazine; Aug. 1770.]

To Lord N[ort]h.

MY LORD,

THERE is not, perhaps, a more exalted and refined pleasure than that which we feel from the contemplation of the great and illustrious characters of antiquity. Indeed, we partake so much in their exploits, and imbibe so much of their virtues, that while we read, we may be said "to live o'er each scene." What threw me into this train of reflection at present, my lord, was reading the history of my favourite prince, Caligula. What a happiness must it have been, my lord, to have lived under the auspicious reign of that emperor, who was as munificent in rewarding merit as he was sagacious in the discovery of it; indeed he took such a fatherly care in providing for the good of his subjects, that at last discovering a genius where it was least expected, in his *horse* I mean, he advanced him to the first honours of the state. The emperor had, no doubt, my lord, suffered by the ignorance and misconduct of former counsellors; and willing to appease the justly incensed people, he did not chuse *anything* for a minister, as some later monarchs have done, but he took to support the weight of government this faithful and generous beast of burden.

This conduct of Caligula, my lord, was perhaps owing to gratitude, as well as to sagacity; the minister in question having long before *firmly supported* him in an *inferior* capacity. That your lordship had attempted something of a like nature, in *doing the business of the crown*, as it is called, is allowed by your enemies; but whether this was sufficient to entitle you to a similar degree of eminence is yet to be decided. We were all, my lord, surprised at your sudden exaltation; nor, I dare say, my lord, when your noble father pressed you to accept of the *premiership*, did your lordship immediately recollect this precedent in your favour.

But to return, my lord. Notwithstanding this prudent choice in Caligula, there were not then wanting in Rome some dangerous incendiaries, who misrepresented this step, painting it in the most ridiculous colours. To all this the minister was silent, not from a consciousness of guilt, but from a natural aversion he entertained to party debate. Indeed it was commonly objected to him, that he was *no speaker* in their house, or senate; but we, my lord, at this enlightened period, cannot sufficiently admire his *dumb administration*.

I am sorry, my lord, history has been defective in many things requisite to be known of this great minister; I mean his birth, progenitors, and education; not that the latter is of much consequence in one placed so near, and in some measure related to the crown. Many, I know, are desirous of being informed of his person and private life, whether he was fitted for a whiskey or a dung-cart; a sprightly nobleman, or a country parson; in short, whether he had good blood in his veins or not. But for my part, my lord, I entertain no doubts on this head: for while I admire his abilities as a statesman, I cannot but allow him the virtues of private life, or horse capacity; much less can I deny him that small addition to his greatness, nobility of blood. I need not further attempt to vindicate his cause, which has already been so strenuously asserted in the person of his descendant, now in the possession of Lord Talbot; this nobleman, who has risked his life in the glorious contest, has silenced the most obstinate of his opponents.

During the whole administration, my lord, of this great statesman, he could not justly be charged with a single *faux pas*, or by any means increasing the murmurs of the people; had he at any time led his royal master into any thing that was *dirty*, he had still abilities sufficient to have carried him through; not leaving him in the mire to which he had brought him, as some later ministers have done.

I am, my lord, &c.,

T. C.[1]

---

[1] "In the Middlesex Journals, for May 3, 17, and 24, 1770, are the following paragraphs, in the notices to correspondents. What the precautions, mentioned in the first of these notices were, I have not been able to ascertain; they may refer to the omission of the names of the individuals satirised.

'Decimus has our sincere thanks, and may depend on our making use of the precautions he requires.

'Decimus may be assured his two last essays are in the Editor's hands, and will be published in due time.

'The address to the Freeholders of Bristol is come to hand.'"—DIX.

THE POLITE ADVERTISER.

[From the Town and Country Magazine, July, 1770.]

To the Printer of the Town and Country Magazine.

July 11, 1770.

SIR,

AS I look upon your Magazine to be the most polite of any published, I should be obliged to you if you would spare half a page once a month to

The POLITE ADVERTISER,
By Sir Butterfly Feather.

WHEREAS a young fellow, whom I have great reason to imagine is either a linen-draper or haberdasher, has had the assurance to tie himself to an unconscionable long sword, thought by Horatio Otranto,[1] the great antiquary, to be three inches longer than the ever-memorable one of the famous earl of Salisbury; this is to inform him, that unless he can wear it, without *fisting* it in the clumsy manner he does, it shall be taken from him.

THE young lady who dropped her garter in the Mall, last Sunday, is desired not to make herself uneasy; for the person who picked it up is threescore and fifteen.

---

[1] Horace Walpole, author of the Castle of Otranto.

Lost, in the parish of St. James's, a parcel of love-letters, most of them beginning with *My dere letele angel*, or *My dear friend;* whoever will bring them to a certain attorney, or destroy them before publication, shall receive a *princely* reward.

A certain academician, who values himself upon his propriety, having painted William the Conqueror with a bagwig and leather breeches, is desired not to exhibit it; as his brethren, though fools enough in all conscience, are not quite so foolish as to think it equal to his transparent paintings.

Wants meaning, every political essay in The Public Ledger.

Wants admiration, Sir Butterfly Feather.

LETTERS

WRITTEN BEFORE LEAVING BRISTOL.

I.

Letter from Chatterton to his friend Baker, in Charles-Town, South Carolina.[1]

March 6, 1768.

DEAR FRIEND,

MUST now close my poetical labours,[2] my master being returned from London. You write in a very entertaining style; though I am afraid mine will be the contrary. Your celebrated Miss Rumsey is going to be married to Mr. Fowler, as he himself informs me. Pretty children! about to enter into the comfortable yoke of matrimony to be at their own liberty: just apropos to the old saw,[3]—but out of the frying pan into the fire! For

---

[1] Reprinted from Southey's edition; vol. iii. p. 413.

[2] Some of the poems addressed to Miss Hoyland; see p. 12, note 1.

[3] For *saw*, Southey prints *law*; perhaps *but* should be omitted.

a lover, heavens mend him; but for a husband! O excellent! what a female Machiavel this Miss Rumsey is! a very good Mistress of Nature, to discover a *demon* in the habit of a parson; to find a spirit so well adapted to the humour of an English wife, that is, one who takes off his hat to every person he chances to meet to shew his staring horns, and very politely stands at the door of his wife's chamber whilst her gallant is entertaining her within. O mirabili! what will human nature degenerate into. Fowler afore-said, declares he makes a scruple of conscience of being too free with Miss Rumsey before marriage. There's a gallant for you! why a girl with anything of the woman would despise him for it. But no more of him. I am glad you approve of the ladies in Charles-Town; and am obliged to you for the compliment of including me in your happiness; my friendship is as firm as the white rock when the black waves roar around it, and the waters burst on its hoary top, when the driving wind ploughs the sable sea, and the rising waves aspire to the clouds, teeming[1] with the rattling hail. So much for heroics. To speak in plain English; I.am, and ever will be, your unalterable friend. I did not give your love to Miss Rumsey, having not yet seen her in private, and in public she will not speak to me, because of her great love to Fowler; and on another occasion. I have been violently in love these three-and-twenty times since your departure; and not a few times came off victorious. I am

[1] Southey prints *turning*, which is nonsense.

obliged to you for your curiosity, and esteem it very much, not on account of itself, but as coming from you. The poems, &c., on Miss *Hoyland*, I wish better, for her sake and yours. THE TOURNAMENT I have only one canto of, which I send herewith; the remainder is entirely lost.[1] I am with the greatest regret going to subscribe myself, your faithful and constant Friend, till death do us part.

THOMAS CHATTERTON.

II.

To his relation, Mr. Stephens, at Salisbury.

[Reprinted from Southey's Edition. Probably written in Aug. 1769.]

SIR,

IF you think vanity is the dictator of the following lines, you will not do me justice. No, Sir, it is only the desire of proving myself worthy your correspondence, has induced me to write. My partial friends flatter me with giving me a little uncommon share of abilities. It is Mr. Stephens alone, whose good sense disdains flattery, whom I appeal to. It is a maxim with me that compliments of friends is[2] more dangerous than railing of enemies. You may

---

[1] This is clearly not the poem called "The Tournament," printed in vol. ii. p. 124, which is complete, but the fragment with the same title printed in vol. ii. p. 247, of which Chatterton said he had "two more cantos," which he in all probability never wrote.

[2] So in the original.

inquire, if you please, for the Town and Country Magazines, wherein all signed D. B. and Asaphides are mine. The pieces called Saxon[1] are originally and totally the production of my muse; though I should think it a greater merit to be able to translate Saxon. As the said Magazine is by far the best of its kind, I shall have some pieces in it every month; and if I vary from my said signature, will give you notice thereof. Having some curious Anecdotes of Paintings and Painters, I sent them to Mr. Walpole, Author of the Anecdotes of Painting, Historic Doubts, and other pieces well known in the learned world. His answer I make bold to send you. Hence I began a literary correspondence, which ended as most such do. I differed with him in the age of a MS. He insists on his superior talents, which is no proof of that superiority. We possibly may publicly engage in one of the periodical publications, though I know not who will give the onset. Of my proceedings in this affair I shall make bold to acquaint you. My next correspondent of note is Dodsley, whose collection of modern and antique poems are in every library. In this city, my principal acquaintance are—Mr. Barrett, now writing at a vast expence an ancient and modern history of Bristol, a task more difficult than the cleansing the Augean stable;[2] many have attempted, but none succeeded

[1] These are the pieces entitled Ethelgar, Kenrick, Cerdick, Gorthmund, and Cutholf; see Southey's edition, vol. iii.

[2] Such a task it proved to poor Mr. Barrett, encumbered as he was by pseudo-antique MSS., so amply furnished to him by Chatterton.

in it; yet will this work, when finished, please not only my fellow-citizens, but all the world; [and] Mr. Catcott, author of that excellent Treatise on the Deluge,[1] and other pieces, to enumerate which would argue a supposition that you were not acquainted with the literary world. To the studies of these gentlemen I am always admitted, and they are not below asking my advice in any matters of antiquity. I have made a very curious collection of coins and antiques. As I cannot afford to have a gordlabine[2] to keep them in, I commonly give them to those who can. If you pick up any Roman, Saxon, English coins, or other antiques, even a sight of them would highly oblige me. When you quarter your arms in the mullet, say, Or, a fess, vert; by the name of Chatterton. I trace your family from Fitz-Stephen, son of Stephen, Earl of Ammerle, in 1095, son of Od,[3] Earl of Bloys, and Lord of Holderness.

I am your very humble servant,
THOMAS CHATTERTON.

---

[1] See note 1, p. 66.

[2] This word (so printed in Southey's edition) is probably merely a printer's error for some such word as *gardrobe*. Cf. Bailey's "*Gardrobe*, a wardrobe, or place to keep clothes in." Or, *Gordlabine* may be merely *good cabinet*, mis-read.

[3] Probably for *Odo;* so also *Ammerle* may be an error for *Aumerle*.

III.

Letter to Mr. Barrett.[1]

SIR,

UPON recollection, I don't know how Mr. Clayfield could come by his letter, as I intended to have given him a letter but did not. In regard to my motives for the supposed rashness, I shall observe, that I keep no worse company than *myself;* I never drink to excess, and have, without vanity, too much sense to be attached to the mercenary retailers of iniquity. No! it is my PRIDE, my damn'd, native, unconquerable PRIDE, that plunges me into distraction. You must know that the 19-20th of my composition is pride: I must either live a slave, a servant, have no will of my own, no sentiments of my own which I may freely declare as such; or DIE! Perplexing alternative! but it distracts me to think of it. I will endeavor to learn humility, but it cannot be here. What it may cost me in the trial, Heaven knows!

I am,

Your much obliged, unhappy
humble servant,

T. C.

---

[1] Reprinted from Southey's edition, and corrected by the MS. in the British Museum. Written early in 1770. A letter addressed by Chatterton to Mr. Clayfield, and containing hints of suicide, had been found on Chatterton's desk by Mr. Lambert, who at once shewed it to Mr. Barrett. The latter remonstrated with Chatterton, who the next day wrote the above letter.

LETTERS

WRITTEN AFTER HIS ARRIVAL IN LONDON.

I.

London, April 26, 1770.

DEAR MOTHER,

HERE I am, safe, and in high spirits.—To give you a journal of my tour would not be unnecessary. After riding in the basket to Brislington, I mounted the top of the coach, and rid easy; and was agreeably entertained with the conversation of a quaker *in dress*, but little so in personals and behaviour. This laughing Friend, who is a carver, lamented his having sent his tools to Worcester, as otherwise he would have accompanied me to London. I left him at Bath; when, finding it rained pretty fast, I entered an inside passenger to Speenhamland, the half-way stage, paying seven shillings. 'Twas lucky I did so, for it snowed all night, and on Marlborough Downs the snow was near a foot high.

At seven in the morning I breakfasted at Speenhamland, and then mounted the coach-box for the remainder of the day, which was a remarkable fine one.—Honest gee-hoo[1] complimented me with assuring me, that I sat bolder and tighter than any person who ever rid with him.—Dined at Stroud most luxuriantly, with a young gentleman who had slept all the preceding night in the machine; and an old mercantile genius, whose schoolboy son had a great deal of wit, as the father thought, in remarking that Windsor was as old as *our Saviour's time*.

Got into London about five o'clock in the evening—called upon Mr. Edmunds, Mr. Fell, Mr. Hamilton, and Mr. Dodsley.[2] Great encouragement from them; all approved of my design;—shall soon be settled.—Call upon Mr. Lambert; shew him this, or tell him, if I deserve a recommendation, he would oblige me to give me one—if I do not, it will be beneath him to take notice of me. Seen all aunts, cousins—all well—and I am welcome. Mr. T. Wensley is alive, and coming home.—Sister, grandmother, &c. &c. &c. remember.

I remain, your dutiful Son,

T. Chatterton.

---

[1] By a singular misconception, Chatterton substitutes this word for *Jehu*.

[2] Mr. Edmunds was editor of the Middlesex Journal; Mr. Fell, of the Freeholder's Magazine; Mr. Hamilton, of the Town and Country Magazine; and Mr. Dodsley, of the Annual Register. See Wilson's Life, p. 249.

II.

Shoreditch, London, May 6th, 1770.

DEAR MOTHER,

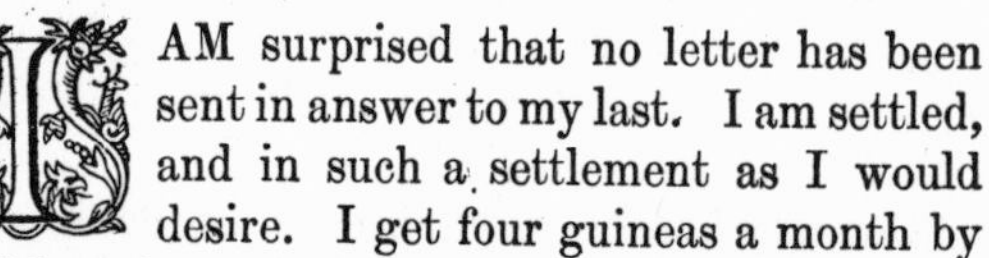

I AM surprised that no letter has been sent in answer to my last. I am settled, and in such a settlement as I would desire. I get four guineas a month by one Magazine: shall engage to write a History of England, and other pieces, which will more than double that sum. Occasional essays for the daily papers would more than support me. What a glorious prospect! Mr. Wilkes knew me by my writings since I first corresponded with the booksellers here. I shall visit him next week, and by his interest will insure Mrs. Ballance the Trinity-House. He affirmed that what Mr. Fell had of mine could not be the writings of a youth; and expressed a desire to know the author. By the means of another bookseller I shall be introduced to Townshend and Sawbridge. I am quite familiar at the Chapter Coffee-house, and know all the geniuses there. A character is now unnecessary; an author carries his character in his pen. My sister will improve herself in drawing. My grandmother is, I hope, well. Bristol's mercenary walls were never destined to hold me—there, I was out of my element: now, I am in it.—London! Good God! how superior is London to that despicable place Bristol! Here is none of your little meannesses, none of your mercenary securities, which disgrace that miserable hamlet.—Dress, which is in Bristol an eternal fund of scandal, is here only introduced as a subject of praise; if a man dresses well, he has taste; if careless, he has his own reasons for so doing, and is prudent. Need I remind you of the contrast? The poverty of authors is a common observation, but not always a true one. No author can be poor who understands the arts of booksellers. Without this necessary knowledge, the greatest genius may starve; and with it, the greatest dunce live in splendour. This knowledge I have pretty well dipped into.—The Levant, man-of-war, in which T. Wensley went out, is at Portsmouth; but no news from him yet.—I lodge in one of Mr. Walmsley's best rooms. Let Mr. Cary copy the letters on the other side, and give them to the persons for whom they are designed, if not too much labour for him.

I remain, your's, &c.

T. CHATTERTON.

P.S. I have some trifling presents for my mother, sister, Thorne, &c.

Sunday morning.

FOR MR. T. CARY.[1]

I have sent you a task. I hope no unpleasing

---

[1] The following list of Chatterton's Bristol friends and acquaintance is given in Southey's edition, vol. iii. p. 494:

T. Skone, a surgeon.
T. Cary, a pipe-maker.
H. Kator, a sugar-baker.

one. Tell all your acquaintance for the future to read the Freeholders' Magazine. When you have anything for publication, send it to me, and it shall most certainly appear in some periodical compilation. Your last piece was, by the ignorance of a corrector, jumbled under the considerations in the acknowledgements. But I rescued it, and insisted on its appearance.

Your friend, T. C.

Direct for me, to be left at the Chapter Coffee-house, Pater-noster-row.

W. Smith, a player [and poet].
Mat. Mease, a vintner [who kept the Nag's Head, Vine Street, Bristol].
Mr. A. Broughton, rector of St. Mary Redcliff.
Mr. J. Broughton, an attorney.
Mr. Clayfield, a distiller.
Mr. Barrett, a surgeon.
Mr. Burgum and *Mr. Catcott*, partners and pewterers.
Rev. Alexander Catcott.
J. Rudhall, apothecary.
E. Gardner.
— *Carty*, a woollen-draper.
— *Hanmer*, a grocer.
— *Ward*, an attorney.
— *Smith*, a surgeon.
— *Capel*, a jeweller.
— *Thistlethwaite*, a stationer.
— *Thaire.*
— *Gaster.*
— *Williams.*
— *Vaughan.*
— *Kalo.*
— *Mason.*
— *Thomas.*

HENRY KATOR.

If you have not forgot Lady Betty,[1] any Complaint, Rebus, or Ænigma, on the dear charmer, directed for me, to be left at the Chapter Coffee-house, Pater-noster-row, shall find a place in some Magazine or other; as I am engaged in many.

Your friend, T. CHATTERTON.

MR. WILLIAM SMITH.

When you have any poetry for publication, send it to me, to be left at the Chapter Coffee-house, Pater-noster-row, and it shall most certainly appear.

Your friend; T. C.

MRS. BAKER.

The sooner I see you the better—send me as soon as possible Rymsdyk's address. (Mr. Cary will leave this at Mr. Flower's, Small-street.)

MR. MASON.

Give me a short prose description of the situation of Nash—and the poetic addition shall appear in some Magazine. Send me also whatever you would have published, and direct for me, to be left at the Chapter Coffee-house, Pater-noster-row.

Your friend, T. CHATTERTON.

MR. MAT. MEASE.

Begging Mr. Mease's pardon for making public use of his name lately[2]—I hope he will remember me, and tell all his acquaintance to read the Freeholder's Magazine for the future.

T. CHATTERTON.

---

[1] Cf. p. 130, last line.
[2] Cf. p. 171, first line, and the note.

Tell Mr. Thaire, Mr. Gaster, Mr. A. Broughton, Mr. J. Broughton, Mr. Williams, Mr. Rudhall, Mr. Thomas, Mr. Carty, Mr. Hanmer, Mr. Vaughan, Mr. Ward, Mr. Kalo, Mr. Smith, &c. &c.—to read the Freeholder's Magazine.

III.

King's Bench, for the present, May 14, 1770.

Dear Madam,

DON'T be surprised at the name of the place. I am not here as a prisoner. Matters go on swimmingly: Mr. Fell having offended certain persons, they have set his creditors upon him, and he is safe in the King's Bench. I have been bettered by this accident: his successors in the Freeholder's Magazine, knowing nothing of the matter, will be glad to engage me, on my own terms. Mr. Edmunds has been tried before the House of Lords, sentenced to pay a fine, and thrown into Newgate. His misfortunes will be to me of no little service. Last week, being in the pit of Drury-lane Theatre, I contracted an immediate acquaintance (which you know is no hard task to me) with a young gentleman in Cheapside; partner in a music-shop, the greatest in the city. Hearing I could write, he desired me to write a few songs for him: this I did the same night, and conveyed them to him the next morning. These he shewed to a Doctor in

Music, and I am invited to treat with this Doctor, on the footing of a composer, for Ranelagh and the Gardens. *Bravo, hey boys, up we go!* Besides the advantage of visiting these expensive and polite places gratis, my vanity will be fed with the sight of my name in copper-plate, and my sister will receive a bundle of printed songs, the words by her brother. These are not all my acquisitions; a gentleman who knows me at the Chapter, as an author, would have introduced me as a companion to the young Duke of Northumberland, in his intended general tour. But, alas! I speak no tongue but my own!—But to return once more to a place I am sickened to write of, Bristol. Though, as an apprentice, none had greater liberties, yet the thoughts of servitude killed me: now, I have that for my labour I always reckoned the first of my pleasures, and have still my liberty. As to the clearance, I am ever ready to give it; but really I understand so little of the law, that I believe Mr. Lambert must draw it. Mrs. L. brought what you mentioned. Mrs. Hughes is as well as age will permit her to be, and my cousin does very well.

I will get some patterns worth your acceptance, and wish you and my sister would improve yourselves in drawing, as it is here a valuable and never-failing acquisition.—My box shall be attended to; I hope my books are in it—if not, send them; and particularly Catcott's Hutchinsonian jargon on the Deluge,[1] and the MS. Glossary,

---

[1] See note 1, p. 66.

composed of one small book, annexed to a larger.[1] —My sister will remember me to Miss Sandford. I have not quite forgot her; though there are so many pretty milliners, &c., that I have almost forgot myself.—Carty will think on me: upon inquiry, I find his trade dwindled into nothing here. A man may very nobly starve by it; but he must have luck indeed, who can live by it.—Miss Rumsey, if she comes to London, would do well as an old acquaintance, to send me her address.—London is not Bristol. We may patrole the town for a day, without raising one whisper, or nod of scandal. —If she refuses, the curse of all antiquated virgins light on her; may she be refused when she shall request! Miss Rumsey will tell Miss Baker, and Miss Baker will tell Miss Porter, that Miss Porter's favoured humble servant, though but a *young* man, is a very old lover; and in the eight-and-fiftieth year of his age: but that, as Lappet says, is the flower of a man's days; and when a lady can't get a young husband, she must put up with an old bedfellow. I left Miss Singer, I am sorry to say it, in a very bad way; that is, in a way to be married. But, mum—Ask Miss Sukey Webb the rest; if she knows, she'll tell ye. I beg her pardon for revealing the secret; but when the knot is fastened, she shall know how I came by it.—Miss Thatcher may depend upon it, that, if I am not in love with her, I am in love with nobody else: I hope she is well; and if that whining, sighing, dying pulpit-fop,

---

[1] This alludes to the important glossary by help of which the "Rowley Poems" were written; cf. p. 348.

Lewis, has not finished his languishing lectures, I hope she will see her amoroso next Sunday.—If Miss Love has no objection to having a crambo song on her name published, it shall be done.[1]—Begging pardon of Miss Cotton for whatever has happened to offend her, I can assure her it has happened without my consent. I did not give her this assurance when in Bristol, lest it should seem like an attempt to avoid the anger of her *furious* brother. Inquire, when you can, how Miss Broughton received her billet. Let my sister send me a journal of all the transactions of the females within the circle of your acquaintance. Let Miss Watkins know, that the letter she made herself ridiculous by, was never intended for her; but for another young lady in the neighbourhood, of the same name. I promised, before my departure, to write to some hundreds, I believe; but, what with writing for publications, and going to places of public diversion, which is as absolutely necessary to me as food, I find but little time to write to you. As to Mr. Barrett, Mr. Catcott, Mr. Burgum, &c., &c., they rate literary lumber so low, that I believe an author, in their estimation, must be poor indeed! But here, matters are otherwise; had Rowley been a Londoner, instead of a Bristowyan, I could have lived by copying his works.—In my humble opinion, I am under very few obligations to any person in Bristol: one, indeed, has obliged me; but as most do, in a manner which makes his obligation no obli-

---

[1] See the Song addressed to Miss P—— L——, of Bristol, commencing with the word *Love*; p. 258.

gation.—My youthful acquaintances will not take it in dudgeon, that I do not write oftener to them, than I believe I shall: but, as I had the happy art of pleasing in conversation, my company was often liked, where I did not like: and to continue a correspondence under such circumstances, would be ridiculous. Let my sister improve in copying music, drawing, and every thing which requires genius: in Bristol's mercantile style those things may be useless, if not a detriment to her; but here they are highly profitable.—Inform Mr. Rhise that nothing shall be wanting, on my part, in the business he was so kind as to employ me in; should be glad of a line from him, to know whether he would engage in the marine department, or spend the rest of his days, safe, on dry ground.—Intended waiting on the Duke of Bedford relative to the Trinity-House; but his Grace is dangerously ill.—My grandmother, I hope, enjoys the state of health I left her in. I am Miss Webb's humble servant. Thorne shall not be forgot when I remit the small trifles to you. Notwithstanding Mrs. B.'s not being able to inform me of Mr. Garsed's address, through the closeness of the pious Mr. Ewer, I luckily stumbled upon it this morning.

THOMAS CHATTERTON.

Monday Evening.

(Direct for me, at Mr. Walmsley's, at Shoreditch —only.)

IV.

Tom's Coffee-House, May 30, 1770.

Dear Sister,

THERE is such a noise of business and politicks in the room, that my inaccuracy in writing here is highly excusable. My present profession obliges me to frequent places of the best resort. To begin with, what every female conversation begins with, dress: I employ my money now in fitting myself fashionably, and getting into good company; this last article always brings me in interest. But I have engaged to live with a gentleman, the brother of a Lord (a Scotch one indeed,) who is going to advance pretty deeply into the bookselling branches; I shall have lodging and boarding, genteel and elegant, gratis: this article, in the quarter of the town he lives, with worse accommodations, would be £50 per annum. I shall have, likewise, no inconsiderable premium; and assure yourself every month shall end to your advantage: I will send you two silks this summer; and expect, in answer to this, what colours you prefer. My mother shall not be forgotten. My employment will be writing a voluminous History of London, to appear in numbers the beginning of the next winter. As this will not, like writing political essays, oblige me to go to the coffee-house, I shall be able to serve you the more by it; but it will necessitate me to go to Oxford, Cambridge, Lincoln, Coventry, and every collegiate church near; not at all disagreeable journeys, and not to me expensive. The Manuscript Glossary, I mentioned in my last, must not be omitted. If money flowed as fast upon me as honours, I would give you a portion of £5,000. You have, doubtless, heard of the Lord Mayor's remonstrating and addressing the King: but it will be a piece of news to inform you, that I have been with the Lord Mayor on the occasion. Having addressed an essay to his Lordship, it was very well received; perhaps better than it deserved; and I waited on his Lordship, to have his approbation to address a second letter to him, on the subject of the remonstrance, and its reception. His Lordship received me as politely as a citizen could; and warmly invited me to call on him again. The rest is a secret.—But the devil of the matter is, there is no money to be got on this side of the question. Interest is on the other side. But he is a poor author, who cannot write on both sides. I believe I may be introduced (and if I am not, I'll introduce myself) to a ruling power in the Court party. I might have a recommendation to Sir George Colebrook, an East-India Director, as qualified for an office no ways despicable; but I shall not take a step to the sea, whilst I can continue on land. I went yesterday to Woolwich to see Mr. Wensley; he is paid to-day. The artillery is no unpleasant sight, if we bar reflection, and do not consider how much mischief it may do. Greenwich Hospital and St. Paul's Cathedral are the only structures which could reconcile me to anything out of the Gothic. Mr. Carty will hear from me soon: multiplicity of literary business must be my excuse.—I condole with him and my dear Miss Sandford, in the misfortunes of Mrs. Carty: my physical advice is, to leech her temples plentifully: keep her very low in diet; as much in the dark as possible. Nor is this last prescription the advice of an old woman: whatever hurts the eyes, affects the brain: and the particles of light, when the sun is in the summer signs, are highly prejudicial to the eyes; and it is from this sympathetic effect, that the head-ache is general in summer. But, above all, talk to her but little, and never contradict her in anything. This may be of service. I hope it will. Did a paragraph appear in your paper of Saturday last, mentioning the inhabitants of London's having opened another view of St. Paul's; and advising the corporation, or vestry of Redclift, to procure a more complete view of Redclift church? My compliments to Miss Thatcher: if I am in love, I am; though the devil take me if I can tell with whom it is. I believe I may address her in the words of Scripture, which no doubt she reveres; "If you had not ploughed with my heifer," (or bullock rather,) "you had not found out my riddle." Humbly thanking Miss Rumsey for her complimentary expression, I cannot think it satisfactory. Does she, or does she not, intend coming to London? Mrs. O'Coffin has not yet got a place; but there is not the least doubt but she will in a little time.

Essay-writing has this advantage, you are sure

of constant pay; and when you have once wrote a piece which makes the author enquired after, you may bring the booksellers to your own terms. Essays on the patriotic side fetch no more than what the copy is sold for. As the patriots themselves are searching for a place, they have no gratuities to spare. So says one of the beggars, in a temporary alteration of mine, in the Jovial Crew:

A patriot was my occupation,
  It got me a name but no pelf;
Till, starv'd for the good of the nation,
  I begg'd for the good of myself.
      Fal, lal, &c.

I told them, if 'twas not for me,
  Their freedoms would all go to pot;
I promis'd to set them all free,
  But never a farthing I got.
      Fal, lal, &c.

On the other hand, unpopular essays will not even be accepted; and you must pay to have them printed: but then you seldom lose by it. Courtiers are so sensible of their deficiency in merit, that they generally reward all who know how to daub them with the appearance of it. To return to private affairs.—Friend Slude may depend upon my endeavouring to find the publications you mention. They publish the Gospel Magazine here. For a whim I write in it.[1] I believe there are not any sent to Bristol; they are hardly worth the carriage—methodistical, and unmeaning. With the usual ceremonies to my mother and grandmother; and sincerely, without ceremony, wishing

[1] See p. 184, note 1.

them both happy; when it is in my power to make them so, it shall be so; and with my kind remembrance to Miss Webb and Miss Thorne, I remain, as I ever was,

Yours, &c. to the end of the chapter,
THOMAS CHATTERTON.

P.S. I am this moment pierced through the heart by the black eye of a young lady, driving along in a hackney-coach.—I am quite in love: if my love lasts till that time, you shall hear of it in my next.

V.

[Tuesday,] June 19, 1770.

DEAR SISTER,

I HAVE an horrid cold.—The relation of the manner of my catching it may give you more pleasure than the circumstance itself. As I wrote very late Sunday night (or rather very early Monday morning,) I thought to have gone to bed pretty soon last night; when, being half undressed, I heard a very doleful voice, singing Miss Hill's favourite bedlamite song. The hum-drum of the voice so struck me, that though I was obliged to listen a long while before I could hear the words, I found the similitude in the sound. After hearing her with pleasure drawl for above half an hour, she jumped into a brisker tune, and hobbled out the ever-famous song, in which poor Jack Fowler was to have been satirized.—" I put my hand into a bush: I prick'd my finger to the bone: I saw a ship sailing along: I thought the sweetest flowers to find:" and other pretty flowery expressions, were twanged with no inharmonious bray. I now ran to the window and threw up the sash, resolved to be satisfied, whether or not it was the identical Miss Hill, *in propria persona*. But, alas! it was a person whose twang is very well known, when she is awake, but who had drank so much royal bob (the gingerbread-baker for that, you know,) that she was now singing herself asleep. This somnifying liquor had made her voice so like the sweet echo of Miss Hill's, that if I had not considered that she could not see her way up to London, I should absolutely have imagined it her's.—There was a fellow and a girl in one corner, more busy in attending to their own affairs than the melody.

[*This part of the letter, for some lines, is not legible.*]

[Returning, in] the morning, from Marybone gardens, I saw the fellow in the cage at the watch-house, in the parish of St. Giles; and the nymph is an inhabitant of one of Cupid's inns of Court. There was one similitude it would be injustice to let slip. A drunken fishman, who sells souse mackarel, and other delicious dainties—to the eternal detriment of all two-penny ordinaries, as his best commodity, his salmon, goes off at three half-pence the piece—this itinerant merchant, this moveable fish-stall, having likewise had his dose of bob-royal, stood still for awhile, and then joined chorus, in a tone which would have laid half-a-dozen lawyers, pleading for their fees, fast asleep: this naturally reminded me of Mr. Haythorne's song of

"Says Plato, who-oy-oy-oy should man be vain?"

However, my entertainment, though sweet enough in itself, has a dish of sour sauce served up in it; for I have a most horrible wheezing in the throat: but I don't repent that I have this cold; for there are so many nostrums here, that 'tis worth a man's while to get a distemper, he can be cured so cheap.

June 29th, 1770.

My cold is over and gone. If the above did not recall to your mind some scenes of laughter, you have lost your ideas of risibility.

VI.

To Mr. T. Cary.

London, ——, 1770.[1]

"Dear Arran! now prepare the smile,
Be friendly, read, and laugh awhile."

* * * * *

BUT, by the Lord, I have business of more importance than poetry.—As I wanted matter for a sheet in the "Town and Country Magazine," you will see this in print metamorphosed into high life.

[1] The date must have been either June 29 or July 1, as he talks of the Magazine (for June) "coming out to-morrow." July 1, 1770, was a Sunday.

You accuse me of partiality in my panegyric on Mr. Allen. Pardon me, my dear friend, but I believe there are very few in Bristol who know what music is. Broderip has no taste, at least no real taste. Step into Redcliff Church, look at the noble arches, observe the symmetry, the regularity of the whole; how amazing must that idea be which can comprehend at once all that magnificence of architecture; do not examine one particular beauty or dwell upon it minutely, take the astonishing whole into your empty pericranium, and then think, what the architect of that pile was in building, Allen is in music. Step aside a little and turn your attention to the ornaments of a pillar of the chapel; you see minute carvings of minute designs, whose chief beauties are deformity or intricacy. Examine all the laborious sculpture; is there any part of it worth the trouble it must have cost the artist, yet how eagerly do children and fools gaze upon these littlenesses. If it is not too much trouble, take a walk to the College-gate, view the labyrinths of knots which twist round that mutilated piece, trace the windings of one of the pillars, and tell me if you don't think a great genius lost in these minutiæ of ornaments. Broderip is a complete copy of these ornamental carvers; his genius runs parallel with theirs, and his music is always disgraced with littlenesses, flowers, and flourishes. What a clash of harmony Allen dashes upon the soul. How prettily Broderip tickles their fancy by winding the same dull tune over again. How astonishingly great is Allen when playing an overture from Handel. How absurdly ridiculous is Broderip when blundering in, and new-modelling the notes of that great genius; how emptily amusing when torturing and twisting airs which he has stolen from Italian operas. I am afraid, my dear friend, you do not understand the merit of a full piece; if you did, you would confess to me that Allen is the only organist you have in Bristol—but of this enough. If you have not music enough to enter into a dispute with me on the merits of Mr. Allen, engage one who has, to throw down the gauntlet, and I shall be ever ready to take it up.

A song of mine is a great favourite with the town, on account of the fulness of the music. It has much of Mr. Allen's manner in the air. You will see that and twenty more in print after the season is over. I yesterday heard several airs of my burletta[1] sung to the harpsichord, horns, flutes, bassoons, hautboys, violins, &c., and will venture to pronounce, from the excellence of the music, that it will take with the town. Observe, I write in all the magazines. I am surprised you took no notice of the last London; in that, and the magazine coming out to-morrow, are the only two pieces I have the vanity to call poetry.[2] Mind the Political Register,[3] I am very intimately acquainted with the editor, who is also editor of another publication. You will find not a little of mine in the "London Museum," and "Town and Country."

---

[1] No doubt "The Revenge;" see p. 207.

[2] See note 1, p. 179.

[3] "The Prophecy" (p. 193) and the Letter to the Lord Mayor (p. 313) both appeared in the Political Register for June, 1770.

The printers of the daily publications are all frightened out of their patriotism, and will take nothing unless 'tis moderate or ministerial. I have not had five patriotic essays this fortnight, all must be ministerial or entertaining.

I remain, yours, &c.,
T. CHATTERTON.

VII.

DEAR MOTHER,

I SEND you, in the box, six cups and saucers, with two basons for my sister. If a china tea-pot and cream-pot is, in your opinion, necessary, I will send them; but I am informed they are unfashionable, and that the red china, which you are provided with, is more in use. A cargo of patterns for yourself, with a snuff-box, right French, and very curious in my opinion.

Two fans—the silver one is more grave than the other, which would suit my sister best. But that I leave to you both.—Some British-herb snuff, in the box; be careful how you open it. (This I omit lest it injure the other matters.) Some British-herb tobacco for my grandmother: some trifles for Thorne. Be assured, whenever I have the power, my will won't be wanting to testify that I remember you.[1]

Your's,
T. CHATTERTON.

July 8, 1770.

[1] These presents were bought out of the five guineas which he received on the 6th of July for his burletta "The Revenge."

N. B.—I shall forestall your intended journey, and pop down upon you at Christmas.

I could have wished you had sent my red pocket-book, as 'tis very material.

I bought two very curious twisted pipes for my grandmother; but both breaking, I was afraid to buy others, lest they should break in the box; and being loose, injure the china. Have you heard anything further of the clearance?

Direct for me at Mrs. Angel's, sack-maker, Brook-street, Holborn.

[Addressed]—Mrs. Chatterton.

VIII.

Dear Sister,

HAVE sent you some china and a fan. You have your choice of two. I am surprised that you chose purple and gold. I went into the shop to buy it: but it is the most disagreeable colour I ever saw—dead, lifeless, and inelegant. Purple and pink, or lemon and pink, are more genteel and lively. Your answer in this affair will oblige me. Be assured, that I shall ever make your wants my wants; and stretch to the utmost to serve you. Remember me to Miss Sandford, Miss Rumsey, Miss Singer, &c.

As to the songs, I have waited this week for them, and have not had time to copy one perfectly; when the season's over, you will have 'em all in print. I had pieces last month in the following Magazines:

Gospel Magazine,

Town and Country, viz.

Maria Friendless,

False Step,

Hunter of Oddities,

To Miss Bush, &c.

Court and City. London. Political Register, &c.

The Christian Magazine, as they are not to be had perfect, are not worth buying.

I remain, Yours,

T. CHATTERTON.

July 11, 1770.

IX.

[*To his Sister.*]

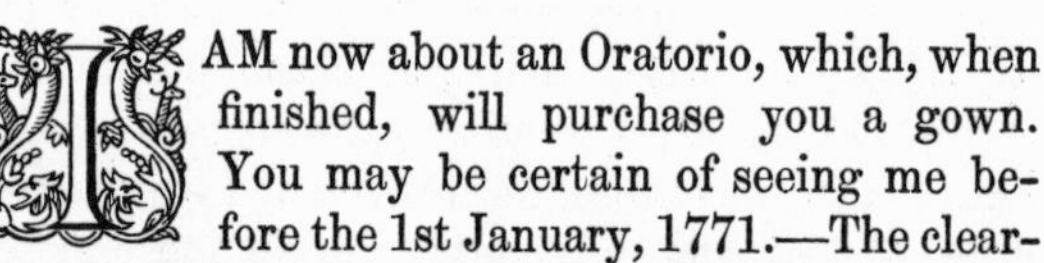

I AM now about an Oratorio, which, when finished, will purchase you a gown. You may be certain of seeing me before the 1st January, 1771.—The clearance is immaterial.—My mother may expect more patterns.—Almost all the next Town and Country Magazine is mine. I have an universal acquaintance: my company is courted every where; and, could I humble myself to go into a compter, could have had twenty places before now:—but I must be among the great; state matters suit me better than commercial. The ladies are not out of my acquaintance. I have a deal of business now, and must therefore bid you adieu. You will have a longer letter from me soon — and more to the purpose.

Yours,

T. C.

20th July, 1770.

X.

To Mr. G. Catcott.

London, August 12, 1770.

Sir,

A CORRESPONDENT from Bristol had raised my admiration to the highest pitch by informing me, that an appearance of spirit and generosity had crept into the niches of avarice and meanness;—that the murderer of Newton[1] (Ferguson) had met with every encouragement that ignorance could bestow; that an episcopal palace was to be erected for the enemy of the Whore of Babylon, and the present turned into a stable for his ten-headed beast— that a spire was to be patched to St. Mary Redcliffe, and the streets kept cleaner, with many other impossibilities: but when Mr. Catcott (the *Champion* of Bristol) doubts it, it may be doubted. Your description of the intended steeple struck me. I have seen it, but not as the invention of Mr. ——. All that he can boast is Gothicising it.

[1] A note in Southey's edition says "Sir Isaac." But of course Chatterton is speaking of Doctor Newton, Bishop of Bristol, author of "Dissertations on the Prophecies," and an Analysis of the Revelation of St. John.

Give yourself the trouble to send to Weobley's, Holborn, for a View of the Church of St. Mary de la Annunciation, at Madrid, and you will see a spire almost the parallel of what you describe. The conduct of [Newton] is no more than what I expected: I had received information that he was absolutely engaged in the defence of the Ministry, and had a pamphlet on the stocks, which was to have been paid with a translation.[1] In consequence of this information, I inserted the following paragraph in one of my exhibitions:[2]

'*Revelation Unravelled, by* ——. The Ministry are indefatigable in establishing themselves: they spare no expence, so long as the expence does not lie upon *them.* This piece represents the tools of Administration offering the Doctor a pension, or translation, to new-model his Treatise on the Revelations, and to prove Wilkes to be an Atheist.'

The editor of Baddeley's Bath Journal has done me the honour to murder most of my hieroglyphics, that they may be abbreviated for his paper. Whatever may be the political sentiments of your inferior clergy, their superiors are all flamingly Ministerial. Should your scheme for a single row of houses in Bridge Street take place, conscience must tell you, that Bristol will owe even that Beauty to avarice; since the absolute impossibility of finding tenants for a double row is the only occasion of your having but one. The Gothic dome I mentioned was not designed by Hogarth.

---

[1] Viz. to a wealthier see.

[2] See pp. 305—309. The dash in the next line of course means *Newton.* Cf. p. 153, note 1.

I have no great opinion of him out of his ludicrous walk—there he was undoubtedly inimitable. It was designed by the great Cipriani. The following description may give you a faint idea of it. From an hexagonal spiral tower (such I believe Redcliffe is) rose a similar palisado of Gothic pillars, three in a cluster on every angle, but single and at an equal distance in angular spaces. The pillars were trifoliated (as Rowlie terms it) and supported by a majestic oval dome, not absolutely circular, (that would not be Gothic) but terminating in a point, surmounted with a cross, and on the top of the cross a globe. The two last ornaments may perhaps throw you into a fit of religious reflection, and give rise to many pious reflections. Heaven send you the comforts of Christianity! I request them not, for I am no Christian. Angels are, according to the orthodox doctrine, creatures of the epicene gender, like the Temple beaux * * *.

I intend going abroad as a surgeon. Mr. Barrett has it in his power to assist me greatly, by his giving me a physical[1] character. I hope he will. I trouble you with a copy of an Essay I intend publishing. I remain,

Your much-obliged Humble Servant,

THOMAS CHATTERTON.

Direct to me at Mrs. Angel's, sack-maker, Brook Street, Holborn.

---

[1] i.e. medical, as at p. 349, l. 6.

OTHER PROSE PIECES.

HE following is a list of other prose pieces by Chatterton, in the order in which they occur in the third volume of Southey and Cottle's edition. See also vol. ii. p. 315.

Ethelgar; a Saxon Poem. (A prose imitation of Macpherson's Ossian; dated Bristol, March 4, 1769; and signed D. B. Printed in the Town and Country Magazine, March, 1769.)

Kenrick; translated from the Saxon. (A similar production, also signed D. B. Printed in the Town and Country Magazine, April, 1769.)

Cerdick; translated from the Saxon. (Dated Bristol, May 20; and signed D. B.; Town and Country Magazine, May, 1769.)

Godred Crovan; a [prose] Poem. (Dated Bristol, Aug. 10, 1769, and signed D. B. Printed in the Town and Country Magazine, Aug., 1769.)

The Hirlas; from the Ancient British. (Dated Jan. 3, 1770; signed D. B. Printed in the Supplement to the Town and Country Magazine, 1769.)

Gorthmund; from the Saxon. (Printed in the Town and Country Magazine, Sept., 1770.)

Saxon Achievements. (A letter to the Town and Country Magazine; dated Bristol, May 15, 1769, and signed D. B. Printed in the May number.)

Anecdote of Chaucer. (Copied from Speght; printed in the Town and Country Magazine, Jan., 1770.)

Anecdote concerning Lord Jefferies. (Said to be "taken from the Records of the Town of Arundel." Printed in the Town and Country Magazine, June, 1770.)

Saxon Heraldry. (A letter to the Town and Country Magazine; dated Bristol, Feb. 4, 1769, and signed D. B. Printed in the Feb. number.)

On an Ancient Manuscript. (A letter to the Town and Country Magazine; dated Bristol, March 4, 1769, and signed D. B. Printed in the March number.)

The following tales, mostly printed in the Town and Country Magazine, and reprinted by Southey and Cottle, were most of them written by Chatterton:

Adventures of a Star. (Town and Country Magazine, Oct. and Nov., 1770.)

Maria Friendless. (Town and Country Magazine, June, 1770.)

The False Step. (Town and Country Magazine, June, 1770.)

Memoirs of a Sad Dog. (Town and Country Magazine, July and Aug., 1770.)

Tony Selwood.

Astrea Brokage. (Town and Country Magazine, Jan., 1770.)

The Hunter of Oddities; several papers. (Town and Country Magazine, 1770.)

On Punning. (Town and Country Magazine, June, 1770.)

The Unfortunate Fathers. (Town and Country Magazine, Jan., 1770.)

The Hirlas; No. 2. (Rather No. 1, as it was written *before* the other piece so called. Dated Bristol, Nov. 17; signed D. B.; and printed in the Town and Country Magazine, Nov., 1769.)

Cutholf. (Another prose poem in the style of Ossian; signed Asaphides; printed in Robinson's Lady's Magazine for Jan. 1771.)

The pieces called Maria Friendless, The False Step, and the Hunter of Oddities are certainly by Chatterton; see p. 358. The remarks about Walpole in the Memoirs of a Sad Dog show that piece also to be his; see Wilson's Life, p. 188.

The only pieces left doubtful are Tony Selwood, Astrea Brokage, and The Unfortunate Fathers. Of these, I am unable to trace the first appearance of Tony Selwood, and do not know on what proof its authenticity rests. Astrea Brokage and the Unfortunate Fathers both have reference to Bristol, and may be Chatterton's. The piece entitled On Punning has evidently been assigned to Chatterton by a mere mistake, from confusion of the initials T. B. and D. B. It is signed "T. B., Berkeley Square, June 16, 1770," and is very stupid. Besides the above pieces, there may have been several others contributed by Chatterton to the various popular magazines, but there is no clue by which they can be detected.

The following is a List of Chatterton's Letters:

To Horace Walpole. (Printed in this edition; vol. ii. p. 282.)

To Horace Walpole. (Printed in this edition; vol. ii. p. 287.)

To Horace Walpole. (Letter dated Bristol, April 8, 1769; two on April 14, 1769; one undated;[1] one dated July 24.)

To Mr. G. Catcott. (His last extant letter; printed in this edition, vol. i. p. 359.)

To Ralph Bigland, Esq. (On heraldry; brief, and valueless.)

To Mr. William Smith. (The curious letter printed *correctly* in this edition, in the Essay on the Rowley Poems, vol. ii. p. xxv.)

To Mr. Stephens; see p. 332.

To Mr. Baker; see p. 330.

To Mr. Rudhall (in Southey's edition, iii. 416).

To Mr. Barrett; see p. 335.

To his mother, sister, &c. (Printed in this volume; pp. 336—361.)

---

[1] This letter was also written on April 14. Only the first of them was sent; the others were withheld, as being less suitable. Chatterton knew that it was a critical moment in his life.

ADDITIONAL NOTES.

HE poems and prose pieces printed in this edition have been compared with the first-printed copies as far as practicable, in order to eliminate the errors that may have crept in from frequent reprinting. The principal sources of information as to the original forms of the poems and other pieces, are the MSS. in the British Museum, The Town and Country Magazine for 1769 and 1770, the Political Register, the North Briton, the Free-holder's Magazine, the Universal Magazine, the Gospel Magazine, the London Magazine, Dix's Life of Chatterton, Sir Herbert Croft's "Love and Madness," &c. These sources are pointed out in nearly all cases in a note subjoined to the title or in a footnote. Where these could not well be consulted, I have in general followed the edition by Southey and Cottle, printed in 1803. The chief difference between the present edition and those of Southey and Willcox is in the punctuation, which I have carefully revised throughout, having found such revision to be very necessary. Many passages have thus been rendered intelligible, which before were meaningless. I have also arranged most of the poems in chronological order, as explained in vol. ii. p. xxxviii. I subjoin a few additional notes upon particular passages.

There is a certain irregularity in English grammar common in old authors, which has hardly received sufficient attention. In many cases, a verb is made to agree with the *nearest* substantive, the ear deciding against the requirements of logic. There are many such instances in Chatterton, but I have not in general considered it necessary to "correct" them, as editors generally take upon themselves to do. Those who read our old dramatists *in old editions* will best understand to what I refer; for the information of readers accustomed only to "edited" texts, I select the following examples from the present volume.

"The wrinkled grass its silver joys *unfold*;" p. 10.

"Displays his bigot blade, and thunders *draw*;" (i. e. draws forth his thunders;) p. 49.

"The greatest of Creation's blessings *cloy*;" p. 67.

"But now my lingering feet revenge *denies*;" p. 88.

"Where ginger's aromatic, matted root
Creep through the mead, and up the mountains *shoot*;" p. 179.

In the last case, *shoot* was put for *shoots* owing to the occurrence of *mountains*, and *creep* was an afterthought. Another peculiarity (of many authors besides Chatterton) lies in the use of a singular verb after singular nominatives connected by the conjunction *and*; as in

"And now the rustling leaves and strengthened cry
Bespeaks the cause of the confusion nigh;" p. 11.

"The distant forest, and the darkened wave
Of the swoln Avon *ravishes* my sight;" p. 58.

Neither does Chatterton stand alone in such peculiarities as the use of *wrote* for the past participle *written* (p. 137); nor in the use of such rimes as *severe, care* (p. 15), *fault, thought* (p. 38), and the like, wherein he only follows the received pronunciation of his day. He always uses *real* as a dissyllable (see p. 30), whilst *satellites* (p. 112) has four syllables, as in Latin.

P. 33. JOURNAL SIXTH. The reason for this title is not clear. It appears from p. 39, that part of it at least was addressed to his friend Baker, concerning whom see p. 12, note 1, and p. 330.

P. 48. *Gloster's bishop* was Warburton; see pp. 147 and 163.

P. 57. POEM ON THOMAS PHILLIPS' DEATH. A facsimile of the copy of this poem in the British Museum, will be found in Willcox's edition, published at Cambridge in 1842.

P. 74, note 2. Besides the misprint of *roar* for *soar* in this place, a few others may be mentioned which are to be found in the editions of Southey and Willcox. For example, in the passage at p. 78, instead of *Waterer* (i. e. Aquarius, as at p. 126), both editions have *water* with a small *w*. Instead of *nightmare* at p. 163, both editions actually have *nightman*. Instead of *peace* in the last line but one on p. 159, the editions have *place*, which destroys the whole force of the allusion; see note 1, p. 160. At p. 147, the title "False Alarm," the name of a work by Dr. Johnson, is printed by Willcox "false alarm," as if it were not a title at all. At p. 150, the name of Home the poet, the well-known author of "Douglas," is printed by Willcox with a small *h*; whilst the word *horners* (p. 152) is unnecessarily spelt with a capital letter. At p. 165, Willcox prints Rambler with a small *r*, thus missing the evident allusion to Johnson's work so called.

P. 82. THE ADVICE. It seems probable that the Miss Rumsey here mentioned is the one who, in March, 1768, was engaged to the poetaster Fowler; see p. 330. She seems to have been still unmarried in 1770; see p. 344. In this case, Fowler is here named Pitholeon; he is elsewhere satirized by Chatterton for his bad poetry; see pp. 34, 38.

P. 91. THE CONSULIAD. Mr. Bell has since ascertained that this piece actually did appear in the Freeholder's Magazine (Jan. 1770), as surmised in the note. The other version, called the Constabiliad, is dated Oct. 30, 1869.

P. 92. Jemmy Twitcher was the popular name for the Earl of Sandwich; see pp. 116-118. "Sandwich acted as public prosecutor in the House of Lords, and the people, taking up a passage in the Beggar's Opera—'That Jemmy Twitcher should peach me, I own surprises me'—nicknamed him Jemmy Twitcher in perpetuity." — J. E. THOROLD ROGERS; *Historical Gleanings, Second Series*, p. 167.

P. 99. THE RESIGNATION. A portion of this piece also appeared in the Freeholder's Magazine. The copy there printed somewhat varies from the one in the editions, but the variations are of little importance. The chief gain is that the correct reading of l. 11, on p. 109, is thus ascertained to be

"Sheltered in the protection of a king."

Towards the end, however, some additional lines appear, and accordingly I subjoin, for completeness' sake, a list of all the various readings.

P. 99, first line of poem, *ambitious* dame.
P. 100, l. 18. *Sudden* instead of *hasty*.
l. 21. The ruins of the pilot us'd to steer.
l. 23. Which doubly dignified the man of place.
P. 101, l. 8. *Shelter such* instead of *save so vile*.
l. 10. *The reigning minister* instead of *each minister of state*.
l. 14. *Rascal libeller should* instead of *lord's exalted but to*.
l. 24. *Hidden* instead of *daily; her* instead of *a*.
P. 102, l. 4. *His* instead of *her*.
l. 7. *Hackney* instead of *subtle*.
l. 18. *Caledonian* instead of *Caledonia's*.
l. 21. *An* instead of *A*.
l. 22. *The* instead of *Its*.
l. 25. *Here Sawney lived* inst. of *Here lived a Laird*.
P. 103, l. 3. *Hebrew* instead of *Latin*.
l. 7. *Book* instead of *crook*.
l. 8. *When to recreation* for *often when to pastimes*.
l. 14. *Scarce* for *just*.
l. 19. *Acts* for *arts;* an obvious improvement.
l. 21. *Dead* for *rent*.
l. 24. *Passions warring* for *warring passions*.
P. 104, l. 4. *Dancing* for *riper*.
l. 17. *To his sight* for *from the hills*.
l. 19. *Pow'r* for *joy*.

P. 104, l. 24. *More enchanted trod the groves of* for *was more pleased with future scenes at.*
last line. *Lengthened out his* for *marked his gladsome.*
P. 105, first line. *Various* for *varying.*
l. 2. *Wish'd* for *great.*
l. 5. *Train of hooting* for *lengthening train of.*
l. 20. *Store-houses* for *hidden cave.*
l. 26. After this line is interpolated the couplet,

With bills for secret services unpaid,
And schemes of future desolation laid.

l. 27. *Pride* for *prize.*
P. 106, l. 11. *Trudging* for *hasting.*
l. 13. *The* for *my.*
l. 16. *Disputes my sov'reign* for *dares contradict my.*
l. 5 from below. *But not* for *Not yet.*
P. 107, l. 17. *Shew his profits, ministry, and pride* for *share the ministry, assist to guide.*
l. 20. *Unowned* (a misprint) for *renowned.*
P. 107, l. 21. *Or* for *and.*
l. 25. *That* for *who.*
l. 27. Thus far was inserted in the Freeholder's Mag. for April, 1770, pp. 105-7.
last line. *The* for *each; bailiff* for *caitiff.*
P. 108, l. 6. After the six omitted another couplet also was added, viz.:

When this their mystic worship they pursued,
'Twas silence and the sleep of solitude.

l. 14. *Birth* for *Bute.*
l. 17. *Wound* for *brand.*
l. 18. *The sting* for *all sense.*
l. 2 from below: *Will you* for *wilt thou.*
P. 109, l. 10. *Known temerity away* for *timid spirit's hasty way.*
l. 11. The first word is *Sheltered.*
l. 17, 18. This couplet is omitted in the Freeholder's Magazine, and the eight lines following are varied considerably, as follows:

Thy ruins on the isles of Thanet built,
The fruits of plunder, villainy, and guilt,

No more shall lull thy conscience into rest,
With dissipation to amuse your breast;
Tho' justice, fett'red in the nets of state,
Still spares your head, and dallies with your fate,
When you presume again to plague the land,
Freedom will place an axe in ev'ry hand.
Contented, &c.

P. 109, l. 4 from below:

Foretell when bustling N[or]th will cease to shine.

l. 2 from below: *Tool* for *fool.*

P. 110, l. 15. Two couplets were inserted before the next line:

He gilds the flying orbs, his venal force
Supports their conscience in the fiery course:
H[o]lland, thy talent wanted no supply,
Thy conscience ne'er gave thy purse the lie.
Your infamy, &c.

l. 19. Whether you shone self-lighten'd, or by Bute.
l. 26. *Race* for *sphere.*
l. 4 from below.

Safe when protected by the Sibyl's swain.

l. 3 from below. *State* for *life.*
last line. *Circumscribed* for *rolled around.*

P. 111. l. 6-8.

Through all the under dignities of place,
Each had in error copy'd from his grace;
The heavy waggon of the state was driv'n
Slow, &c.

l. 15. *The plots* for *each plot.*
l. 17. And ruined ev'ry measure Bute could frame.
l. 19. After this line the following twenty lines were inserted:

Bute from the summit of his glory spy'd
His glaring inability to guide;
And must'ring ev'ry rascal of his gang,
(Who might for merit altogether hang,)
From the black catalogue, the worthy crew,
The jesuitical and scheming few,

Selected by the leader of the clan,
Receiv'd instructions for their future plan;
And, after proper adoration paid,
Were to their destin'd sphere of state convey'd,
To shine the minister's satellites,
Collect his light, and give his lordship ease;
Reform his crooked politics, and draw
A more determin'd weapon on the law;
Settle his erring resolutions right,
And give in just proportion day and night.
Alas! the force of Scottish pride is such,
These mushrooms of a day presum'd too much;
Conscious of cunning and superior arts,
They looked contempt on Gr[a]ft[o]n's trifling parts.

The above and all from p. 107, line 28, were published in the Freeholder's Magazine for May, 1770, pp. 162-3, with a note [*To be continued*]; but no more appeared, and the Magazine itself does not appear to have been published after the following August.

P. 136. Kew Gardens. The MS. notes quoted in the footnotes are written below the MS. copy of the poem in the British Museum. They are surely *not* Chatterton's, as Willcox asserts, but are probably due to Mr. Isaac Reed, in whose handwriting the transcript is written.

P. 138, l. 15. The name intended by the asterisks is certainly Barrington; see the description of picture No. 13 on p. 307. See also p. 106.

P. 148, l. 5. By Horne is meant John Horne, better known as Horne Tooke. Cf. p. 163.

P. 150, l. 5 from bottom. The asterisks no doubt stand for Junius. Cf. p. 92, l. 7.

P. 152, l. 6 from bottom. The last word in the line should be *Creech*.

P. 155, l. 7. Colonel Luttrell contested Middlesex against John Wilkes, and was declared member, though Wilkes had a large majority. "His lordship" is Lord Mansfield.

P. 168, l. 3. The name signified by the asterisks, is Kenrick. Southey prints this line (vol. i. p. 177)

"Kenrick disdains to p—s upon the Dead."

P. 185. Happiness. This piece, dated 1770 in Southey's edition, is dated 1769 by Sir H. Croft.

P. 189. *Pulvis* is intended for Dr. Barrett, author of The History of Bristol.

P. 262. On Immortality. I have no doubt that this poem was suggested to Chatterton by reading Night VII. in Young's Night Thoughts; in which we find such lines as these :—

Our heads, our hearts, our passions, and our powers,
Speak the same language, call us to the skies.—
His immortality alone can solve
That darkest of enigmas, human hope.—
'Tis immortality deciphers man,
And opens all the mysteries of his make.—
Why happiness pursued, though never found ?—
— these, and a thousand pleas uncalled
All promise, some ensure, a second scene; &c.

That Chatterton had read this poem is proved by his quotation from it, in his poem called The Resignation, stanza 5; the original of which is

Heaven is all love; all joy in giving joy;
It never had created but to bless.

P. 277. Christmas Games. A few words occur in this essay which may, perhaps, require elucidation by help of Chatterton's favourite book, Bailey's Dictionary. They are explained by Bailey as follows:

"*Wastel-Bread,* the finest sort of white bread or cakes."

"*Kichel,* a kind of cake."

"*Deis* [for *Dais*], the upper table in some English monasteries." It is not "the upper *seat* of the table," as Chatterton says.

"*Fortuny,* a tournament."

"*Mummery,* masquerading, buffoonery."

"*Henchman,* a footpage."

The quotations from Speght's Chaucer agree with two of those printed in vol. ii. pp. 307 and 308. Short as they are, they afford evidence of Chatterton's entertaining the idea that the way to make old English look older is to spell a common word like *that* either *yatte* or *thatte,* spellings which do *not* occur in MSS. of any pretensions to accuracy or antiquity.

P. 364. The piece signed "Tony Selwood" first appeared in the Town and Country Magazine for August, 1770. There is nothing to connect it with Chatterton.

Abstract of the MSS. in the British Museum.

The Chatterton MSS. in the British Museum are the Additional MSS. 5766, A, B, and C. A complete description of them would take up a considerable space, but the following abstract will give a sufficient clue to their contents.

5766 A. A large thin portfolio, containing the original drawings and MSS., on parchment and paper, which Chatterton asserted to be the productions of Thomas Rowley, and which manifestly are *not* of the fifteenth century, but of modern fabrication. The contents of this volume are described in Southey's edition, vol. iii. pp. 497—515. The principal pieces are as follows:—

1. A parchment fragment, containing the first thirty-four lines of the poem, beginning "Anent a brooklette," printed in vol. ii. p. 211.

2. A fragment called the "Yellow Roll," containing drawings of coins.

3. A fragment called the "Purple Roll," of which a facsimile was given in Willcox's edition, but there wrongly entitled the *Yellow* Roll. It is valueless and nearly illegible, and, though the *largest* of all the fragments, measures only 13 inches by 10 inches.

4. "The Rolle of Seynte Bartholomew's Priorie."

6. Small fragment containing the Lines on W. Canynges Feast, described in Additional Notes, vol. ii. pp. 343 and 344.

7. The life of Sir Simon de Burton, printed in vol. ii. pp. 122 and 123.

8. Account of St. Mary's Church of the Porte. Beneath it, on paper, a copy of the Epitaph on Robert Canynge, printed in vol. ii. p. 273. This copy differs slightly from that printed in this edition, having *Nee* and *dye* for *Ne* and *die* in l. 10, *reyse the Soule* for *rize the Soulle* in l. 11, and *theyr* for *yer* in l. 12.

9. A fragment about the "Knights Templars' Churche."

10—33 (also No. 5) are valueless scraps of drawings or writings, some of which are engraved in Barrett's History of Bristol.

33 *a*. Memoranda of events from A. D. 1340—1374; printed by Southey, vol. iii. p. 373.

34—42. Chiefly worthless scraps, many of them either illegible or containing merely some rude drawing. No. 41 contains four portraits, which are actually pasted down on to a portion of a *genuine* document, dated 10 Hen. IV., consisting of a quit-claim from Will. Penesford to Thos. Botiller, burgess of Bristol in Temple Street. This suggests that whatever genuine documents Chatterton ever saw were probably of a purely legal character, such as old deeds, and the like; most of which, in all probability, he could not read.

The above pieces and scraps belonged to Mr. Barrett and were given subsequently to Dr. Glynn, who bequeathed them to the British Museum, together with the other papers and transcripts which follow in parts B and C.

5766 B. 1. A Chronycalle of Brystowe; printed in vol. ii. p. 268.

2. Hereaudyn; printed in vol. ii. p. 273.

3. Painter's Bill; printed in Southey's edition, iii. 303.

4. The Parliament of Sprites; printed in vol. ii. p. 228; also the poem on The Dedication of Our Lady's Church, in vol. ii. p. 225.

5, 6, 7. To Johne Ladgate, Songe to Ælla, and Ladgate's Answer; vol. ii. pp. 116—119.

8. Account of the Mayor's first passing over the old Bridge; vol. ii. p. 279.

9. Songe of Seyncte Warburghe; vol. ii. p. 262; see note 1.

10. Letters between Canynge and Rowley; printed in Southey's edition.

11—35. Various transcripts of pretended deeds and letters. Fictitious list of mayors and bailiffs of Bristol. Also the accounts of the churches of Greater St. John, St. Thomas, St. Peter, St. Philip, All-hallows, St. Owden, St. Mary of Redcliffe, St. John, St. Lawrence, St. Mary Magdalen, St. Stephen, St. Leonard, St. Michael, &c.; printed in Southey's edition, vol. iii. No. 21 is the deed printed in vol. ii. p. 299.

36. Proclamation of Wm. Canynge; vol. ii. p. 296.

37. Anecdote of Chaucer; printed in Southey's edition. It is merely the short story, copied from Speght, about Chaucer beating a Franciscan friar. It first appeared in the Town and Country Magazine (Jan. 1770), to which no doubt Chatterton sent it.

38, 39, 40. Drawings of a monument and gates.

41, 42. Life of Canynge, and more letters between Rowley and Canynge, printed by Southey.

43. The first twelve lines of "The World;" vol. ii. p. 243. The fourth line slightly varies, having *guiled* for *gilded*, and *her* for *his*.

44. Plan of Bristol, by Rowley.

45. Letters of Rowley; see Southey's edition, iii. 331—345.

46. Scraps printed by Southey; vol. iii. 370—372.

47. The Hirlas; see Southey's edition, iii. 46. (There are two pieces thus named; see pp. 362, 364. The one here meant is the one dated Jan. 3, 1770.)

48. The original letter on "The Ryse of Peyncteynge in Englande;" see vol. ii. p. 282, and additional notes, p. 344.

49. Second original letter on "The Hystorie of Peyncters in Englande;" vol. ii. p. 287.

50. A third letter to Walpole, never sent. See Southey's edition, iii. 399.

51. Another letter to the same, copied out by Mr. Barrett; never sent. See Southey's edition, iii. 401.

52. Articles of Belief of Thos. Chatterton; see p. 276.

53. On Mercy. A poem. This poem and the two next following are perhaps in Chatterton's handwriting, though this has been doubted. They are of small merit.

54. A poem entitled "Love and Beauty. A Dialogue."

55. A poem entitled "To a Young Lady."

56. Fragment of a satirical poem, in a dialogue between Hobbinol and Thyrsis. Of no merit.

57. A poem entitled "Journal Sixth;" vol. i. p. 33.

58. Poem to Mr. Clayfield; see vol. i. p. 57; note 1.

59. Elegy on the death of Thomas Phillips; only the three first verses. See vol. i. p. 50.

60. Elegy on the death of Thomas Phillips; vol. i. p. 50.

61. Happiness; a Rhapsody; vol. i. p. 185.

61 *a*. The Constabiliad; see note 1 on p. 91. (Omitted in the B. M. Catalogue.)

62. A New Song; vol. i. p. 76.

63. Extracts from Speght's Chaucer; vol. ii. p. 307.

64. Resignation; vol. i. p. 99.

65. A coat of arms, coloured.

66. Elegy on Mr. William Smith; vol. i. p. 261.

67. Elegy on the demise of a great genius; forming part of the poem called February; vol. i. p. 126.

68. Amphitryon; a Burletta. See vol. i. p. 207; note 1.

69, 70, 71. Extract from Ælla. Notes of arms, &c.

72. The Freere of Orderys Whyte; vol. ii. p. 251.

73. Sketches of coats of arms.

74. A few lines of two poems. (1.) "There was a Broder of Orderys Blacke;" (2.) "In the merye, merye vale." Worthless fragments.

75. Original letter from Chatterton to Mr. Barrett. Printed at p. 335.

76. Letter from a female to Chatterton, with an objectionable paraphrase by himself. Worthless.

77. Coats of arms of the Chatterton family, &c.; see vol. ii. p. 314.

78—100. Drawings of buildings, sketches of coats of arms, drawings of monumental effigies, &c.

5766 C. A thin octavo volume, containing "The Rolle of St. Bartholomeweis Priorie," printed in Southey's edition, vol. iii. and in Barrett's Bristol, p. 428; also drawings of gates, chapels, tombs, &c.

NOTE.

It should be here particularly observed that the four poems following, viz. "To Miss Hoyland" (vol. i. p. 22), "To Miss C." (vol. i. p. 24), "To Mr. Powel" (vol. i. p. 30), and "Clifton" (vol. i. p. 61), are said by Southey and Willcox to be printed from MSS. in the British museum. This is an oversight, there being no such MSS. in existence. All four poems (and only these four of Chatterton's) are to be found in a book called "Miscellanies in Prose and Verse, by Edward Gardner," printed at Bristol in 1798. Gardner says that he received these poems from Chatterton, indirectly, about a month before his unfortunate journey to London. It was Edward Gardner who lent Chatterton Watson's Translation of Horace; see vol. i. p. 256.

MSS. in the Bristol Library.

The following extract from the Catalogue (p. 311) of the Bristol Library, in Queen's Road, is of interest.

"Chatterton. The Battle of Hastings. Extracts from Craish's Heraldry. The Tournament. Fragment of a Poem (framed). A letter to Bp. Newton. A letter to George Catcott, Aug. 12, 1770. In the handwriting of Thomas Chatterton.

"Transcripts of Poems attributed to Rowley; by Geo. Catcott and others.

"Correspondence of Geo. Catcott and others concerning Rowley's Poems.

"Miscellaneous Papers relating to Thomas Chatterton, (including the 'Exhibition;' 440 lines)."

Most of these papers were presented to the Library by Mr. Richard Smith; see vol. ii. p. 323. The "Fragment of a Poem" is a part of the Merrie "Trickes of Laminge-towne," as explained in Mr. R. Smith's letter. The letter to Mr. Geo. Catcott is the last Chatterton ever wrote, of which the whole contents are certainly known. His mother is said to have received one a few days later. See p. 359, and cf. Wilson's Life, p. 297.

The original MS. of Chatterton's Will is now in the library at the Philosophical Institute, Bristol.

THE END OF VOL. I.